The Golden Stool

The Golden Stool

Some Aspects of the Conflict of Cultures in Modern Africa

EDWIN WILLIAM SMITH

ISBN: 9789389545982

First Published 1926, reprint 2016 in India by

Facsimile Publisher
12 Pragati Market
Ashok Vihar, Ph-2
Delhi - 110052, India
books@facsimilepublisher.com
www.facsimilepublisher.com

AFRICA

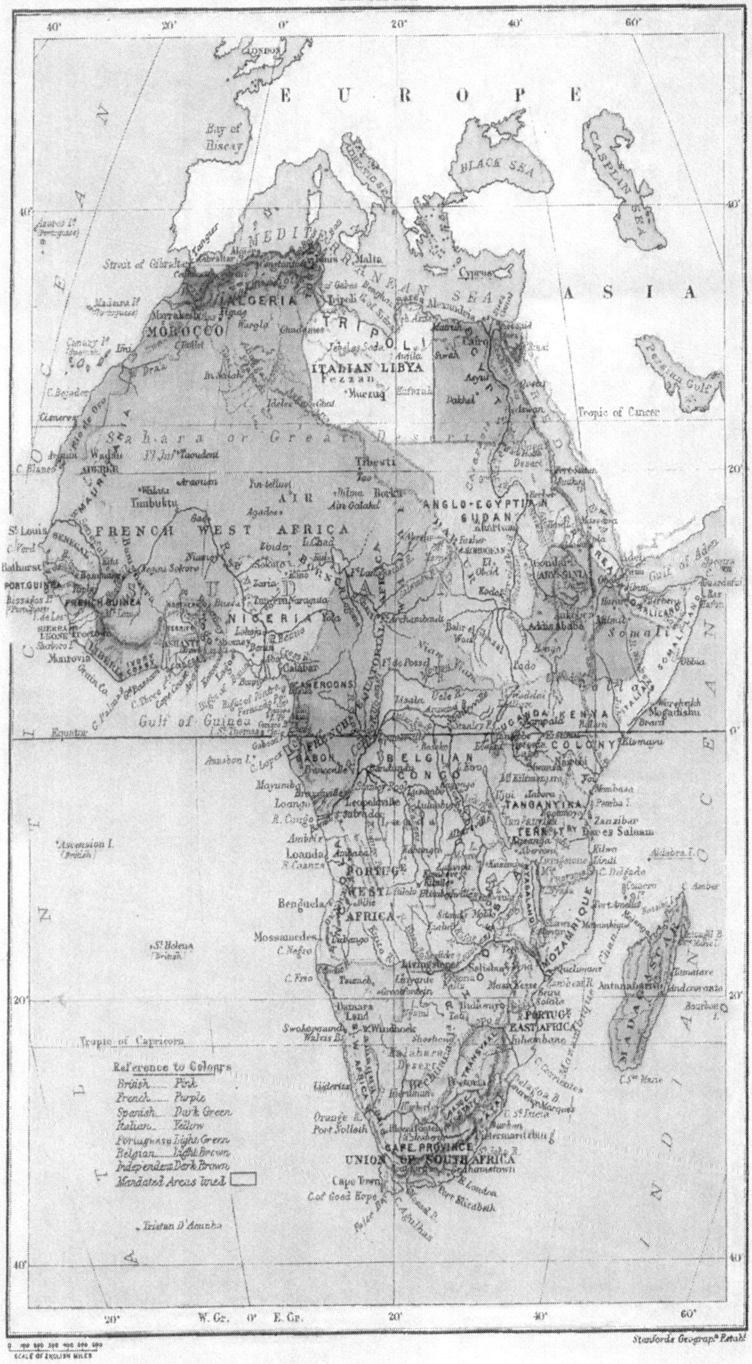

E U R O P E
A S I A
Bay of Biscay
BLACK SEA
CASPIAN SEA
MEDITERRANEAN SEA
Strait of Gibraltar
Malta
Cyprus
ALGERIA
MOROCCO
ITALIAN LIBYA
Fezzan
Murzuq
Persian Gulf
Tropic of Cancer
Sahara or Great Desert
Timbuktu
FRENCH WEST AFRICA
AIR
L. Chad
ANGLO-EGYPTIAN SUDAN
Gulf of Aden
ABYSSINIA
Addis Ababa
PORT. GUINEA
FRENCH GUINEA
NIGERIA
Monrovia
IVORY COAST
Gulf of Guinea
CAMEROONS
FRENCH EQUATORIAL AFRICA
Calabar
UGANDA
KENYA COLONY
Equator
GABON
BELGIAN CONGO
Loango
Leopoldville
Loanda
TANGANYIKA TERRITORY
Zanzibar
Dar es Salaam
Ascension I.
PORTUGUESE WEST AFRICA
Benguela
Mossamedes
St. Helena
MOZAMBIQUE
MADAGASCAR
Antananarivo
Tropic of Capricorn
PORTUGUESE EAST AFRICA
Kalahari Desert
TRANSVAAL
Walvis B.
Lüderitz
Delagoa B.
Durban
Pietermaritzburg
CAPE PROVINCE
UNION OF SOUTH AFRICA
Cape Town
C. of Good Hope
C. Agulhas
Port Elizabeth
Tristan D'Acunha
Reference to Colours
British ... Pink
French ... Purple
Spanish ... Dark Green
Italian ... Yellow
Portuguese Light Green
Belgian ... Light Brown
Independent Dark Brown
Mandated Areas lined
W. Gr.
E. Gr.
SCALE OF ENGLISH MILES
Stanfords Geograph. Estabt.

TO THE MEMORY

OF

ANDREW DALE

(Sometime Magistrate in Northern Rhodesia)

AND

MUNGALO

(AN AFRICAN CHIEF)

MEN I WAS PRIVILEGED TO CALL MY FRIENDS

FOREWORD.

By the Right Hon. SIR F. D. LUGARD, G.C.M.G.

(Formerly Governor-General of Nigeria).

OF the making of books on Africa there is no end—especially of the travel and tourist type—but books which combine half a lifetime of the closest contact with, and work among Africans with a profound study of the best English and French authors on the subject are as rare as they are welcome.

Born in South Africa and with seventeen years' experience as missionary and pioneer, Mr. Smith has shown himself in his already published works to be a competent student of African languages and of African mentality, while the extent of his reading, as evidenced by the references in the present modest volume, is amazing. He reviews the complex problems which face the Administrator and the Missionary with a breadth of view and an insight which command admiration, even if in rare instances the reader may not wholly share his conclusions. His study of Islam in Africa is particularly liberal and illuminating.

I can heartily recommend this little volume to those who desire to get at the facts and I know of none which I have found more instructive.

F. D. LUGARD

AUTHOR'S PREFACE.

"I BEG to direct your attention to Africa."

These words, so strangely unemotional to our ears, were spoken by David Livingstone to members of the University of Cambridge on December 4th, 1857. His journey across Africa had made his name famous. On his return to England, universities and learned societies vied with each other in doing him honour. At Cambridge the Vice-Chancellor presided over the meeting in the venerable Senate House which was crowded with graduates, undergraduates and visitors. The plain, single-minded missionary was accorded a reception that an Emperor might envy. And at the conclusion of his address he launched an appeal which was destined to have a tremendous effect upon men and movements in after days: "I beg to direct your attention to Africa. I know that in a few years I shall be cut off in that country, which is now open; do not let it be shut again! I go back to Africa to try to make an open path for commerce and Christianity; do you carry out the work which I have begun. I leave it with you."

For as long as I can remember, David Livingstone has been my hero—my master. And when the

Primitive Methodist Conference did me the honour of appointing me to this lectureship, I felt that in the choice of my subject I could not do better than follow his lead and direct your attention to Africa. I was born in Africa and the happiest years of my maturity have been spent there. To study its history and its peoples has always been my delight. My thoughts naturally gravitate thither. And in these days when the problems arising from the contact of races and cultures cause grave concern to all thinking men, there are reasons why, apart from my personal predilections, your attention should be directed to Africa. I fear that my treatment of the subject may be summary. The space at my disposal does not admit of detailed examination of all the questions. Some indeed, the problems caused by the immigration of Indians, for example, must be passed over entirely; and others, such as the liquor-traffic, can be barely mentioned. But so far as the limits allow I shall endeavour to state the problems fairly and to indicate where in my judgment the solution is to be found.

So, I beg to direct your attention to Africa.

EDWIN W. SMITH.

Walton-on-Thames,
February 27th, 1926.

ACKNOWLEDGMENTS.

I AM grateful to gentlemen, experts in their several departments, who after reading chapters of my book in manuscript have favoured me with valuable suggestions: to wit, Sir Humphrey Leggett, D.S.O., chairman for the past six years of the East African section of the London Chamber of Commerce, and Mr. H. Worsley, General Manager of the British Cotton Growing Association, who have read Chapter V; Dr. J. Howard Cook, formerly of Uganda, who has read Chapter VI; Sir Godfrey Lagden, sometime Resident Commissioner in Basutoland, who has read Chapter VII; the Rev. W. W. Cash, D.S.O., author of *The Moslem World in Revolution* and general secretary of the Church Missionary Society, who has read Chapter IX; and Major Hanns Vischer, secretary of the Colonial Office Advisory Committee on Native Education, who has read Chapter XI. Needless to say, none of these gentlemen is responsible for the opinions I have expressed. My friends and colleagues, the Revs. J. C. Mantripp, C. P. Groves, B.D., and H. B. Hardy, M.A., have read the entire manuscript and helped me materially by their criticisms. I also wish to thank the able custodians of the magnificent library of the Royal Colonial Institute who have always been ready and courteous in their assistance.

I ought to add that the substance of Chapter VIII appeared as an article in *The East and The West* for April, 1924; and part of Chapter X in the International Missionary Review for January, 1922. The Editors have kindly given permission for me to use these.

Lastly and supremely, I thank Sir Frederick Lugard, who, in the midst of his abundant labours, has kindly given time to read the book and to write an Introduction. Sir Frederick's connexion with Africa dates back to 1885, when as a young soldier he went to the Sudan. Since then he has occupied many responsible positions, culminating in the Governor-Generalship of Nigeria. Now as a member of the Mandates Commission of the League of Nations, and in other capacities, he is doing work for which we all honour him.

E. W. S.

CONTENTS.

CHAPTER IV.

CHAPTER V.

CHAPTER VI.

CHAPTER VII.

CHAPTER VIII.

CHAPTER IX.

CHAPTER X.

CHAPTER XI.

EPILOGUE

THE GOLDEN STOOL

—o—

CHAPTER I.

WHEREIN, FOR REASONS WHICH WILL PRESENTLY APPEAR, IS TOLD THE STORY OF THE GOLDEN STOOL OF ASHANTI.

I.

IN the interior of Gold Coast Colony, West Africa, lies the land of Ashanti, known to our fathers as the seat of a fierce barbarism that had its centre in the capital—Kumasi. The Wesleyan missionary, Thomas Birch Freeman, styled it "that bloody city."

Early in the 18th century there came to the court of Osai Tutu, the fourth King of Ashanti, a celebrated magician named Anotchi, who announced that he was specially commissioned by Onyame,

Note.—My authorities for this chapter are W. W. CLARIDGE, *A History of the Gold Coast and Ashanti* (1915) ; *Ashanti, Report for* 1921 (Colonial Reports, No. 1142) ; R. S. RATTRAY, *Ashanti* (1923), Chapters XXIII and XXIV.

the God of the sky, to make Ashanti a great and powerful nation. In the presence of the King and a great multitude he drew down from heaven a black cloud from which issued the rumblings of thunder and a wooden stool. The stool sank slowly through the air till it rested upon the King's knees without touching the earth. Except for the gold which partially covered it, the stool was such as Africans commonly use. Anotchi proclaimed that it contained the *sunsum* (the soul) of the Ashanti people, that with it was bound up their power, their honour, their welfare, and that if ever it were captured or destroyed the nation would perish.

Thereafter the Stool was cherished as the most sacred possession of the tribe. It was never allowed to touch the ground. On the rare occasions when it was brought out, it was placed on an elephant skin spread upon the ground and was covered with a cloth of a special kind. Not even the King ever sat upon it. Whenever on great occasions its power was evoked the King would pretend three times to sit upon it and would then seat himself upon his own stool and rest his arm upon the Golden Stool. Once a year it was carried in solemn procession, under its own umbrella and accompanied by its own attendants who in pomp and number exceeded the attendants of the King who walked behind it.

When, some time after the appearance of the Stool, the King of Denkyira, who claimed the over-lordship of Ashanti, sent to collect the customary tribute, consisting of a brass pan filled with gold dust, together with the favourite wife and the favourite son of every chief, the Ashanti people, emboldened by possession of the Golden Stool, resisted his demands. In the war which followed, the King of Denkyira and his Queen were captured and beheaded and the golden fetters they had worn were taken to embellish the Golden Stool. Later on, the chief of a neighbouring territory arrogantly made for himself a replica of the sacred emblem. The King of Ashanti led an army against him, cut off his head, and melted the gold that adorned the rival stool. The gold was cast into two masks representing the face of the impious chief and these were hung as trophies upon the Golden Stool.

As time went on the power of the King of Ashanti increased enormously and every victorious advance added to the prestige of the Golden Stool. The extension of their dominions brought the Ashantis in the early years of last century to the sea-coast, where English forts had been built. Much of the subsequent history of the contact between the two races must be passed over. Frequent conflicts took place, culminating, in 1873, in the march of Sir Garnet Wolseley to Kumasi. After capturing and burning the town he concluded a treaty with the King. Fourteen years later Prempeh became King of Ashanti and in the early years of his reign peace and prosperity returned. But in 1893 trouble arose again and because Prempeh would not accept a British protectorate over his country, nor stop the raiding of the coast tribes by his people, nor grant facilities for trade, an expedition was sent against him under Colonel Sir Francis Scott, who in 1896 occupied Kumasi with his troops. There was no fighting on this occasion. Not a shot was fired. At the time this was put down to the promptitude with which the British forces carried out the operations, but we know now that the Ashantis feared to take the Golden Stool to a war in which they were sure to be defeated, and had therefore decided to offer no opposition. King Prempeh was sent into banishment from which he was not allowed to return until 1925.

Men of the King's bodyguard who were the custodians of the Stool carried it off into the forest after Prempeh's arrest and deposited it at the village of Wawase, where a special hut was built for it. Guardians were appointed to secure its safety. The British resident at Kumasi, who regarded the Stool as the symbol of the Ashanti kingly power, wished very much to gain possession of it, but all attempts failed to discover its whereabouts.

In December, 1899, an Ashanti youth offered to reveal its hiding-place to Sir Frederick Hodgson, the Governor of the Gold Coast. A small force of Hausa troops went with the Governor's private secretary, Captain Armitage, to bring in the trophy. They disguised the traitor as a soldier and when they came to a village put him into a hammock and caused porters to carry him so that he might pass as an invalid trooper. It is uncertain whether the youth had really been sent, as he professed, by the guardians of the Golden Stool, or whether, having discovered the stool, he was acting on his own initiative because he had some motive for betraying its position. Perhaps he was merely deceiving the Governor. However that may be, the nearer they approached their destination the greater became the nervousness of the unhappy youth. One night he escaped and took refuge with a chief to whom he revealed the purpose of the expedition. Captain Armitage discovered him next morning, and learning what had taken place tried to persuade the chief that the youth was mad and that his ravings were not to be believed. Recovering their guide they went on and finally near a village some twenty-five miles north-east of Kumasi the boy led them by night along a path which he said would take them to the Golden Stool; but his nerve failed at that point; neither persuasion nor threats could induce him to guide the party farther, and they were compelled to return empty-handed.

In March, 1900, Sir Frederick Hodgson visited Kumasi with the intention of clearing up the mystery of the Golden Stool. He summoned the chiefs and people to a meeting to be held on the 28th, and they came—outwardly submissive, but inwardly boiling over with indignation. Captain Armitage's expedition, artfully conducted as it was, had aroused the nation's suspicions. It needed but a spark to set the land ablaze.

That spark was supplied by the Governor. He addressed the assembly through an interpreter, and, after telling them that King Prempeh would not be allowed to return to Ashanti, proceeded to make several demands, the principal being for the delivery of the Golden Stool.

According to a transcript of his speech forwarded by him to the Colonial Secretary this is what Sir Frederick Hodgson said:

> " There is one matter which I should like to talk to you about. I want first to ask a question of the King of Bekwai.[1] King, I want to ask you this question. You were put on the stool not very long ago. What would you have done to a man sitting on your right hand who kept back part of the stool equipment when you were enstooled ? "
>
> *King of Bekwai* : " I have no power myself ; my power is the government."
>
> *Hodgson* : " Then you would have reported the matter to me to deal with."
>
> *King of Bekwai* : " Yes."
>
> *Hodgson* : " And you would have expected me either to get you the equipment or to punish the man ? "
>
> *King of Bekwai* : " Yes."
>
> *Hodgson* : " Now, kings and chiefs, you have heard what the King of Bekwai has said upon the point I raised. What must I do to the man, whoever he is, who has failed to give to the Queen, who is the paramount power in this country, the stool to which she is entitled ? Where is the Golden Stool ? Why am I not sitting on the Golden Stool at this moment ? I am the representative of the paramount power ; why have you relegated me to this chair ? Why did you not take the opportunity of my coming to Kumasi to bring the Golden Stool and give it to me to sit upon ? However, you may be quite sure that although the Govern-

[1] This was a local chief ; they were called kings in those days.

> ment has not yet received the Golden Stool at your hands, it will rule over you with the same impartiality and with the same firmness as if you had produced it."

A singularly foolish speech! An excellent example of the blunders that are made through ignorance of the African mind! The Governor regarded the Stool as a kind of Stone of Scone upon which the kings of Ashanti were seated at their accession, a symbol of supreme authority, and hence, as the representative of Queen Victoria, he naturally expected to have it brought out as his throne. As a matter of fact, no King of Ashanti had ever sat upon it. It was held in reverence by the people as being, not an appurtenance of the kingly office, but the embodiment of the nation's soul. If the Governor had known the real significance of the Stool in the mind of the people he would not have reproached the chiefs in this manner. This much may be said in his defence—he blundered in ignorance.

The speech was received by the assembly in silence. But the chiefs returned home to prepare for war. Within a week fighting had commenced.

II.

The meeting described was held on March 28th. Three days later the Governor sent Captain Armitage with forty-five soldiers to get possession of the Golden Stool. The wretched youth already mentioned led the party along a faintly visible track in the forest and brought them to a hut beneath whose floor, he declared, the sacred emblem lay buried. It was not there, however, and evidently the soil had never been disturbed. The discomfited party set out to return to Kumasi, were ambushed on the road, and had to fight their way through. Within a very short time Kumasi was completely beleaguered by the insurgent Ashantis. Reinforcements came up from the coast and increased the garrison to seven hundred: twenty-nine Europeans, including four women, and the remainder native troops and camp-followers. Towards the end of June the Governor, with some European officers and 600 Hausa soldiers, fought his way through the besiegers to the coast, leaving three European officers and a hundred Hausas to carry on with three weeks' rations. Not until July 15th did the relieving column under Colonel James Willcocks succeed, after a magnificent march from the coast amid appalling difficulties, in raising the siege. There is no need to dwell upon the terrible sufferings endured by the tiny garrison, most of whom were found too weak to stand when relief arrived. Fighting went on until towards the end of December. The total casualties in this little war numbered 1,007 on the British side. Of our British officers, nine were killed, six died of disease, and forty-three were wounded. How many of the Ashantis were killed and wounded is not known. What the affair cost in money I do not know. Certainly it was a heavy price to pay for a blunder.

Ashanti was formally annexed as a British

possession. In the settlement nothing was said about the Golden Stool.

III.

Twenty years later, a quarrel arose over the ownership of land at the village of Wawase where, apparently, the Stool had been hidden all this time. The Chief Commissioner—as the British official was styled—thought it well to make an inspection before giving a decision in the dispute. He had no idea, it is evident, that he was going to where the Stool was kept, but the guardians of the Stool were not convinced on this point and as soon as they heard of his intention of proceeding to Wawase they conveyed their charge secretly to a place called Abuabugya.

In August, 1920, a chief named Esubonten desired to have a new road made between Abuabugya and a neighbouring town, and the British Government undertook the work. At a certain point the overseer-in-charge saw that by diverting the road in a fresh direction the construction would be rendered easier. He gave his orders accordingly. The native headman of the place (a man named Danso) was greatly perturbed by this change of plan. As a matter of fact, he was in charge of the Golden Stool and had buried it thereabouts, but owing to the clearance of some bush, could not distinguish the exact spot where it lay. His fears were not unwarranted. One of the workmen drove his pick into a box hidden in the soil, and his exclamations of surprise drew his mates to the place. Danso hastened thither and tried hard to get them away, but their curiosity was aroused and it was not until he assured them that the box contained a smallpox fetish that they would leave it alone. They were, however, only half-convinced by what he said.

That night Danso, with the help of some old men, put the Golden Stool into a tin trunk and carried it off to the house of a man named Yankyira. They took a solemn oath not to reveal the secret to others. But the road-makers had seen too much, and evidently subsequent reflection led them to realise what had happened. Perhaps they babbled. Three days later a man named Seniagya, who by descent was a Stool Carrier and had become a Christian, turned up at the village. What arguments he employed are not known, but he persuaded Danso and Yankyira to strip the Stool of its gold and golden ornaments and to share the booty with him. Another young man named Yogo, who chanced to pass at the time, claimed and received a share.

The desecration of the Stool soon became known to the chiefs of Kumasi. They discovered that a certain native goldsmith had received and melted down one of the Golden Bells and that the Golden Fetters had been pawned for thirty shillings. Most of the rest of the gold had disappeared.

When it gradually spread abroad the news caused great excitement among the people. At first it seemed incredible to them that their own fellow-countrymen should have perpetrated such an atrocious deed; when they could no longer doubt, their anger against the impious culprits waxed hot and had not the police hurried the men off to gaol they would have been torn limb from limb. Wisely determining to leave the case in the hands of the chiefs, the Government limited its action to seeing fair play and to having the last word in determining what punishment should finally be inflicted upon the prisoners.

The provincial chiefs, summoned to the capital, conducted a public inquiry which lasted several days. They invited the ministers of various religious denominations to be present. The result of the inquiry was drawn up in terms which are worth quoting. The court found that the men named—Seniagya, Danso, Yankyira, Yogo, together with Kujo-Roku, the goldsmith—"being natives of Ashanti and subjects of the Gold Stool of the Ashanti nation, did expose, steal, destroy and otherwise unlawfully deal with and use the said Gold Stool, thereby betraying the said Ashanti nation and laying it open to disgrace and ridicule, and debasing the name and fame of Ashanti, much to the annoyance and provocation of all people, young and old, thereby giving occasion for disturbance and bloodshed, but for the intervention of Government."

The chiefs recommended that these men should be put to death, but the Government substituted banishment for the supreme penalty. Esubonten, whose duty it had been to guard the Stool, was found guilty of negligence and was deposed from his chieftainship and banished. Of eight other persons who were accused of buying the ornaments of the Stool, five were acquitted and the other three were ordered "to swear fetish" before the chiefs, and were fined. One of them agreed forthwith to pay £100 and the chiefs were so pleased by his ready compliance that they reduced the fine to £70, one sheep and two bottles of whiskey.

The fines having been paid, the ceremony of the oath followed. The "Fetish" was brought in, attended by its own retinue and carried beneath the umbrella that always figures in Ashanti ceremonials. It was treated, in fact, as if it were a Chief of high standing. When the expensive carpet covering it was removed, the "Fetish" was revealed to be a couple of brass bells of unequal size. They were probably bells that had been attached to the Golden Stool.

Two of the chiefs came forward and after removing their head-gear, each laid a hand on a bell. A third chief then removed one of his sandals and ordered one of the guilty men to put his foot upon it. Placing his foot upon the man's, the chief administered the oath in these terms: "I swear by the great oath Kromanti that if I am in possession of any of the ornaments of the Golden Stool, or have given possession of them to any person to hold in trust for me, may the Fetish kill me!" The chief then held the larger of the two bells to the man's mouth and he touched it with his tongue three times while one of the attendants kept ringing the second bell. After invoking some spirit the chief placed the large bell three times on the man's head, and again the other bell was rung. A fresh bottle of whiskey was then opened and a wineglassful was handed to the chief who spilt three drops on the ground and emptied the remainder on the man's head.

The two other men undertook to find sureties for the amount of the fine inflicted upon them.

IV.

Why, it may be asked, did not the Government, which in times past had tried so hard to secure the Golden Stool, take this opportunity of seizing it? The answer to this question provides one of the most interesting features of the whole affair.

In earlier days the authorities blundered through sheer ignorance. But recently they had appointed an anthropologist whose business it was to study Ashanti customs and beliefs, and this officer, Captain Rattray, a man of conspicuous ability and long experience, endowed with much tact and wholly sympathetic in his attitude towards the people, had investigated and reported on the history of the Stool. What he said enlightened the Government as to the true nature of the reverence in which the Ashantis held this ancient shrine—the shrine of the nation's soul. Every native of Ashanti believes that a stool is the repository of a man's soul. They place miniature fetters around the central support of a stool, "to chain down the soul to it." The Golden Stool holds the soul, not of any individual but of the nation. The idea may seem fantastic, but it can be readily understood why, believing as they do, the Ashantis revere the Stool so highly, and why they went to war with Britain rather than surrender it. They would have gone to war again in 1920 had the Government taken advantage of the opportunity to seize the Stool. From such a conflict the timely researches of Captain Rattray saved Britain and Ashanti. For, realising at last what the Stool stood for, the Government made it known that so far as it was concerned there was no longer any need to conceal the Stool, and that no attempt would be made in future to interfere, so long as the Ashanti did not make use of it for seditious purposes.

No declaration of the British Government, perhaps, was ever received with such joy by the Ashantis as was this.

When the women of Ashanti wished to offer Princess Mary a wedding present, their gift took the form of a Silver Stool, a replica of one that belonged to their principal Queen Mother. At a great public assembly this venerable lady presented it to Lady Guggisberg, the wife of the Governor, for transmission to the Princess. In her speech she said :

"I place this stool in your hands. It is a gift on her wedding-day for the King's child, Princess Mary. Ashanti stool-makers have carved it, and Ashanti silversmiths have embossed it. . . It may be that the King's child has heard of the Golden Stool of Ashanti. That is the Stool which contains the soul of the Ashanti nation. All we women of Ashanti thank the Governor exceedingly because he has declared to us that the English will never again ask us to hand over that stool. This stool we give gladly. It does not contain our soul as our Golden Stool does, but it contains all the love of us Queen Mothers and of our women. The spirit of this love we have bound to the stool with silver fetters just as we are accustomed to bind our own spirits to the base of our stools. . . We pray the great God Nyankopon, on whom men lean and do not fall, whose day of worship is a Saturday and whom the Ashanti serve just as she serves Him, that He may give the King's child and her husband long life and happiness, and finally, when she sits upon this silver stool, which the women of Ashanti have made for their white Queen Mother, may she call us to mind."

V.

It must now be explained why this tale has been told at such length. The story is romantic in itself, but it has been told for a purpose.

The title of this lecture will have reminded my readers of the famous Golden Bough. In writing the book which bears that title, Sir James Frazer started from the legend of the priesthood of Nemi—the beautiful lake in the neighbourhood of Rome. The rule of the priesthood was that whoever aspired to the office had first to attempt the life of the actual holder of it; having slain him he succeeded to the office and held it until he himself was slain in turn by a stronger or craftier man. The candidate had to break off a bough from a certain tree which grew within the sanctuary at Nemi. This fateful branch, according to ancient opinion, was that Golden Bough which Virgil tells us Æneas plucked before he essayed his perilous journey to the world of the dead.

It is a strange story, and the illustrious author, when he sought for an explanation of it, was led from point to point till he had filled seven large volumes with an enormous collection of facts—to say nothing of interesting theories—concerning primitive society and religion.

Now the Golden Stool might lead on to as far-reaching an inquiry as the Golden Bough led Sir James Frazer. But this lecture is limited to one small volume.

There is here in miniature the story of a conflict of cultures. People of an advanced civilization encounter a barbaric nation, many of whose customs bewilder and shock them. War ensues. The white men show themselves ignorant of the black man's beliefs, beliefs which they label as superstitions. The black man treasures his ancient heritage and is prepared to suffer and to die rather than surrender it. Blunders are committed which can only be remedied by the aid of anthropology. Learning by experience to respect the African outlook upon life, the British authority wins the loyalty of its subjects. But the African social system suffers in the conflict that has taken place. The King is deposed and his authority is invested in the British

Crown. Limits are placed upon the authority of the native chiefs. They retain the semblance of power, under the supervision of the suzerain, but are not allowed to inflict capital punishment. Meanwhile other forces are at work. Christianity enters and gains considerable influence. In the story of the Golden Stool, the villain of the piece is a Christian, who shows himself so far emancipated from the ancient restraints that he robs the sacred emblem of his nation. Here are disintegrative forces at work. What is taking the place of the old social bond now crumbling before the advance of the alien culture? That new habits are being formed, which cannot be for the welfare of the people, is seen in the incongruous use of whiskey in an ancient religious rite.

Thus the history of the Golden Stool brings us face to face with some of the many problems arising out of the conflict of cultures in Africa.

CHAPTER II.

Wherein are set forth Some of the Conditions in the New Africa, in the form of a Contrast between 1876 and 1926.

I.

IN 1876, David Livingstone, " the greatest Christian of the nineteenth century," had been dead three years. During his lifetime, and largely through his own explorations and the stimulus he gave to other travellers, the African continent became known, as it had never been known before, to the outside world. In the early years of the century Arrowsmith presented the African Exploration Society with a map from which all hypothetical features had been removed and which showed the interior as a blank. European enterprise had been busy upon the West Coast since the fifteenth century, in South Africa since the seventeenth, but it was not till the thirties of last century that the geographical problem of the Niger was solved, and not until the fifties was the Zambezi explored. By 1873 many of the chief features of the continent had been revealed, but some were still obscure,

In 1874, soon after Livingstone's body (minus the heart, which remained in Africa) was laid to rest in Westminster Abbey, Henry M. Stanley, who had been fired by the news of Livingstone's death with a resolution to continue his work, was asked by the Editor of *The Daily Telegraph* what remained to be done. He replied: "The outlet of Lake Tanganyika is undiscovered. We know nothing scarcely—except what Speke has sketched out—of Lake Victoria; we do not even know whether it consists of one or many lakes, and therefore the sources of the Nile are still unknown. Moreover, the western half of the African continent is still a white blank."[1] Under the auspices of *The Daily Telegraph* and *The New York Herald*, Stanley set out a few weeks later to settle these problems, "and to investigate and report upon the haunts of the slave-traders." With one possible exception, namely, Livingstone's journey across Africa in 1853-6, Stanley's expedition, which in 999 days traversed the continent from east to west, surpassed all others in importance for the future history of Africa. In June, 1876, Stanley was circumnavigating Lake Tanganyika. When he emerged from the mouth of the Congo in 1877 the last of the great geographical secrets had been wrested from the Dark Continent.

Since that date much has been done to fill in the details of the map. A great deal still remains to be accomplished in the way of accurate survey, but

[1] H. M. STANLEY, *Through the Dark Continent* (1878), Vol. I, p. 3.

now it can be said that Africa is known through and through.

II.

Speaking of his great journey Stanley said :[1]

> " I declare solemnly to you that, from a distance of ten miles from Bagamoyo, my starting place on the east coast of Africa, until I sighted an English flag at the mast-head of a merchant river steamer on the Congo, along a journey of 7,600 miles, I never saw a flag, or an emblem, or symbol, flagstaff, erection of wood, stone or iron, to indicate that I had come across civilized, or semi-civilized, power or authority ; the authority I encountered everywhere being the authority of independent native chiefs, exacting tribute on the eastern half, and opposing violence on the western half."

In this respect the map of Africa presents a very striking contrast to-day. In 1876 the modern scramble which has resulted in parcelling out almost the entire continent among the Powers of Europe was only on the eve of beginning.

This, in brief, was the situation in 1876. Egypt was still under the suzerainty of Turkey ; the country was bankrupt and this year saw the beginning of the Dual Control which lasted with some interruption for six years, when France retired and Great Britain was left alone to pursue, through Lord Cromer, the beneficent work which transformed Egypt into a prosperous country. From

[1] At the Berlin Conference. H. M. STANLEY, *The Congo and the Founding of its Free State* (1885), Vol. II, p. 411.

about 1819 Egyptian authority had been extending south along the Nile up to the Albert Nyanza. The Mahdi had not yet appeared on the scene, but the slave-trading and misgovernment against which General Gordon, then in Egyptian service as Governor-General of the Sudan, was heroically and vainly struggling, were sowing the seeds of the revolt which broke out in 1881.

In 1876 the Suez Canal had been opened seven years. This was an event of the highest consequence for the future development of East Africa, since the protection of the great line of communication between the metropolis and India became of paramount interest in British policy.

Italy had not set foot on African soil in 1876. Tripolitania and Tunisia (later to come under the control respectively of Italy and France) still formed part of the Ottoman Empire.

Of all the European Powers France only at that time had embarked upon a policy of appropriation with definite ends in view. Ever since she had lost her colonies in the Napoleonic wars her eyes had been fixed on Africa as the region which afforded the best opportunities of regaining an Empire. In 1830 she began to take possession of Algeria—an acquisition which, up to 1864, is said to have cost her 150,000 men and £120,000,000. With the appointment in 1854 of General Faidherbe as Governor of Senegal began the era of conquest which has secured to France the largest share of North Africa—a conquest which the French regard as the means for creating a more harmonious order. France had also secured ports on the Red Sea. Her policy received fresh impetus when after the war of 1870 she felt greater need of recouping herself in Africa for her losses in Europe.

As early as 1415, Portugal had begun the modern partition of Africa by the capture of Ceuta; she had built forts on the West Coast in the 15th century and had established herself on the East Coast in the 16th. In 1876 she held territory at Cape Verde on the West Coast, and along the shores of Angola south of the Congo. By arbitration she had secured in 1875 the very useful port of Delagoa Bay.

In 1876 Spain was in possession, as now, of Fernando Po.

The only other European flag which flew over African soil in 1876 was the Union Jack. For the previous eighty years British explorers had been busy on the Niger, but no territory in the interior had been occupied. Only small patches at Sierra Leone, on the Gambia and on the Gold Coast, and the port of Lagos were in British possession. Great Britain had no intention, no desire, to extend her dominions in West Africa. The policy formulated by a Parliamentary Committee in 1865 was still in force: all further extension of territory or assumption of government, or new treaty offering any protection to native tribes, was held to be inexpedient. In South Africa, the borders of Cape Colony did not extend much beyond the Orange River. The area of the diamond fields around Kimberley was acquired in 1876 by arrangement with the

Boers and Griquas. Cecil Rhodes had then been six years in Africa, and, in the intervals of making money out of diamonds, was dreaming of painting red most of the map of the world. Bechuanaland had not yet come under British rule, nor Zululand, nor the Transkeian territories. Basutoland had been taken under our protection in 1868. Natal was a British colony, but south of the island of Socotra which was occupied in 1876 there was no other British possession along the east coast.

The two Dutch republics, the Orange Free State and the Transvaal, were independent in 1876. So were Liberia and Abyssinia.

To sum up. The total area controlled by Europeans in 1876 did not exceed one-tenth of the continent. All the rest of Africa was held by independent African, or semi-African, states and tribes. Now, in 1926, barely one-tenth of Africa is free from European domination. Indeed if we remember that the republic of Liberia is controlled financially by the United States, and that Egypt, while nominally a sovereign power, is still garrisoned by British troops, we must conclude that Abyssinia, covering an area of 350,000 square miles, is the only entirely independent State left in Africa.

How this startling change has taken place during the fifty years since 1876 has often been told,[1] and the story need not be repeated here at any length. Stanley's great journey precipitated the

[1] See J. S. Keltie, *The Partition of Africa* (1893+); Sir E. Hertslet, *The Map of Africa by Treaty* (3rd Edition, 1909); Sir H. H. Johnston, *A History of the Colonization of Africa by alien races* (1899), *The Opening Up of Africa* (1911).

scramble. King Leopold took the initiative by calling the Brussels Conference of 1876—a conference which might have led to international agreement and to something like a system of Mandates such as regulate the holding of the late German colonies to-day under the League of Nations. An International African Association was actually formed, but it soon became evident that each nation would, like Hal o' the Wynd, fight for its own hand. The Congo State, founded for the International Association, became, for all intents and purposes, the private domain of King Leopold, and its government a scandal to Christendom until Belgium took it over as a colony. Germany, unified after the war of 1870 and enriched with a rapidly developing industry, entered suddenly into the scramble by raising her flag, first in Damaraland and then in East Africa in 1884. By this action France was spurred to fresh activities. Great Britain saw that if she did not bestir herself she would be left behind in the race, and urged on by commercial companies, missionary societies and enterprising individuals, intervened at last—tardily, but very effectively. Portugal awoke out of a long period of dormancy and succeeded in establishing some of her fanciful claims based upon real and alleged discoveries in the past. Italy came in later and acquired Eritrea, part of Somaliland, Tripolitania and Cyrenaica. Her ambitions concerning Abyssinia met with a rude check on the battlefield of Dogali in 1887. Spain also entered into the competition and gained 70,000 square miles of the Sahara and the region on the Muni river, south of the Cameroons. Later her protectorate was recognized over a narrow strip of Morocco which in recent years has cost her heavily in men, money and prestige.

The motives underlying this partition of Africa need not be described here at any length : we shall understand them better when we have reached a later chapter of this book. A French writer says that the European invasion was guided one-tenth by civilizing zeal and nine-tenths by the bait of gain. Commercial, strategical and philanthropic reasons entered into it. It must be remembered that in the nineteenth century the population of Europe increased threefold, and that this meant an enlarged demand for food, for more abundant supplies of raw materials, and for new markets for the products of the factories. The improving standard of living led to a call for such luxuries—pneumatic tyres on cycles and cars, for example—as only the tropics could supply. No government could allow traders to enter the almost unknown and savage lands of Africa without affording them protection ; nor could any humane government allow the peoples of Africa to be exploited by uncontrolled and irresponsible European citizens. To such considerations must be added the fact that the conscience of Europe had been aroused to the iniquity of the slave-trade, and it soon became apparent that the healing of this open sore of the world (as Livingstone called it) could not be accomplished by treaties made in Brussels or Berlin, nor by patrolling the coasts with gunboats; there must be active intervention in the interior, which again meant commerce and government control. Cynics may sneer at this alleged philanthropic motive, and it cannot be denied that sometimes it has been little more than a cloak for sinister deeds, but it was a real motive. Humanitarian and religious sentiment has generally supported intervention. At certain critical moments the Christian public of England urged their government with persistence and success along this path. It cannot be denied that other motives have been operant. The French have undoubtedly been stimulated by a consciousness that North Africa supplies fine recruits to supplement her decreasing man-power for the defence of her home frontiers.

Whatever the motives, and whatever the results, the last fifty years have drawn Africa into the orbit of European politics. For good or evil, the vast majority of African peoples has been brought under the sway of white men.

III.

Commerce has been referred to and we must return to it later. Here it will be sufficient to note that the opening up of Africa by the explorers, great and small, has revealed the vast wealth, actual and potential, of the continent. It is now known that it is far from being what Defoe said of it, " the most desolate, desert and inhospitable country in the world, even Greenland and Nova Zembla not excepted." On the contrary, its mineral and agricultural opulence makes it one of the most valuable quarters of the globe. During these fifty years much has been done to turn its resources to account—and only a beginning has been made as yet. A few figures to show the growth of commerce with Africa are all that are needed here to point the contrast between 1876 and 1926. It is said that in 1815 the total value of the commerce (including slaves) did not exceed £30,000,000. Of this amount the exports formed one-half, and fifty per cent. of them came from Egypt and other Mediterranean countries. In 1876 these figures were doubled. In 1925 the total value of the commerce was not less than £600,000,000.

It can with safety be foretold that this striking increase in the economic value of Africa to the outside world will grow more and more in years to come.

IV.

When my parents landed at Algoa Bay, South Africa, in May, 1874, it took them, with delays on the road, twenty-six days to reach Aliwal North by coach—a distance of 300 miles. In 1876, the year of my birth, only 109 miles of railway were open in Cape Colony and only a short narrow-gauge line of two miles (the first railway in Africa) in Natal. The other railways in Africa at that time were the Egyptian (less than 1,000 miles), and the Algerian (about 300 miles). At present there are some 35,000 miles of railways in the whole continent.

These lines have been built partly for strategic or military purposes, but mainly to provide highways for commerce. The mines have acted as magnets, drawing the railways farther inland. The revolution that they have caused in the life of Africa is beyond all measurement.

Let us visualise one picture.

Here in 1876 is Henry M. Stanley crossing the continent from Zanzibar to the mouth of the Congo. He travels on foot, except when he can launch on some lake or navigable river the teakwood boat which his men carry laboriously in sections. He engages 300 men to carry 18,000 pounds weight of stores—beads, wire, medicines, provisions, calico, tents, and other articles. With the wives of some of the men and a small armed escort, his attendants number 356 in all—very few of whom will survive to see their homes again: death by disease, accident, and hostile spears will take the majority. At an average rate of seven miles a day they reach the southern shore of Lake Victoria, after passing through thirst and famine belts, and encountering what Stanley calls "bellicose exhibitions" on the part of unfriendly natives who try to block his way. After visiting Uganda, he strikes south to circumnavigate Lake Tanganyika, and thence crosses to Nyangwe on the Congo—the point at which Livingstone was compelled to turn back. He constructs canoes, launches his boat, mans them with the remnant of his followers, and boldly strikes out along the unknown highway which no white man has ever travelled before. Whenever they reach the rapids the little fleet is painfully hauled over the rocks and launched again. Now they paddle between banks lined with cannibals who shout, Meat! Meat! and then pursue them in their canoes. Stanley fought thirty-two small battles on the Congo, the only alternative being, as Holman Bentley said, "to walk quietly into their cooking-pots and submit to dissection and the processes of digestion." So he wins his way with indomitable energy and all the while he is dreaming. Looking upon the undeveloped wealth of the country, the fine promise of some tribes, the hideous barbarity of others, he sees visions of a time when "all the land will be redeemed from wildness, the industry and energy of the natives stimulated, the havoc of the slave-trade stopped and all the countries round about permeated with the nobler ethics of a higher humanity." What Africa needed, he said, was railways—he called them "a tramway"—to be "an iron bond, never to be again broken, between Africa and the more favoured continents."

Finally, Stanley and his followers stumble, haggard, crippled, diseased, to the Atlantic shore, after 999 days of travel. That was in 1877. Any tourist of to-day who wishes with a minimum of fatigue to cross Africa from west to east, or from east to west, will have a choice of easy routes. He can accomplish the journey with no more exertion than is involved in walking from one vehicle to another—and in something less than a month. If he wishes to go from Cape to Cairo, it will take longer, but it will be scarcely more arduous; by railway, motor car and river steamer he can cover the 7,000 miles in forty-five days,[1] if he is lucky enough to catch all the connections. He will probably grumble if a shower-bath and plenty of ice are not available every day!

It should be added that the motor-car is playing an enormous part in the opening up of Africa. Even the Sahara is being conquered by it. In 1922-3 two Frenchmen drove a car from Algeria to Timbuktu; in 1924 another Frenchman made the journey in sixty-four hours. Early in 1925 six cars crossed the Sahara, from Tunis to Lake Chad; and another French expedition traversed Africa, at almost its broadest part, from Donakry on the Atlantic to Massawa on the Red Sea, a distance of nearly 3,750 miles. In December, 1924, startling advertisements appeared in the papers inviting us to cross the Sahara in comfort: "London to Timbuktu in twelve days! Enjoy the most wonderful of journeys and the most thrilling of holidays!" and although this tourist scheme had to be abandoned on account of threatened raids by desert nomads, nobody doubts that the desert has been conquered, so far as motor-transport is concerned. The camel has had his day in the north, as the ox-wagon has had its day in the south. In

[1] *South and East African Year Book and Guide* for 1925, p. 362. As the crow flies the distance is about 4,200 miles. This route is *via* Albertville, Mwanza, etc.

1925 a gallant French officer and his wife motored across the continent from Algiers to Cape Town and an English officer and his wife from Cape Town to Cairo. Ten thousand cars a year are imported into South Africa. Nearly every farmer of importance possesses one and can get about easily: a fact which facilitates the exchange of ideas and stimulates progress—or the reverse. Everywhere in Africa the petrol-driven car is working a quiet (or perhaps not altogether quiet) revolution in travelling and transport of goods.

The aeroplane has also invaded Africa. In 1919 an air route was laid out by British officers between Cairo and Cape Town, aerodromes being built at twenty-four places. The following year two gallant South African officers (Van Ryneveld and Brand) flew over the route in seventy-two hours, forty minutes. During the winter of 1925-6 Mr. Alan Cobham, who had already proved it possible to breakfast in London and dine in Africa on the same day, accomplished the flight from England to Cape Town in ninety "flying hours," and flew back from Cape Town to Cairo in nine and a half days. In 1902 it took Mrs. Smith and myself fifty-three days to travel from Bulawayo to the Zambezi in an ox-wagon; Mr. Cobham covered the same distance, in the reverse direction, in two hours, forty minutes. In 1925 a scheme was launched by which it is hoped eventually to bring East Africa within six days of London, by way of the Nile. The first regular African air-service was established on the Congo, between Stanley Pool and Stanleyville, a distance of 1,000 miles, in 1921. The aeroplane has already been pressed into the service of the Missions. We may live to see our missionaries carried from London to the Kafue by aeroplane or airship.

The telegraph has also been extended in Africa. Its range in 1876 was extremely limited. By 1903 it had been carried northward from Cape Town to Ujiji on Lake Tanganyika. Since then it has gone south from Egypt across the Sudan and penetrated in all directions. In 1876 Stanley was out of the world when he reached the Victoria Nyanza. In 1914, the very day war broke out, two British officers were killed there in battle in response to telegraphic orders from London and Berlin to commence hostilities.

And "wireless," which during the war played a prominent part in Africa, is now breaking down the isolation of life in the interior. Already at the time of writing (early in 1925) news comes that in Nyasaland they are listening-in to places in South Africa. People in Nigeria hear songs that are sung in London. What will it not mean to solitary exiles to be able to hear a concert, or sermon, broadcasted from England? It is theoretically possible, if not as yet practicable, for my old colleagues in Northern Rhodesia to listen to this lecture delivered in Manchester. This certainly was never dreamt of in 1876!

The continent of Africa has shrunk to smaller dimensions—reckoned in time.

V.

Another most important fact must be noticed: the progress that has been made in conquering African diseases. Here again an effective contrast may be drawn between 1876 and 1926.

The early records of West Africa make very depressing reading. In 1823 seven schoolmasters, five of them accompanied by their wives, landed at Sierra Leone (well-named "the White Man's Grave"), in the service of the Church Missionary Society; six out of the twelve died that year, and four more within eighteen months. In twenty-five years, 109 men and women died on that mission. The Wesleyan Mission on the Gold Coast went through similar experiences: the first man who was sent out in 1835 died within six months, the next two within four months, and the next two within a month. The ill-fated Niger Expedition of 1841 lost forty-two men out of 150 within two months.

This heavy mortality has continued into more recent times. A grim story (perhaps apocryphal) is told of a newly-appointed Governor of one of the West Coast possessions, who, being a careful man, asked whether the government would pay his fare home when his time expired. After some delay he was told that the question had never previously arisen. Canon Robinson tells that when he was on the Niger in 1894 the average length of a white man's life was reckoned at two years. Miss Kingsley, writing of about the same period,[1]

[1] MARY KINGSLEY, *Travels in West Africa* (1897), pp. 681, 690.

declared that there was no other region in the world that could match West Africa for the steady kill, kill, kill that its malaria worked on the white men : eighty-five per cent. of them, she reckoned, died of fever or returned home with their health permanently wrecked.[1] The West Coast, perhaps, provides the extreme example of the unhealthiness of Africa, but in varying degrees much the same must be said concerning other tropical portions of the continent : they have levied a very heavy toll on the white race. To adapt Rudyard Kipling—"If blood be the price of *Empire*, we ha' bought it fair." "The ruby crown that Britannia wears is jewelled with British blood."

It is a truth that makes one glow with pride that even in those deadly times, there was never any lack of men and women to answer the call of duty—whether traders, officials, soldiers, or missionaries. When in the fifties John Bowen was chosen as Bishop of Sierra Leone—where his two predecessors had died within two years of their consecration—and some of his friends urged him to refuse, he replied : "If I served in the Queen's army and refused to go to a post of danger I should be dis-

[1] Roman Catholic missionaries are expected to stay out on the West Coast at least ten years at a time. A pamphlet published some seven or eight years ago entitled, "The Epic of the Dark Continent," said, "The terrible death-rate of our own Irish priests and nuns in that fateful area helps one to understand why thirty-five is the average limit of the workers' lives." Since missionaries do not go out much before they are twenty-five, it would appear that in reality ten years were the average expectation of life by the Roman Catholic missionaries on the West Coast. *West Africa*, September 5th, 1925.

graced in the eyes of men. Were I offered a bishopric in England, I might feel at liberty to decline it; one in Sierra Leone, I must accept." Two years later he was dead. This is typical of the spirit that has made possible the penetration of Africa.

What is the cause of this heavy mortality amongst white men in tropical Africa? It has generally been ascribed to "climate" and the "climate" of Africa has been held to be so bad as to rule out any prospect of successful European colonization, so far as the tropics are concerned. Mr. Benjamin Kidd said in 1898, "the attempt to acclimatize the white man in the tropics must be recognized to be a blunder of the first magnitude. All experiments based upon the idea are mere idle and empty enterprises foredoomed to failure."[1] But much research has been carried on since that time, and, while few would presume to dogmatise on the subject, the trend of expert opinion[2] seems to be towards the conclusion that not climatic factors—heat, humidity combined with heat, tropical sunshine—but rather disease is the obstacle in the white man's path. And the discovery of paramount importance that has marked the last fifty years is that these tropical diseases are preventable. The discoveries as to malarial fever, for example, which date from about 1897 and are due to such benefactors of the human race as Laveran, Manson and Ross, have entirely

[1] BENJAMIN KIDD, *The Control of the Tropics* (1898), p. 48.

[2] J. W. GREGORY, *The Menace of Colour* (1925), Chapter VIII, "Can the white man colonize in the tropics?"

altered the prospects of life in Tropical Africa We are now aware of the simple truth that if a man is never bitten by a mosquito he will never suffer from malaria: and the problem of living in the tropics has largely resolved itself into the problem of getting rid of or circumventing the particular mosquito which conveys the infection.

Other diseases endemic in the tropics, the presence of which is one of the chief causes of the Africans' backwardness, are under investigation, with promising results. It is now known that leprosy and sleeping sickness are, to some extent at least, curable and that the latter is preventable; yaws and syphilis can be cured; smallpox has been eradicated wherever vaccination has been practicable; typhoid fever and dysentery are known to be avoidable by inoculation; ankylostomiasis and other parasitic diseases can be prevented.

The impression must not be conveyed that Africa has been turned into a health resort. Far from it. But proof is forthcoming that wherever sanitary measures founded upon these modern discoveries have been properly taken, there the rate of mortality among Europeans in Africa and among Africans themselves has decreased considerably. West African conditions have changed so greatly that Sir Gordon Guggisberg, the Governor of the Gold Coast, was able in 1924 to say: "If statistics don't lie West Africa is a healthier place than London." Probably he did not intend this to be taken *au pied de la lettre*, for in another place[1] he declared that

[1] SIR GORDON GUGGISBERG, *The Keystone* (1924), p. 10.

"the married European with children has not and never will have a real home life in West Africa." This, of course, is the vital question: can Europeans live in Tropical Africa, maintain their physical and moral vigour, and rear families there equal in stamina to the parent stock, in the neighbourhood of black people of a much lower standard of civilisation? This remains to be proved, or disproved, but the statement is warranted that in view of physiological discoveries that have been made, and that are still being made, it is hazardous to affirm that white men can never acclimatize in Tropical Africa. At any rate, so far as disease is concerned, there seems to be no insuperable reason why that region should not become the home of a vigorous European population—if only they will obey the laws of health.[1]

VI.

Henry M. Stanley's starting point on his transcontinental journey of 1874-7 was Zanzibar, where he found Bishop Steere at work "almost single-handed" and where the Cathedral Church was already built on the site of the old slave-market. At Bagamoyo, on the mainland opposite Zanzibar, a Roman Catholic mission was founded, but from that point onward he encountered neither missionary nor mission station. Had he taken the northerly route to Victoria Nyanza he would have found two or three stations near the coast, but no more.

[1] But compare pp. 63, sqq., *infra*.

Now, as for some years past, a chain of mission stations extends from the east to the west coasts with but a break of three hundred miles in the centre, and by the time this lecture is printed, it is possible that this gap will have been closed. Krapf's seventy-year-old dream of an Apostles' Way across Africa will then have been fulfilled.

One day, when they were paddling down the Congo in January, 1877, Stanley's English companion, Francis Pocock, began to sing sadly :

> " The home land, the fair land,
> Refuge for all distressed,
> Where pain and sin ne'er enter in,
> But all is peace and rest."

Stanley bade him choose some more cheerful tune, so he sang :

> " Brightly gleams our banner,
> Pointing to the sky,
> Waving wanderers onward
> To their home on high."

These were the first Christian hymns sung (so far as there is any record) on the Congo. It was not until two years later (1879) that the Baptists commenced their mission near the coast in Congoland. In subsequent years they worked their way into the centre ; in 1926 they report one hundred and two foreign agents ; 914 African workers (679 of them paid by the Native Church) ; a Christian community of 33,889 ; 992 elementary and other schools (including four training and eleven industrial institutions) with 28,335 scholars. Many of these converts were gathered from among the tribesmen who in 1877 greeted Stanley with their cannibal cry, "Meat! Meat!" There are many other missions at work in this region.

An even more remarkable change has taken place in Uganda. In 1875 Stanley taught the king, Mtesa, his first lessons in Christianity, and fondly believed that he had made a convert of him. "Oh! that some pious, practical missionary would come here!" he wrote in his journal. "Here, gentlemen, is your opportunity!" He entrusted a letter to a Belgian officer, who was travelling home from Uganda, appealing for a mission to be established in the country—a letter which was found on the murdered body of this officer, forwarded to England by General Gordon, and published in *The Daily Telegraph* on November 15, 1875. A week later—they wasted no time in those days—the Church Missionary Society accepted the challenge, and in April, 1876, Alexander Mackay and the rest of the first party started on the long, wearisome journey to Uganda. In 1884 there were thirty-eight Baganda Christians. To-day, in the whole Protectorate of Uganda there are 500,000 Christians, Protestant and Catholic. The Anglicans have 400 schools, with 117,000 scholars; 2,000 places of worship; and a native clergy—canons and rural deans among them.

In October, 1875, the pioneers of the Livingstonia Mission steamed into Lake Nyasa. When the Jubilee was celebrated in 1925 the Mission reported a European staff of seventy-seven, a native staff of 1,120, not including 1,551 teachers, a Christian community of 58,861, 772 schools, 43,492 primary and middle school pupils, besides 126 college and High School students. One member of the original band—Dr. Laws—still remains at his post. Few living men have witnessed such changes as he has seen in the life of a people. They are so great and have come so rapidly that the younger generation know nothing of what things were like in their fathers' days. When the Livingstone film was shown in Blantyre last year, with its realistic pictures of slave-raiding, of the burning of villages, of the long lines of victims marching with yokes on their necks, it all seemed as remote to them as it did to English people. Only a few were old enough to remember the horrors of those days.

The Nyasaland mission of the Church of Scotland reports over 15,000 baptized Christians, and 300 schools with 15,000 scholars.

The story of the penetration of Africa by Christian missions cannot be continued further in these pages. The progress made is remarkable. In 1876 Christian missions had more or less occupied South Africa. In North Africa practically nothing had been done to win the Moslem population—the North African Mission was not started till 1876. Along the West Coast, from the Gambia to the Congo, Anglicans, Methodists, Presbyterians, Lutherans, and Baptists were at work. The Primitive Methodists had succeeded the Baptists on the island of Fernando Po in 1870. None of the missions had penetrated far into the interior. The Christianization of the continent can hardly be said to have begun fifty years ago. The progress that these years have witnessed is so great that Sir Harry Johnston, one of the greatest living authorities on Africa, is justified in saying : " before long, so energetic are the missionaries, the whole of Central Africa will have been Christianized, excepting along the east coast where the Arab influence is too strong to be uprooted."[1]

Testimony to this remarkable advance is borne by the records of Bible translation in Africa. In 1876 some portion of Holy Scripture had been translated into fifty of the languages : to be exact, the whole Bible into seven, the New Testament into nine others, some book of Scripture, or books, into twenty-three, and selected passages into eleven more. In 1926 translations have grown to 244, of which 180 appear on the British and Foreign Bible Society's list. The figure is made up as follows : twenty-eight complete versions of the Bible, and fifty-nine New Testaments ; some book or books in 138 other languages, and selected passages in nineteen more. That is to say, 194 translations have been issued since 1876. During the last fifty years, an average of nearly four new versions has been published every twelve months. An astonishing result when it is remembered that the existence of most of these languages was unknown in 1876. Moreover, an examination of the list in 1876 reveals the fact that, as might be expected, the languages in which translations had been made

[1] Sir H. H. Johnston, *The Backward Peoples and our Relations with them* (1920), p. 29.

were almost entirely spoken in the coastal regions. Languages of the far interior were absent from the list. Now every part of the continent is represented.

This extension of Christianity is not the least significant of the points of contrast between 1876 and 1926.

CHAPTER III.

Wherein our Problem is Stated in General Terms and an Attempt is Made to Draw up a Debit and Credit Account.

I.

WHAT do the facts set out in Chapter II mean to the Africans? It can be said, in general, that European activities during the last fifty years have created a new environment for them. The white man has arrived and has dug himself in. Year by year it is becoming less possible for the African to live in isolation from the outside world.

An American anthropologist speaks of Africa as having been from the earliest times "the battle-ground between the lighter and darker races."[1] Whether it was the cradle of the human race as some experts assert may be a matter for argument, but there is every reason to believe that a very large portion of the continent was in Palæolithic times the home of ancestors of the Negroes of to-day. Then, perhaps twenty-five thousand years

[1] R. B. Dixon, *The Racial History of Man* (1923), p. 190.

ago, perhaps ten thousand years ago, invaders belonging to the Caspian type, "white" men, began to enter Africa from the north-east, to blend with, or displace, the Negroes of the Nile valley, and to permeate large regions of north and central Africa with their superior culture.[1] Egypt had become a "white" man's country seven thousand years ago. How far the astonishing civilization of Egypt influenced the rest of the continent we do not yet know with any certainty, but there are indications that it permanently affected some remote African peoples. Unmistakable evidence of this is to be found in Nigeria.[2] The Fulani, whose origin is wrapt in mystery, trace to Egypt their fashion of hairdressing, and it is an interesting fact that the long side-locks which they wear are almost identical with those pictured on Egyptian and Cretan monuments. Certain burial practices, beliefs about the soul, the manufacture of glass, and many other things in Nigeria and elsewhere all seem to point to Egypt—though in these matters we may yet come to the conclusion that the Egyptians derived more from the Negroes than the Negroes derived from the Egyptians. Carthaginian merchants traversed the Sahara and while trading with the peoples of the Niger undoubtedly introduced elements of their civilization. The Yoruba tribes of Nigeria claim descent from them. There are traditions which seem to indicate a Persian

[1] Sir H. H. Johnston, *The Opening up of Africa* (1911), Chapters I-IV.

[2] C. K. Meek, *The Northern Tribes of Nigeria* (1925), Vol. II, pp. 160, sqq.

invasion of West Africa, and some anthropologists explain the apparent mongoloid elements in certain African tribes by imagining that Chinese led expeditions into the Sudan. More possibly the Romans left some traces of themselves during their incursions. It is difficult not to see the civilizing hand of Phœnicians or other pre-Islamic Semites in the stone buildings of Southern Rhodesia and their associated gold-diggings and irrigation works. Still later, in the seventh century of our era, came the Arabian followers of Muhammad who profoundly affected the African culture wherever they penetrated.

The extent of this foreign influence must not be exaggerated, but all these movements prove that before the European invasion Africa had not been completely isolated from the world outside. Neither the barren wastes of the Sahara (at one time very much less barren than now), nor the dense Equatorial forests, nor the sudd of the Nile, have proved insuperable barriers to the immigration of foreigners of more advanced culture than the Negro. Whatever may have been the colour of their skin, many of these invaders are classified "white" by anthropologists. To this day certain of the peoples of Africa are as much "white" as "black." The Bantu, who cover an immense area south of the Sudan, are differentiated from the true Negroes largely by the trace of Caucasian blood that they inherit. Many of the languages and much of the culture of the Africans are shot through with foreign elements. The conflict of cultures we are witnessing to-day is in fact no new thing. The ancient infiltration was, however, spasmodic and partial, compared with the modern. The events of the past fifty years have more profoundly influenced the African than the events of any previous thousand or even ten thousand years.

It is with this modern phase of the age-long impact of the white man upon the black that this book is concerned.

II.

The startling and bewildering feature of this modern invasion of Africa is the rapidity with which it is being effected. We are not speaking of a gradual permeation extending over hundreds and thousands of years, but of changes that have taken place within the lifetime of many—changes that are going on under our eyes at this moment.

Three or four brief sketches will suffice to illustrate what is meant.

In 1896 British officers saw the grove at Kumasi where the remains of human sacrifices were flung: "the ground here was found covered with skulls and bones of hundreds of victims."[1] King Prempeh,[2] exiled after the war of 1895-6, returned in 1925 as a private citizen and a Christian to the city which no longer deserves the epithet "bloody"; he who once presided over human sacrifices now

[1] R. S. S. Baden-Powell, *The Downfall of Prempeh* (1898), p. 24.

[2] See *ante*, p. 4.

serves on a sanitary board and takes the chair at missionary meetings in the Wesleyan Church. He may well have gasped with astonishment as he drove in a motor car around the place, looking in vain for old landmarks. He saw fine parks which have taken the place of malarious swamps. "A 'Burlington Arcade' of European shops, with residential flats above, now stands on ground where twenty years ago naked savages still led the life of primitive man."[1] Passing along a street adorned with buildings that would not disgrace the more popular thoroughfares of London or Paris you may see African gentlemen possessed of legal, medical or theological degrees won at British or American universities, and African ladies dressed in London or Paris frocks, tripping along in silken stockings and high-heeled shoes. The older generation is there too—grey-haired Ashanti aristocrats looking like Roman senators in bronze, dressed in their beautifully woven locally-made togas; men who once took part in some of the terrible deeds under the old regime.[2] A Wesleyan chapel was built under the shadow of the "execution tree." And now a great college, solidly built of stone, has been erected by the Wesleyans on land given by the Ashanti chiefs and with money largely contributed by the people. Telephone wires run through the city, and the skilled operators in the exchange are African girls. Sir. R. Baden-Powell, when he

[1] G. Ward Price, *With the Prince to West Africa* (1925), p. 115.

[2] I have borrowed some phrases from Captain R. S. Rattray's description in *The Times Trade and Engineering Supplement*, March 21, 1925.

marched his native levies into Kumasi, surely never dreamed that in thirty years' time the great educational movement he was to launch would extend to Ashanti and that King Prempeh's son would become a scout-master. Nor did he imagine that a Kumasi cricket team would ever beat white opponents.

Outside Kumasi motor cars run over fine metalled roads. And a railway, bringing the town within twelve hours of the coast, runs through that dark and pestilential forest where for long weeks at the end of 1895 British soldiers and Native levies clambered over giant tree-roots or splashed through the sucking mud.

Kumasi is the capital of Ashanti which forms part of Gold Coast Colony, a land made so prosperous by the industry of the natives under British administration that no direct taxes are levied. Out of the revenue derived from local products, over £220,000 has been spent in building a hospital. From the same source is coming the money to build the college at Achimota which is to cost £400,000. Here one sees British rule at its best. An African has written thus about it: "The Gold Coast African finds himself to-day a happy and loyal citizen in the British Commonwealth. He is happy because every moiety of his land is his alone, and he is loyal because he knows that that right will never be outraged."[1]

What a change from the condition of things in 1895!

On March 12th, 1877, when descending the

[1] J. B. WANQUAH in *West Africa*, March 21, 1925.

Congo, H. M. Stanley found that the mighty river suddenly expanded into a lake, which at the suggestion of his companion, Francis Pocock, he named "Stanley Pool." On the right towered a long row of cliffs, white and glistening, which at once reminded the intrepid voyagers of Dover. On the left bank they found populous settlements of the Nshasa and other tribes. On the shores of the Pool a modern city named Kinshasa has now been built as the capital of the Belgian Congo. Where twelve years ago all was bush, land for building is now worth 10,000 francs a hectare, and rents vary from 1,100 to 1,500 francs a month. River steamers are moored at the quayside; and aeroplanes start from and land at the aviation camp. A railway runs from the town past the unnavigable stretch of the river to the mouth. The population comprises 1,200 Whites of various nationalities, and 15,000 Blacks most of whom are drawn from far-distant regions to work in the Lever soap-factories and in other industries. Here you may see half-naked savages from the Equatorial forest mingling with more civilized Africans who ape the Europeans in their dress. Here too are African women arrayed in gaudy frocks, with naked feet thrust into patent leather high-heeled shoes, costing eighty francs a pair. In the clubs on Sunday evening you will find black men and women dancing the most modern dances—the gentlemen in white or khaki, the ladies in fashionable European attire. Very few of the labourers bring their wives to Kinshasa. They live detached from tribal restraints. Their rapid industrialisation gives them a totally fresh view of life, and on their return to their distant villages they carry home a new restlessness, new ambitions, new hunger for things unobtainable. The change gives point to M. Wauters' question: "What would Stanley say?"[1]

In 1901—the year before I went to Northern Rhodesia—Mr. George Grey (brother of Earl Grey of Falloden) led an expedition through that country prospecting for copper, the rumour of its existence in the Katanga district of Belgian Congo having been reported by Commander Cameron in 1876. Mr. Arnot was probably the first Briton actually to reach the Katanga (1889) where he established the Garenganze mission; Belgian explorers had visited it since then, but when Mr. George Grey revealed the immense mineral wealth of the country it was still an almost unknown land and the people were almost entirely barbarous.

The plan of the township that has now arisen near the site of Mr. Grey's camp brings vividly to mind the thriving city of Eden which started such bright hopes in the breasts of Martin Chuzzlewit and Mark Tapley. Here it is on paper, with its broad avenues, its Palais de Justice, its cathedral, its prison and barracks, its parks and factories, all beautifully planned in symmetrical fashion. It is not credible, one thinks, that such a city can exist where, so few years ago, barbarism reigned. But

[1] JOSEPH WAUTERS (ex-minister of Labour, Belgium). *Le Congo au travail* (1924), pp. 86 sqq.

this city of Elisabethville actually exists. The site was chosen in 1910, and twelve years later was occupied by 2,000 Europeans, while the adjoining *ville indigène* accommodated 12,000 Natives. The beautiful streets and boulevards are there—so is the cathedral; substantial houses, fine hotels, excellent shops—all lit by electricity. Mr. Robert Williams, the eminent railway engineer, tells us[1] that in 1923 he was lodged in "a residence as comfortable as my home in London."

He continues:

> "I visited the school for native workmen at the railway works there. I watched the natives being trained as locomotive drivers and was deeply interested in hearing one of them describe to his teacher the names and functions of all the parts of a sectional drawing of a locomotive. There was no lack of understanding and intelligence there, I assure you. . . . . And here I may say that most of the drivers, stokers, signalmen, pointsmen, porters, telegraph clerks, and even station-masters in Katanga, are natives. One black station-master whom I met spoke both English and French, and was evidently a well-educated man."[2]

No other region in the world, perhaps, possesses such vast potential wealth as the Katanga. It produces about two thousand tons of copper a week and is capable of producing a thousand tons a

[1] ROBERT WILLIAMS, *More Milestones in African Civilization*. In *United Empire*, February, 1924.

[2] The Belgian authorities recognize no colour-bar in the industrial world. M. Franck, the Belgian Colonial minister, says: "Ce serait une injuste expropriation du plus respectable de tous les droits: le droit de faire tout ce dont l'indigène est capable, dans le domaine de la production économique." He tells that when South African agitators came to preach the colour-bar doctrine in the Katanga they were immediately expelled.—*Études de colonisation comparée*, 1924, p. 127.

day. Cobalt, the valuable metal used in making special steels, is found there in great quantity. Sufficient radium is being extracted from the uranium of Katanga to meet the world's present needs. The opening of these mines gives employment to many thousands of Africans, some of whom come from distant places. The educated men to whom Mr. Williams refers have been trained at the Belgian schools at the works, or at the mission schools, such as Livingstonia and Blantyre in far-off Nyasaland. Many of them are natives of Congoland, and the point to which attention should be principally given is that here are Africans who had never seen an engine until the railway reached Katanga in 1910, and who are now driving locomotives and handling railway signals.

As in Congoland, so in Kenya, Rhodesia and elsewhere important townships are arising where Europeans and Africans intermingle and influence each other. Bulawayo, Salisbury, Livingstone, Fort Jameson, Blantyre, Nairobi—even Johannesburg—have all made their appearance since 1876.

Nor is it in the towns alone that changes are taking place, the rapidity and the results of which are bewildering; the Natives who live away from European settlements are also being affected. Major St. Orde Browne has described, as he saw it, the advent of civilization among certain East African tribes. In 1909 many of the natives of Kenya had seen no white man except himself.

"Communities among which the war-horn and the poisoned arrow were quite the possible form of greeting were five years later thoroughly used to Europeans, buying and selling in coin, going away to work, and using piece-goods, steel tools and matches as if they had known them all their lives."[1]

The profound, incalculable transformations that are being so rapidly produced in Africa will be studied in subsequent chapters. It is the relative suddenness of the change that is so disturbing. But yesterday the vast majority of Africans lived in a secluded world, as their forefathers lived before them, with the very dimmest notions of any more spacious universe. Now among them the energetic white man has forced his way, with his railways and motor cars, his flying-machines, his passion for precious metals, his hunger for land, his need for trade, his desire for rapidly and easily acquired wealth, his ardour for putting things right in this crooked world. No wonder if the African feels that he is being hustled. The pace is too rapid. Changes that normally take hundreds of years are being brought about in a generation. The African is being called upon to take a prodigious leap out of the prehistoric age into the twentieth century.

An eminent French savant hardly exaggerates when he writes:

> "Among a European people a revolution represents a brusque and perhaps a brutal acceleration of the evolution which is normally in course of development, but always in conformity with the mentality of that people. On the contrary, among African or Asiatic peoples, a revolution, when it results from contact with Europeans, is a cataclysm."[2]

[1] G. St. J. Orde Browne, *The Vanishing Tribes of Kenya* (1925), p. 9. [2] Louis Vignon, *Un programme de Politique coloniale* (1919), p. 160.

III.

The main concern of this study is with the effect on the Africans, but it must not be forgotten that when a higher civilization impinges upon a lower both sides are affected. A double diffusion takes place. The barbarian learns many of the vices, and also, we may hope, many of the virtues of the civilized man, who in his turn is enriched in proportion as he serves the barbarian and debased in so far as he descends to his level. Africa has increased the moral wealth of Great Britain by providing the circumstances that have called forth the courage, humanity, and endurance of our Livingstones, our Gordons, our Cromers, our Lugards, our Moirs. But it would be folly to ignore that there is another side of the question.

Seton Merriman pictured in Victor Durnovo[1] a man who believed that there were no laws in Central Africa except the laws of necessity, that the best thing to do was to make hay while the sun shone and then to clear out of the country. Africa made of him a worse man than Nature had originally intended. The Irritability of Africa—" which makes honourable European gentlemen commit crimes of which they blush to think in after days "—descended upon this half-breed. Africa has been the scene of some of the most revolting cruelties known or unknown to history. The enervating climate, the madness caused by fever-germs rioting in the blood, the loneliness which dooms a man to

[1] In *With Edged Tools.*

live for long months without seeing a companion of his own colour, the continual down-drag of a barbarous environment, the sense of being of a superior race, the possession of power over weaker peoples,—these go far to explain, if they do not excuse, the loathsome deeds done under the tropical sun. Unfortunately many Europeans have not the moral stamina to withstand the corruptive influence of life in Africa, which at times makes savages even of highly-born, educated Englishmen: of the perpetrators of the vile deeds described by Dr. Norman Leys one was the son of a bishop and the other the son of a peer. Pages of this book could easily be filled with descriptions of acts that would make the readers' blood curdle with horror and boil with anger.

It is more germane, however, to point out that prolonged contact with African barbarism produces permanent effects upon European groups. This has been proved abundantly in South Africa.

> "Our society," writes Dr. Edgar Brookes,[1] "has come to represent that of the Athens of Pericles—an educated democracy, resting upon a foundation of what, when all hypocritical periphrases are swept away, is really slave-labour. Our whole cultural and social milieu is coloured by that fact. Where our common habits and our common modes of thought differ most profoundly from those of the races overseas from which we spring, the explanation of that difference is largely to be sought in our Native Problem.

[1] Dr. Brookes is Head of the Department of Politics and Public Administration at Transvaal University College, Pretoria. The quotation is taken from his paper, "The Economic Aspects of the Native Problem," read before the South African Association.—*South African Journal of Science*, Vol. XXI, November, 1924.

> The young South African commonly possesses, along with a genuine passion for equality and fraternity as regards his white fellow-Afrikanders—a robust democracy that distrusts knighthoods and looks with suspicion even on a harmless O.B.E.—the additional characteristic of a born aristocrat, with the vices as well as the virtues of an hereditary aristocracy, as regards the Native peoples among whom he lives. This peculiarly Spartan ethos, so unlike that of almost every country in the world (except perhaps the Southern States of America) marks us out as a distinct nation, with a distinct civilization—and it is entirely the product of the despised black man who has influenced our development, even as we have influenced his."

Had there been no aboriginal peoples in South Africa it is probable that the white immigrants would have worked with their own hands—as they do in Australia and Canada. The experience of Queensland—where the climate is more tropical than in most of South Africa—has abundantly proved since the Kanakas were excluded from the sugar plantations in 1901 that white men can work in torrid regions and produce larger crops than the black man.[1] If white men can work in Queensland, they can work in the salubrious regions of South Africa. But the presence of the black has caused the white man to regard himself as an

[1] J. W. Gregory, *The Menace of Colour* (1925), Chapter IX. "The Australian adoption of White Labour for its sugar plantations has been the greatest contribution yet made to the practical solution of the problem whether the white man can do agricultural work in the tropics. The development of the plantations during the past twenty-four years shows that white labour can be employed successfully in such an ultra-tropical industry as sugar cultivation in even the ultra-tropical climate of the Queensland coastlands, provided the workers are protected from infectious disease and from the competition of people with lower standards of life." (pp. 223, 224).

aristocrat. As early as the first decade of the Dutch settlement the farmers, who were intended to be peasant proprietors, tilling the ground chiefly with their own hands, began "to aspire to a position in which their work would consist merely in directing others," and they demanded that the Government should provide them with cheap labour.[1] Slaves were introduced and for 177 years slave-labour formed the economic basis of colonial life. Since the emancipation in 1834, free labour has taken its place. There is much truth in Dean Inge's biting words: Our countrymen in South Africa sit under a tree and hire a coloured man to work for them.[2] The psychological effects are incalculable. South Africans are not weaklings; they come of some of the finest stocks the world has known. Manual work in itself is not degrading—to ply spade and pick, hammer and chisel, never lowered any man. But because many kinds of work have been done for generations by black men, it has come to pass that they are regarded as derogatory to the dignity of the white man. The finest race will deteriorate when such a notion becomes a rule of life. As Mr. Dawson truly says: "The existence of a large and practically inexhaustible supply of Blacks, ready to be engaged for the cost of horses' feed, with worse than horses' quarters, is a standing temptation to slackness, and the draw that way, once encouraged, is difficult to check."[3] Hence,

[1] G. McCall Theal, *History of South Africa* 1486-1691 (1888), pp. 112, 113.

[2] *Outspoken Essays*, second series, p. 225.

[3] W. H. Dawson, *South Africa* (1925), p. 343.

too, that "boss spirit," so characteristic of South Africans. Even the children become infected by it : if a boy drops his cap he may be heard to call a black to pick it up, and it is not unknown for school-children to have black servants to carry their books and slates.

The land system has created a class of *by-woners*—"hangers-on"—who, because the farmers insist upon having cheap black labour, and because these unfortunate whites can neither obtain land nor have ever been accustomed to work, are forced into the towns, there to swell the ranks of the unemployed and unemployable. They form the class of Poor Whites. The evils of slumdom as we know them in England are being repeated under the blue South African sky. In Port Elizabeth and elsewhere thousands are herded in single-room tenements. Mr. Ambrose Pratt describes what he saw in Johannesburg:

> "Dirty, mean little houses, broken, almost impassable roadways, squalor unspeakable. And these streets stretch out for miles. Here is the quarter of the 'poor whites,' wretched victims of the Kaffirs' monopoly of the unskilled labour market, who derive an infamous living by the laundry labour of their wives, the prostitution of their daughters, and by selling liquor in secret to the native hordes."[1]

Things have grown worse since those words were written in 1913. In 1916 there were said to be 106,000 Poor Whites; in 1922 it was estimated that every twelfth white person in South Africa might be so classed. The offspring of educated,

[1] AMBROSE PRATT, *The Real South Africa* (1913), p. 149.

respectable citizens are adding to the number. Only fifty per cent. of the boys leaving school can now be placed in employment.[1] No wonder that South Africans have become alarmed at the double trend of events—the decreasing efficiency of a large section of the whites, and the increasing efficiency of a section of the blacks. The latter have for long borne the burden of unskilled labour, and are ready to push their way into skilled trades wherever the opposition of organized Labour cannot exclude them. Mentally, morally, and physically many of the Blacks are far superior to many of the degenerate Whites. What their wiser leaders pointed out long ago has now become evident to South Africans generally: the most serious of their problems lies in the rapid deterioration of large numbers of the Whites. Many of these are the victims of circumstances, but the root of the evil is to be found in that long-established prejudice against manual toil.[2] The Government is doing its best to get these people employed[3]—even at the expense of the Blacks, e.g.,

[1] Edgar Brookes, *op. cit.*, pp. 658, 659.

[2] Sir W. Hely Hutchinson (Governor of Natal, 1893-1900; then of Cape Colony) said: "The poor white problem is one of the most pressing of South African problems. It is in a sense the direct result of native and coloured environment."

[3] In 1925 two railway lines were opened, in the construction of which over 1,000 Poor Whites were employed. The substitution of White for Black labour increased the cost of one line by £20,000. The Auditor-General of the Union is reported to have declared that this employment of Whites instead of Blacks on railway work is not in conformity with the principles of the Constitution, because the law lays down that railways shall be administered on "business principles," and it is not business to spend so much money unnecessarily.

by turning off old and industrious employés from the railways and substituting less competent Whites. Many are advocating the displacement of black by white labourers in the mines and industries. The problem will never be solved until the idea of manual toil being ignominious because it is "Kaffirs' work" is abandoned, and until the standard of living among the Blacks is raised by education so that they cannot undersell the Whites on the labour market, but are paid equal wages when they do the same class of work. This would mean a revolution in the economic life of South Africa.

The civilized community in contact with a barbarian either raises it to its own level, or sinks.

IV.

South Africa has much to teach other communities in the continent about the effect upon the white man of this contact between civilization and barbarism. But our concern here is with the effect upon the black man.

Lord Bryce, one of the wisest teachers of our age, said: "whoever examines the records of the past will find that the continued juxtaposition of two races has always been followed either by the disappearance of the weaker or by the intermixture of the two."[1] If this rule is to hold good in Africa, then one of two things will happen: either the African, or the European in Africa, will disappear;

[1] JAMES (VISCOUNT) BRYCE, *The American Commonwealth* (1911), Vol. II, p. 532.

or Africa will one day be inhabited by a mixed Afro-European race.

The latter alternative means that Africa will follow the example of a large area of South America where an amalgamation is taking place of the aboriginal survivors with the imported negroes and the Portuguese and Spanish colonists. Professor Gregory, like others who have examined the question, concludes that the European race, as a race, has no chance of permanence in most of South America.[1] Is a similar hybridization to occur in Africa? The process has certainly begun.

In South Africa public opinion both among Blacks and Whites is against miscegenation. Intermarriage is forbidden by law in the Transvaal and the Orange Free State. But illicit unions of white men and black women are common, and not alone in the lower grades of society. Some South Africans, both White and Black, would make such cohabitation a criminal offence,[2] but so long as the races come into contact it will go on. The 500,000 "coloured" people within the Union represent various degrees of intermixture of the many races who live in the country—white, black, yellow and brown. Writers who are anxious to preserve the

[1] *The Menace of Colour*, p. 237. "The proportion of South Americans who are counted as white is estimated as from one-third to one-tenth; but even the lower of these estimates includes many who are only partly white. The number free from any Indian intermixture is probably less than one-tenth and the proportion of Iberian blood is dwindling." p. 118. Lord Bryce was much of the same opinion.

[2] A Bill was to be introduced into the 1926 session of the Union Parliament punishing offenders by imprisonment and flogging.

purity of their stock regard with apprehension the growth of this element. Mr. Stevens is very outspoken on the subject. "In a century or two," he admonishes his fellow South Africans, "the South African schoolboy will listen with mouth agape whilst his master traces his descent from the ancients of Europe, of Asia, and of Africa—and those European progenitors, courteous reader, will be you and I."[1]

In the rest of British Africa the same kind of coalescence is slowly going on. In the French, Portuguese, Belgian and Italian territories, where pride of race is not so strong as among ourselves, these unions are more common and are more frequently acknowledged. There the white man is not ashamed to own his children and may even send them to be educated in Europe, a thing few Britons would dream of doing. "A Frenchman the more!"—is the attitude the French take. Some people regard this hybridization as the best solution of the colour-problem. There seems to be only one obstacle to the growth of a very large Afro-European population, namely the relative paucity of white men.

Considering the stir they make, it is startling to discover how few the Whites are.[2] In the whole of British Africa there are only 1,617,300 people of European stock, and of these 1,519,500 live within the Union of South Africa. All British East Africa

[1] E. J. C. STEVENS, *White and Black*, p. 40.

[2] SIR LEO CHIOZZA MONEY, *The Peril of the White* (1925), Appendix, "The World's Population in 1921."

(Tanganyika, Zanzibar, Kenya, Uganda, Nyasaland and Northern Rhodesia) contains only 18,000; and British West Africa only 7,400. The French African Empire contains 1,222,300 people of European stock and of these 1,191,000 reside in Algeria, Morocco and Tunis, and 17,200 in Madagascar, leaving only 14,100 in the remainder of the vast area of French Africa. In other European territories there are: Italian Africa, 48,700; Portuguese, 24,600; Spanish, 12,900; Belgian, 10,000. The whole continent contains 3,112,800 Europeans, as against 126,301,900 non-Europeans.

What prospect is there of an increased European population? At present, the countries which enjoy a salubrious climate (South Africa, S. Rhodesia, Kenya) are calling for settlers, but only for such as possess capital—and these are not numerous to-day. Other colonies do not as yet ask for more than sufficient men to direct industries. Even though science should make it possible for Europeans to colonize Africa in the real sense of the term—as Canada is colonized—seeing that our birth-rate is diminishing[1] and that there is so much room in other parts of the Empire, it seems very unlikely that British Africa will be much more fully occupied by white men fifty years hence than it is now. Nor will it be otherwise in other territories. It is probably true that European emigration on a large scale will only take place to

[1] The birth-rate in England and Wales fell from 23.9 in 1912 to 18.8 in 1924 (in 1925, 18.3); in France it rose from 18.9 in 1912 to 19.2 in 1924. CHIOZZA MONEY, *op. cit.*, p. 136.

the countries where manual labour by Europeans forms the basis of industry, and that while white men in Africa act only as overseers of black labourers no very great addition to their numbers is to be expected.

One effect of the modern invasion of Africa has undoubtedly been to decimate the black population in many regions.[1] Nowadays most people who have interests in Africa are greatly concerned about the depopulation: they see that no profit is really made if you kill the goose that lays the golden eggs. Efforts are being made to stay the death-rate. The Africans possess considerable resilience and soon begin to increase when favourable conditions are established. If the rate at which they have multiplied in South Africa during the last thirty years be maintained for another fifty years,[2] the Blacks will then number 16,500,000; and if the annual rate should increase from two to three per cent., as it may easily do if certain hygienic measures are adopted, they will number 24,000,000. If the European population continues to grow as at present, by immigration and naturally, it will reach 6,500,000 fifty years hence. The moral of these figures has been pointed out by Mr. C. W. Cousins, the Director of Census, 1921. Twenty-five years, he says, will probably decide the question whether the white race is to have any part in the ultimate development of South Africa. Failing

[1] See later, Chapter VI.

[2] Between 1891 and 1921 the Whites of South Africa increased by 500,000; non-Europeans by 2,630,000—notwithstanding the influenza which swept off 500,000 natives in 1918.

accessions from abroad, "it must for ever abandon the prospect of maintaining a white civilization except as a proportionately diminishing minority and in the face of an increasing, and at last an overwhelming majority. It may then be forced to abandon its domination, or even to abandon the country."

In South Africa, as in some other regions, there is no likelihood that the Africans will share the fate of the aborigines of Tasmania and Newfoundland, who died out long ago; nor that they will dwindle in number like the Maoris of New Zealand. If the European powers are faithful to the principle of Trusteeship an increase of the population may be seen in those regions where of late years it has declined. In that case it is possible that when they are educated and their race consciousness is fully developed, the Africans will one day be successful in regaining their own country.

From these considerations it is by no means certain that the African is the "weaker" race of Lord Bryce's dictum. It may be the white man that will disappear, though in many regions he will by that time have intermingled his blood largely with that of the blacks, and in that sense will remain. Some people who have studied the question have no doubt on the matter. Professor Gregory, for example, thinks that "the ultimate supremacy of the Negro over most of the continent appears inevitable."[1] He would apparently exclude South Africa. If, as some writers prognosticate, the

[1] *The Menace of Colour*, p. 237.

Whites cannot retain their footing even there, then Professor Gregory's conclusion appears incontrovertible.

V.

These are matters that the future will decide. Our concern now is with the present time. The end is not yet, but can a kind of interim balance sheet be drawn up to show where the African has gained and where he has lost through his contact with the Whites?

If a glance is taken beyond the modern period, it is seen that the African's debt to the Caucasian is tremendous. The Negro, it would seem, never domesticated any of the wild animals that lived around him in such varied abundance: at any rate only the ass and the cat come to us from Africa. The Negro's oxen came to him from Asia, as also his pigs, goats and domestic fowls. His sorghum was probably introduced from Arabia, his eleusine and millet from Syria. Various lentils, peas and melons, the castor-oil plant and the banana, all came into Africa from the East.[1]

In modern times Africa has been further enriched from abroad. The Portuguese have been among its greatest benefactors in material things. During the 16th and 17th centuries they introduced tobacco, sweet potatoes, maize, wheat, ground-nuts, sugar-cane, manioc, the paw-paw, orange and pineapple.

[1] Sir H. H. Johnston, *The Opening up of Africa*, p. 48 sqq.

These are substantial items to be placed to the white man's credit.

An endeavour must be made to arrive at a fair estimate in this matter.

When in 1925, by a majority of 3,820,000 votes to 79,000, the Trade Union Congress passed a resolution declaring that the domination of non-British peoples by the British Government is a form of capitalist exploitation having for its object the securing for British capitalists cheap sources of raw materials, the right to exploit cheap and unorganized labour and to use the competition of that labour to degrade the workers' standards in Great Britain—the Congress, notwithstanding Mr. J. H. Thomas's warning, made itself ridiculous. That there has been exploitation of the native races, and that this still exists few would question. Something must be said about it in subsequent chapters. But there is another side of the matter which is totally ignored in this resolution. From personal observation, I bear testimony to the services rendered to the African by high-minded British soldiers, traders, and administrators. Nobody who knows anything of the history of the Gold Coast, Nigeria, Sudan, Uganda (to name no others) can doubt for an instant that the Africans have gained in many directions from their contact with Europeans. To see nothing but "capitalist exploitation" is grossly unjust.

It must be admitted on the other hand that certain evils have attended the European invasion; in some instances as a direct result of selfish policy, in others as a consequence of ignorance and shortsightedness; and often contrary to our intention, as if some malignant Fate were dogging our steps.

Europeans may pride themselves upon having put a stop to intertribal warfare. It is no longer possible for a Chaka to devastate vast regions and cause the death of two million people. On the other hand—to say nothing of various unjust wars waged against the Africans—Europeans were not content to fight their battles in Europe but must needs carry the great War into Africa. Almost the whole continent was directly affected by their action. Thousands of willing Africans were enlisted to fight on both sides and also hundreds of thousands (538,570 on the British side in the East African campaign alone)[1] to carry food and ammunition. It is not known how many of these carriers died—certainly a large proportion: "in tens of thousands," says Mr. Hobley. Nor does any one know how many of the non-belligerents perished in their villages through famine and disease.[2] It was a shameful thing to thrust an unnecessary war upon Africans—

[1] British East Africa (now Kenya) furnished 201,431; Uganda, 178,819; Nyasaland, 123,320; Nigeria, 35,000. (*The Empire at War*, edited by Sir Charles Lucas, Vol. IV.) Nothing is said of Northern Rhodesia, but we know that one district provided, for various kinds of work, 6,500 men per annum out of 7,400 able-bodied male adults. (F. H. MELLAND, *In Witch-bound Africa*, (1923) p. 27.)

[2] Germans shot down carriers when these were too exhausted to march further. One of their officers wrote in a private letter: "Our road is paved with corpses of the natives we have been obliged to kill." (G. L. BEER, *African Questions at the Paris Peace Conference*, pp. 44, 45, quoting Cd. 8689 (1917).) Entire areas in East Africa were depopulated by the retreating German armies which compelled women as well as men to act as carriers.

unnecessary, for the issue was decided in Europe. It is perhaps no exaggeration to say that during the four years more Africans lost their lives than in all the inter-tribal wars of the previous fifty years.

White men—the British in particular—have put down the slave-traffic at very great cost to themselves in blood and treasure; but they ought not to be over-complacent about it, since, if they did not start it, they carried it on for about four hundred years.

We have built railways and hospitals. Our doctors have spent years, and, in many instances, have sacrificed their lives while investigating tropical diseases. As a result of their labours millions of Africans will benefit. On the other hand, it must not be forgotten that by opening up Africa Europeans have introduced new diseases and made possible the spread of others. Sleeping sickness had been endemic for centuries in West Africa, but it was only when travellers, accompanied by great bands of porters, began to ascend the Congo that it was carried eastwards. The people of Uganda, where the disease destroyed 200,000 persons, blame Europeans for the calamity and we cannot disclaim responsibility. Influenza killed 500,000 black people in South Africa and 155,000 in East Africa—to say nothing of other regions—and but for Europeans it would probably never have touched them. If it is true that syphilis was introduced by Arabs, and in more virulent form by Indians, it is also true that tuberculosis was taken to Africa by Europeans.

It is a fact that in some regions Europeans have

brought the Africans the blessings of good government, of education and the Christian religion ; but on the other side must be placed the inhuman cruelties practised at the expense of the Africans in Belgian Congo (under the Leopold regime) and in the German and Portuguese colonies. Nor is the British record clean in this respect. Moreover, it cannot be questioned, that contact with Europeans has caused debasement of African character in some respects,[1] while awakening their intellect and kindling their ambition.

The African has received the products of our European factories (including our cast-off garments and alcohol) ; but at the same time many an interesting African industry has been destroyed.

The European places a high estimate on the value of his civilization—and has a corresponding contempt for African barbarism. But the African may be excused if he wonders how far he is better off under our rule than he was under his own. His old social system is being rapidly disintegrated. He is no longer free as he was. From hunter and warrior, he is reduced (as he thinks) to earning

[1] The painful description penned by Dr. Allegret of the effect upon the character of Africans in French West Africa applies also, in greater or less degree, to other parts of the continent : " A new spirit of acquisitiveness has been awakened, new vices have replaced, or have been superimposed upon the old. By civilizing the natives we have increased their power to take action and have put new tools in their hands without having trained their reason or their conscience. We have, so to speak, increased tenfold the power and the speed of the locomotive without repairing the line upon which it is to run. . . . The black race is in danger, physically and morally ; its normal and progressive development is threatened."—*International Review of Missions*, April, 1923.

wages from one white man that he may pay taxes to another. He is compelled to spend long months apart from wife and children that he may satisfy the exigent white stranger's hunger for precious metals. No wonder that many a woman lives to curse the day that reft her of her man and carried him off to township and mine—curse it for a home-breaker, for a destroyer of health, for a murderer of unborn babes ![1]

If only we Europeans do our duty in a Christian way, the Africans will be the ultimate gainers from this invasion. But as regards our interim balance sheet, it must be confessed that were any one to say that the account is against Europe it would be difficult to contradict his statement.

[1] G. E. TILSLEY, in *World Dominion*, December, 1925, p. 19. Some other effects of the advent of Western civilization are not so apparent to us, but they are very real to the Africans. There is, for example, the cleft driven between the old and young members of families and tribes—a feud created between those who look back on yesterday, with its stability and ordered life, and those who are all for the new ways.—Some of the statements made above do not apply in equal degree to every part of Africa. Certain of them would not be accepted by any one who was familiar only with British West Africa. There, however, the absence of some unpleasant effects of European invasion is counterbalanced by the ravages of the liquor traffic and by the long-enduring effects of the slave trade. As Sir C. Lucas says, the slave trade made West Africa "the darkest and most degraded part of the world."—*A Historical Geography of the British Colonies*, 2nd Edition (1890), p. 77.

CHAPTER IV.

WHEREIN AN ATTEMPT IS MADE TO ESTIMATE THE AFRICAN'S WORTH.

I.

UNFORTUNATELY no record is available of what the Africans thought concerning the first white men who arrived on their coasts to carry them into slavery. It is known, however, that in other parts of Africa the Natives regarded the earliest European visitors as supernatural beings. Their appearance was looked upon as a portent. "There was a pretty general fear that disease and death would follow," says Dr. Bentley of his arrival in Congoland. The fears of the Negroes pictured Mungo Park in the flowing robes of a tremendous spirit: one of them said that when the white man appeared a cold blast of wind poured down upon himself from the sky, like so much water. When Natives of Nyasaland first saw a steamer on the lake they were terror-stricken and said: "It is God. He walks on the water." When they beheld the white skin of the man who landed they said: "It is surely God. He has come to us in the likeness of men." When he ate some bananas in their presence, they said: "No, not God, but a friend of His." It is widely believed that white men come out of the sea—this has been said in my presence in the far interior by men who had never seen the sea. Their wonderful possessions are supposed to have been picked up on the ocean shore, or on the ocean-bed—so easily obtained, so niggardly imparted! Some even think (a curious reminiscence of slavery-days) that they compel the spirits of black men to manufacture these things for them beneath the sea or under the earth; and that tinned meats are really the flesh of those black captives! The white man is considered a magician of very extraordinary gifts: probably few Europeans who travel in Central Africa escape from having the power attributed to them of making or of withholding rain. Everything about them is wonderful, uncanny.

In some districts the European's white skin is taken as proof of his favour with the Creator, for white is the African's emblem of happiness and blessedness, as black is their emblem of sadness and misfortune.

So is built up the white man's prestige; and it is upon this, rather than upon actual force, that his power chiefly rests. There is always a machine gun in the background, of course, but it is not this that counts most. Apart from the sentry at the district gaol, and except at the capital, which was also the headquarters of the native police, I very rarely saw an armed policeman in Northern Rhodesia. The whole of Nigeria, an area equal to that of Germany, Holland, Belgium, and two-thirds of France, with over 18,000,000 inhabitants, is governed with the aid of 2,500 African troops, officered by white men : and the Political Officers average only one to every 70,000 Africans.

This prestige is not based solely upon a reputation for thaumaturgy. Though for long years the African may retain an uneasy sense of the European's magic, he does at last discover him to be a man like unto himself. It is commonly believed that he admires and respects brute strength above all else but a study of his folk-tales proves the contrary. He is a very shrewd judge of men. The profound esteem with which David Livingstone was regarded, and the reverence in which his name is still held by those who remember him, should in itself be sufficient to show that the African recognizes and appreciates nobility of character. He may, and in many instances he does, begin by crediting the European with magical power, but in the long run it is such virtues as kindliness, humanity, courage, justice, truthfulness, cheerfulness, that he looks for and admires. It is a circumstance of great value to their successors that, over a vast area, the first Europeans exhibited those virtues in an eminent degree.

It comes as a shock to the African to discover that white men are not all immaculate. He quickly loses respect for them when they fall below the standard he has set up. It is to be feared that over a large part of Africa they are not respected as they were. "Let it be repeated," says Mr.

D. K. Mackenzie,[1] "to the younger generation the white man is no longer a little tin god, or any other kind of god." Instead of regarding him with awe as a supernatural being, as their fathers did, they make fun of him. Young Africans are terrible mimics, and in hundreds of villages to-day the white man and his ways form the subject of acted comedies. To laugh at a man is of course compatible with respect and affection, and these comedies are not in themselves proof that Europeans are no longer reverenced. But they do mean that Europeans are discovered to be human and as such must prove themselves worthy of respect.

That the war has lowered the white man's prestige is the testimony of many observers.

> "The effect of the war upon the Native was in almost every way most unfortunate, quite apart from the loss of life and damage to property," writes Major Orde Browne.[2] "It is true that he gained an enormously increased respect for the power and resources of the mysterious European, which must serve as a great deterrent to any idea of armed movements; but against that advantage must be set the effect upon the native mind of seeing the previously all-wise European embark upon a bitter and prolonged war of an extent and duration utterly beyond African experience. . . . . . To the more intelligent such a revelation must have had a marked effect in making them doubtful whether the white man's ways were really preferable to their own. Of necessity, in a campaign very many ugly things have to be done, while the stripping off of many of the restraints of civilized life left the ruling race only too often in a most unprepossessing light."

[1] D. K. Mackenzie, *The Spirit-ridden Konde* (1925), p. 159.

[2] G. St. J. Orde Browne, *The Vanishing Tribes of Kenya* (1925), p. 271.

This estimate is confirmed by another experienced East African official—Mr. C. W. Hobley, who writes :—[1]

> "The black troops soon came to realize the physical disabilities of the Europeans and their vulnerability. They saw Europeans shot down and even bayoneted by enemy black soldiers, they realized that very few Europeans were crack shots, they noted the inferior marching capacity of the white man, his inability to find his way about in the bush unaccompanied by a native guide, and in some cases they even saw that the courage of the white was not greater than that of the black. After all this can it be wondered that the prestige of the white race has suffered in the war? Is it surprising that the attitude of many of the blacks to the white man has altered?"
>
> Mr. Hobley adds: "It is doubtful if the old traditional wide respect of white by black can ever be entirely restored."

Apart from the effects of the war, a very serious aspect of the subject must be reckoned with. Large numbers of Africans have undoubtedly, and not without reason, come to question the white man's equity. Some writers exaggerate the extent to which, largely under the stimulus of certain Afro-American agitators, the national sentiment has arisen, with its cry "Africa for the Africans"; but undoubtedly it exists in some quarters, and it feeds upon every instance of the white man's injustice and cruelty. The European's reputation is at stake.

> "By all ye cry or whisper,
> By all ye leave or do,
> The silent, sullen peoples,
> Shall weigh your Gods and you."

[1] C. W. Hobley, C.M.G., *Bantu Beliefs and Magic* (1922), p. 287. See R. St. Barbe Baker's article in the *Empire Review*, November, 1924: "It is difficult to estimate the damage to European prestige as the result of the last war."

II.

Lord Bryce demonstrated that race sentiment is a comparatively recent growth. It emerged when peoples began to realize themselves as nations and came into contact and competition with others.[1]

It was not until modern times that Britons came into touch with Africans. In the Middle Ages the strangest notions, coming down from Greek geographers, prevailed concerning them. Ethiopia was "the blue men's land."

> "In this land," wrote Bartholomew the Englishman, in the 13th century, "be many nations with divers faces wonderly and horribly shapen. . . And other as Trogodites dig them dens and caves, and dwell in them instead of houses; and they eat serpents, and all that may be got; their noise is more fearful in sounding than the voice of other. . . . There be other that be called Bennii, and it is said, they have no heads, but they have eyes fixed in their breasts. And there be Satyrs, and they have only shape of men, and have no manners of mankind. . . Other men of Ethiopia live only by honeysuckles dried in smoke, and in the sun, and these live not past forty years."[2]

Such were the ideas generally held when Englishmen began to frequent the western shores of Africa. In what degree was Shakespeare's knowledge more accurate?

He makes Othello tell Desdemona:

> ". . . of the cannibals that each other eat,
> The Anthropophagi, and men whose heads
> Do grow beneath their shoulders."

Desdemona was not alone in feeling the fascination

[1] VISCOUNT BRYCE, *Race Sentiment as a factor in history* (1915).

[2] *Mediæval Lore* (King's Classics), pp. 88-90.

of an opening world. That Elizabethans were intensely curious as to the peoples of the new lands we may gather from Trinculo: "When they will not give a doit to relieve a lame beggar, they will lay out ten to see a dead Indian." Shakespeare took Othello, a black man, as the hero of his greatest tragedy, and perhaps none of his characters shows more supremely "the mastery of his genius and of his power over the human heart." The Moor's blood is highly inflammable, but his nature is noble, confiding, tender and generous,[1] and shows up well against that of the detestable Iago, whom Shakespeare uses as a foil. Othello is thoroughly human: we pity him as he becomes entangled by circumstances; we do not hold him in contempt. If the prejudice against colour had emerged in Shakespeare's day, he did not share it. Indeed it is more than likely that *The Tempest* voices his protest against the brutalities inflicted by the Whites of his day upon the Blacks. Here is perhaps the earliest treatment in English literature of the conflict of cultures in Africa. Trinculo and Stephano, who swear by the bottle, are of the type that has too frequently represented European civilization. Caliban is the "half-devil and half-child" of the later Kipling. He embodies, perhaps, the Elizabethan conception of the African:

> "A devil, a born devil, on whose nature
> Nurture can never stick."

But the penetrative insight of Shakespeare reveals

[1] The adjectives are Hazlitt's.

that he too is human. He is gross, uncouth, wild, but, as Hazlitt says, his figure acquires a classical dignity in comparison with the drunken sailors. Shakespeare shows him to be sensitive to the white man's injustice.

> "When thou camest first,
> Thou strok'dst me, and mad'st much of me. . .
> . . . and then I lov'd thee,
> And shew'd thee all the qualities o' th' isle. . .
> Curs'd be I that I did so! . . .
> . . . here you sty me
> In this hard rock, whiles you do keep from me
> The rest o' the island."

With a fidelity that excites our admiration Shakespeare limns in a few sure words Caliban's swift and pathetic trust in "the brave god"—"Hast thou not dropped from heaven?" He is indeed "a most ridiculous monster, to make a wonder of a poor drunkard." But, passion'd like ourselves, he is not to be fooled all the time: he awakes at last to the true character of those men who have excited his wonder:

> " . . . . . what a thrice-double ass
> Was I, to take this drunkard for a god,
> And worship this dull fool!"

And if in this respect Shakespeare correctly reads the savage's mind, he is no less prophetic in his estimation of that spiritual faculty which enabled this poor clod to sense that the isle was full of noises,

> "Sounds, and sweet airs, that give delight, and hurt not."

It is nothing short of marvellous that, at a time

when the barbarian (whether African or other) was so little known, Shakespeare should, while exaggerating his brutishness, have interpreted his soul so well.

III.

For a long period the African has been looked upon as an inferior being, and even as sub-human. This finds frequent utterance. "The negro," says Mr. R. C. F. Maugham,[1] "was sent into the world for one end and for one end only—viz. manual labour." Many men voice the sentiment more tersely when they speak of "the damned nigger." Even when not expressed, the disdain is too often apparent in the white man's attitude. If this contempt did not originate with the enslaving of the African it was greatly reinforced by that traffic. On the whole the European did not find it difficult to carry Negroes into slavery and it was easy to argue from this fact that the African was a slave by nature. To-day, the need for the labour of the black man forms the basis of the argument that the black man is fitted only for manual and menial toil. The slave-trade inflicted a terrible wrong upon the Negro: and it requires little effort to hate a man whom you have wronged. "Half of his worth doth Zeus the far-seeing take from a man when the

[1] *Portuguese East Africa* (1906), p. 302. The Portuguese who have never viewed the African except as *mão d' obra* ("labouring hand"), "have always known how to deal with the negro," says Mr. Maugham.

day of slavery catcheth him," said Homer, and to this day the feeling remains that a slave is only half a man, if so much. The contempt felt for slaves was by association extended to the whole African race. It became natural for the upholders of slavery to speak of the Africans in this way: "stupid and unenlightened hordes; immersed in the most gross and impenetrable gloom of barbarism, dark in mind as in body, prodigiously populous, impatient of all control, unteachably lazy, ferocious as their own congenial tigers, nor in any respect superior to these rapacious beasts in intellectual advancement but distinguished only by a rude and imperfect organ of speech, which is abusively employed in the utterance of dissonant and inarticulate jargon."[1] It must be remembered too, that these men only knew negro slaves and there is this much truth in Homer's dictum: the slave loses the dignity and self-respect that he possessed as a freeman; the mentality of a slave is a characteristic quality. In the same way, men judge the African wrongly to-day when they see him out of his natural environment. In European townships and labour-camps, and even in schools, he often suffers from what the psychologists call an "inferiority-complex," which makes him an unpleasant person.

The colour prejudice is not, I believe, instinctive. Here as elsewhere I agree fully with Mr. J. H. Oldham.[2] I had an African nurse and was

[1] From a pamphlet, *Slavery no Oppression*, quoted by R. COUPLAND, *Wilberforce* (1923), p. 115.

[2] J. H. OLDHAM, *Christianity and the Race Problem* (1924). pp. 31-33.

surrounded by black folk in my youth; I cannot recall that their colour ever aroused in me any repugnance. But it is unquestionable that the physical dissimilarities do account for much of the aversion that people feel for the African. The coal-black faces and bodies, the odour, and the simian features, to which Mr. Putnam Weale refers,[1] are taken by many Europeans as marks of the beast. Such terms, of course, are exaggerations, for many Africans, though black or chocolate in colour, are decidedly good-looking: on coming back to England my own feeling was that on the average they were more handsome than English people. The odour is not always noticeable and Africans have told me that the odour of white people is unpleasant to them. A missionary's wife once declared confidently in my hearing that the black skin was a sign of God's curse on the African. Here the laws of association play a part. The Africans associate white with good fortune; we associate black with dirt, soot and the devil. Many good people find it difficult to believe that a man with a black skin can be other than black-hearted.

The dissimilarities between white and black do not stop at physical features. The ordinary traveller, ignorant of the language and constitutionally unfitted to see any good in un-British ways, is struck with the tremendous difference between the African's life and his own and can hardly help feeling the Africans to be inferior.

[1] B. L. Putnam Weale, *The Conflict of Colour* (1910), p. 228.

It cannot be denied that closer acquaintance may, with more reason, deepen the impression. No small part of the unenlightened African's life is extremely repulsive to a decent European—the uncleanly habits, the infanticide, the lack of humanity, the sacrifice of human beings, and so on; only a rose-pink sentimentalism could be blind to such things. They do foster a sentiment of superiority in the white man. But it is well to recall that a decent Roman citizen probably had much the same feeling when he first came into contact with the early inhabitants of Britain—"those ferocious islanders," Tacitus calls them, "a fierce and savage people, running wild in woods." We can see that while the Roman historian's judgment was true superficially it erred in not taking all the facts into consideration. We know now that the prideful Roman was not essentially superior to the Britons whom he conquered, and it may be that history will in like manner correct hasty judgments pronounced upon the Africans.

It would be easy to compile a long list of these superstitions about the Africans, but reference to some recent statements will be sufficient as an illustration.

"Family responsibilities count not at all" with the Bantu, says a semi-official handbook published in South Africa.[1] The same publication repeats the hoary libel uttered *ad nauseam* at missionary meetings, that the Africans purchase their wives. One statement is as false as the other.

[1] *South African Year Book and Guide*, 1925, p. 195.

> "In Africa," writes the English wife of a French doctor, "there are no hereditary beliefs, customs or rites such as would serve to keep the family together. Wives are bought, daughters are sold, and it is only the money or exchange transaction which keeps the tie good. . . Their minds are empty of any sort of religious idea or conviction. The Congolese neither play, talk, nor work. . . But the primitive blacks have acquired a complicated mentality where reason has no place."[1]

There is no need to enter here into a refutation of all these errors. The last mentioned, however, merits brief examination.

A medical man who lived in South Africa for a short time has said that the brain of the Black is different from the White's, not in degree of quality, but in kind. If the divergence were so great as he imagined, it would be difficult to understand how it is possible for the African to learn our language, and for us to learn his. It is a common idea that the African's mind works so diversely from the European's that to think black is, and must always remain, an impossible achievement for the White. A school of anthropologists, of which M. Lévy-Bruhl is the chief spokesman,[2] claims to have discovered that "primitive" man (including modern barbarians) is incapable of dispassionate and consistent observation, is devoid of the power of abstraction, unable to draw any benefit from experience and cannot construct or comprehend even the most

[1] GABRIELLE M. VASSAL, *Life in French Congo* (1925), pp. 91, 97, 149.

[2] L. LÉVY-BRUHL, *Les Fonctions mentales dans les sociétés inferieures* (1918), English translation, *How Natives think* (1926); *La Mentalité primitive* (1922), English translation, *Primitive Mentality* (1923).

elementary laws of nature. He is in a pre-logical stage of mentality. These conclusions have recently been controverted brilliantly by Dr. Malinowski,[1] who shows that "every primitive community is in possession of a considerable store of knowledge, based on experience and fashioned by reason." It cannot be denied that it is difficult for civilized men to understand the uncivilized. But that is not because the mind of the latter works differently from ours. Dr. McDougall is unquestionably right in saying that the interval between the modern man of scientific culture and the average citizen of our modern states is far greater than that between the latter and the savage.[2] "The English and Welsh country-side," says another scholar,[3] "preserve, for those who have eyes to see them, very many customs and prejudices which presuppose savage mentality"—which is to say that the difference between cultured Europeans and barbarian Africans is one of education, not of mental structure; it is a matter of disparity in dominant traditional ideas. The Africans, so far from lacking reasoning powers, are ruthless in their logic. Starting from the belief in the survival of the human personality, for example, they argue that a Chief requires a retinue in the spirit world, and they reach the terrible conclusion that therefore men and women must be slain that they may accompany him.

[1] Essay in *Science, Religion and Reality* (1925), pp. 21 sqq.

[2] W. McDougall, *The Group Mind* (1921), pp. 75, 76.

[3] H. J. Rose, *Primitive Culture in Greece* (1925), p. 2.

My experience leads me to confirm what Mr. Peter Nielsen, an experienced observer, has written :

> "I have listened to thousands of old Native men of many different tribes in my time, I have heard them speak their inmost thoughts, not through interpreters—who ever learned anything through an interpreter ?—I have studied these people in and out of Court, officially and privately, in their kraals and in the veld during many years, and I say that I can find nothing whatever throughout the whole gamut of the Native's conscious life and soul to differentiate him from other human beings in other parts of the world."[1]

Perhaps the greatest mistake that is made in regard to the Africans is to argue from their actual achievement as a race to their natural ability as individuals : that is to say, because the Negroes have done so little as a race in the past, we infer, a priori, that the Negroes of to-day are defective mentally.

That many Africans show remarkable capacity cannot be doubted. The Negro did not change his race when he was exported to America and his progress there since his emancipation from slavery has been truly astonishing. To give one instance only : a Negro who was born in slavery has achieved an international reputation by his researches in chemistry. In British, American and South African Universities African students have taken excellent degrees. A few years ago, a full-blood Congo Negro[2] was awarded the Goncourt prize in literature in competition with some of the

[1] Peter Nielsen, *The Black Man's Place in South Africa* (1922), p. 81.

[2] René Maran, author of the prize novel *Batouala* (1921).

leading writers of France. Many other examples might be given, but it will be sufficient to relate the following experience of a South African judge, Sir Thomas Graham:

> "Speaking with his wide experience as a Judge, he said that he had formed the definite conviction that there was no substantial difference in natural ability between the White and the Black. At Port Elizabeth a short time before he had tried an action, arising out of a labour dispute, in which the principal witness on one side was the Native secretary of an organization representing 14,000 Bantu workers. This man was highly intelligent and gave his evidence with the utmost clearness and confidence; though he had a large number of intricate figures and details to deal with he never hesitated a moment or made a single mistake. After the trial the Judge called the man to him and ascertained that he came from Nyasaland. 'That alone,' added the Judge, 'was a remarkable thing—a Native coming down from Nyasaland and taking charge of an organization of Coloured and Native people in South Africa, and this man had been educated from a state of semi-savagery in a single generation.' "[1]

It may be objected that Africans who have shown such outstanding ability are so few in number that one cannot argue from these particular instances. Yet that some Africans have climbed so high surely proves that the mere fact of a pure African ancestry is not of necessity a bar to mental and cultural advance. Apparent racial inferiority may be due, not to a permanent organic disability but to relatively superficial factors such as social inheritance and lack of opportunity. One must remember the very short time that the advantages

[1] W. H. Dawson, *South Africa* (1925), p. 173.

of education have been offered to the Africans. And the fact must not be overlooked that in the past "uneducated" Native chiefs and others have shown very remarkable ability. Whatever may be said of them in other respects (and some of them were men of considerable character) such men as Moshesh, Sebituane, Msidi, Khama, Chaka, Lobengula, and Lewanika certainly did not lack in intellectual power. Of Lewanika I was told by a British administrator that, all things considered, there was no abler diplomat in Europe.

Why then have the Africans never developed a higher civilization?

"The Negroes have no chapter in the history of the planet," says M. Louis Vignon.[1] Mr. Putnam Weale says that the Asiatic has contributed immensely to the civilization of the world, has founded every great religion that exists. "Not so the black man. He is the child of nature—the one untutored man who was a helot in the days of Solomon, as he is still a virtual slave."[2] Such writers imply that the world owes nothing to the African—and never will owe anything to him. This exaggerated statement must not be allowed to pass unchallenged. Eminent authorities like Sir James Frazer are coming to the conclusion that European culture owes more to the Africans than has yet been acknowledged. It is highly probable that Africans

[1] *Un Programme de Politique Coloniale* (1919), p. 41.

[2] *Op. cit.*, p. 233. How untrustworthy a guide this author is in things African is shown in his statement that while Christianity succeeds in Uganda it fails in South Africa because the people there are Bantu. The Baganda are also Bantu.

discovered the process of smelting iron.[1] In many regions of the continent a civilization of a relatively high character had been developed before the Europeans came, and apart from Islamic influence—civilization quite as high as the Romans found in Britain.

Yet it must be conceded that as a whole the Africans never progressed very far. They never, for example, invented a system of writing.[2] Why is it? To this various answers may be given, such as the deadening effect of disease carried by insects. If, as has been alleged, the mosquito was one cause of the degeneration of the Greeks, may it not also have been a factor, coming at an early stage, in hindering the further evolution of the African? But perhaps the chief reason was that the conformation of the African continent has always made intercourse with the outside world difficult. History proves that peoples advance under external stimulus and stagnate when that stimulus ceases to operate. Peoples do not rise

[1] E. TORDAY, *Journal of Royal Anthropological Institute*, Vol. XLIII, p. 414: "I feel convinced . . . that we are indebted to the Negro for the very keystone of our modern civilization and that we owe him the discovery of iron." He gives his reasons in *Causeries Congolaises*, pp. 230 sq. In his latest work Sir James Frazer suggests that the story of the Fall of Man contained in Genesis was derived by the Hebrews from the negroes, "with whom they may have toiled side by side in the burning sun under the lash of Egyptian taskmasters." *The Worship of Nature*, (1926) Vol. I, p. 223 sq.

[2] This needs a slight modification, for two African peoples have possessed such a system. See M. DELAFOSSE, *Civilisations Négro-Africaines* (1925), pp. 127-8. This highly experienced administrator demonstrates the existence of a definite African culture.

independently to a high degree of culture: "civilization is a plant much oftener propagated than developed." Our British culture is an outstanding example.

In a previous chapter allusion was made to the invasions of "white" peoples in Africa. Unquestionably these did stimulate the Negro race to a limited degree, but the stimulus was not continuous and when it ceased the Negro, and even the Negroid who had absorbed foreign blood, sank into stagnation again. Many of the Africans were never affected by this stream from abroad, and others only to an infinitesimal extent. This in itself is sufficient to account for the position in which the Africans were found by Europeans. And there is the further fact that for thousands of years they have been oppressed by various fears and psychologists make clear how these phobias may adversely affect the whole life of the people.

But, we must not commit the error of inferring from their past and present state that the Africans have no capacity to advance. The limits of a people's power of adaptation and of progress cannot be determined from any consideration of their history before the stimulus to adaptation occurred.[1] Under the new conditions a real awakening of mind, a definite naissance, is taking place. And the advance made by so many

[1] This is quoted from PROFESSOR L. T. HOBHOUSE by the REV. J. W. PRICE in his remarkable article, "The Cultural Possibilities of the Negro and Bantu" in the *Holborn Review*, October, 1925. He develops fully the argument of these paragraphs.

individual Africans under European guidance may be taken as a promise of greater things to come.

General Mangin, the famous French commander of African troops, bears this testimony:

> "The Negro is probably as competent as the white man to handle the scientific instruments of civilization. . . . . I do not deny that he has still to be educated. What I do maintain is that he has qualities of head and heart which ought not to be treated as negligible. He is by nature good and faithful and endowed with a sense of honour, and if he is really given the chance, he will reach a high level. There is an *élite* in the black world capable of excelling in all regions of human intelligence."

IV.

In earlier days there was some excuse for despising the African. Europeans were necessarily ignorant of his languages and they had not studied the social customs and beliefs. Jean Jacques Rousseau, writing in 1754, said: "The whole of Africa and its numerous inhabitants, singular alike in their character and in their colour, have still to be examined; all the land is covered with peoples of whom we know nothing but their names: and yet we presume to judge concerning the human race!"[1] We remember how John Morley describes the way in which people of the 18th century talked of *l'homme naturel*—"one who had watched bees or beetles for years could not give us a more full or confident account of their doings." In the absence of facts, philosophic conjectures took their place

[1] *De l' inegalité parmi les hommes*, p. 112.

The inductive method is now applied to the study of man. And one of the distinguishing features of the last fifty years has been an industrious, painstaking collection of the facts concerning the African. In this study missionaries and government officials have taken the leading share. There remains a great amount to be done, but to-day we know the Africans as our fathers did not know them. And the hopeful thing is that the more we have come to know about them, the more we have learnt to respect them. We have discovered to be true of them what Rousseau predicted falsely would be discovered about the gorillas and orang-outangs whose existence had been reported in his time: he said that they would prove *ni des bêtes ni des dieux, mais des hommes*. Never before, it may be safely said, were there so many people convinced of the real worth of the African— not as a labourer, but as a man. And that conviction is based, not upon sentimental considerations, but upon actual knowledge. "Les connaître, c'est les aimer," truly says Mr. Torday.[1]

It is no accident that the post-war period has witnessed a greater interest in Africa—and the Africans. The loyalty and generosity of the Natives during that conflict struck deep into the hearts of the British people. While the war diminished in some degree the prestige of the Whites, it enhanced the prestige of the Blacks. Men who fought with and against African troops were loud in their praises. "As far as actual fighting is concerned,"

[1] E. TORDAY, *Causeries Congolaises* (1925), p. 9.

said one distinguished English general, "the West Africans would be fit to fight alongside any troops in the world." "Just as good as the best Indian soldier when properly trained and officered," said another. It is the way of the British soldier to admire bonny fighters whatever side they may be on—as Kipling recorded after the Sudan campaign :

> "An' 'ere's to you, Fuzzy-wuzzy, with your 'ayrick 'ead of 'air—
> You big black boundin' beggar—for you broke a British square !"

So men came back from the war with a new respect for the African and a determination to see justice done to him.[1] East may be East, and West, West,

> "But there is neither East, nor West, Border, nor Breed, nor Birth,
> When two strong men stand face to face, though they come from the ends of the earth."

[1] CAPTAIN W. D. DOWNES, *With the Nigerians in German East Africa* (1919), pp. 288, 289 : "The Empire owes more recognition than has up to date been given to the negro soldier for all that he has had to endure and all the appalling hardships in East Africa and the Cameroons he has gone through for the sake of the Empire. Their deeds have not been done in the limelight and the public have heard very little of their doings . . . but, my reader, they have fought and conquered, suffered and died, for the British Empire. . . I sincerely hope that all the negro has done for the British race will not be forgotten, and that the welfare of the African will be one of Britain's first considerations after the war."—Some of those who had to do with the Carrier Corps had the same feeling. MR. F. H. MELLAND, after giving the figures already quoted (p. 68, footnote) writes : "Perhaps the reader will now understand a little why we are rather proud of our natives ; and one reason why we would like to do a little more for them, which we cannot do unless the people at home will take some interest in them. On their war record alone they seem to have earned that interest."—*In Witch-bound Africa*, p. 27.

The new attitude is one of respect rather than pity. Pity for what old missionaries called "the perishing progeny of Ham" comes at times perilously near contempt. Respect means that we honour whatsoever there is of good in the African's life, and that we desire to help him to make that good better, not by supplanting it with an entirely exotic culture, but by stimulating him to develop his culture according to his own genius.

This new attitude of respect underlies Article 22 of the Covenant of the League of Nations, which is rightly considered the Black Man's Magna Charta. It reads:

> "To those colonies and territories which as a consequence of the late war have ceased to be under the sovereignty of the States which formerly governed them, and which are inhabited by peoples not yet able to stand by themselves under the strenuous conditions of the modern world, there should be applied the principle that the well-being and development of such peoples form a sacred trust of civilization and that securities for the performance of this trust should be embodied in this covenant."

This article (to use Burke's words about another document) provides "a real chartered security for the rights of man." True, at first sight it does not bear the significance here attributed to it. But to say "not yet able to stand by themselves" implies a conviction that some day they will be able to stand by themselves—that they possess qualities which can be developed under sympathetic guidance to a high level. It is true, again, that the Article refers specifically only to the territories surrendered by Germany. But the principle of Trusteeship here laid down is of universal application, and the British Government has definitely extended it to embrace all its African dependencies. In 1923 it said : "As in the Uganda Protectorate, so in the Kenya Colony, the principle of trusteeship for the natives, no less than in the mandated territory of Tanganyika, is unassailable." The Memorandum of the Advisory Committee on Education (accepted in 1925 as a statement of Government policy) draws no distinction between West and East Africa in referring to the responsibility of the Controlling Power as trustee "for the moral advancement of the native population."

These official documents contain a progressive definition of trusteeship—an advance from "well-being and development," and "protection and advancement," to "moral advancement." The Report of the East Africa Commission (1925) recognizes that the status of trusteeship "imposes upon the trustee a moral duty and a moral attitude." This represents a wonderful progress from the time when the exploitation of the African in the form of slavery was the dominant purpose of Britons. It is a triumph of Christian principle in the realm of high national policy. It looks upon the African as primarily a man—not a labourer. He is a ward whose guardians pledge themselves to care for and educate, imparting to him what they possess to the full extent of his present capacity to receive ; and looking to the future when he will be able to manage his own affairs. Once adopted such a principle can never be abandoned for a less worthy ideal. Trusteeship involves a duty that is not limited to agents of the Imperial Government and to missionaries; as the East Africa Commission declare, it "lies really upon the shoulders of every man and woman of European race in Africa." Every action of Europeans in Africa must be tested by this principle as a touchstone.

Respect for the African's manhood involves the adoption of what Sir Frederick Lugard, in oft-quoted words, calls the true conception of the inter-relation of colour: "complete uniformity in ideals, absolute equality in the paths of knowledge and culture, equal opportunity for those who strive, equal admiration for those who achieve; in matters social and racial a separate path, each pursuing his own inherited traditions, preserving his own race-purity and race-pride; equality in things spiritual, agreed divergence in the physical and material."[1]

This is the attitude adopted throughout this book. It is a position far removed alike from that taken by the "damned nigger" people and from that of a certain writer who seems to think that Pope Gregory's *non angli sed angeli* was a declaration of the Almighty, and who declares "the *Evangelization* of the world can only come about as a result of the *ev-Anglo-isation* of the world." The African is being cut away from his old moorings. Contact with western civilization makes it for ever impossible that he should remain as he is, or get back again to where he was. But he is not to be regarded

[1] *The Dual Mandate in British Tropical Africa* (1922), p. 87.

as a European who happens to be born with a black skin. It must be frankly recognized that he possesses aptitudes and traditions which, though they may differ from those of Europeans, are still worth conserving. The Africans must be enabled to build something new upon the sound elements in their individual character and social system. For its enrichment humanity needs, not black Europeans, but Africans true to their racial ethos.

What Robert Bridges writes of nations of advanced culture is true also in a measure of Africans :

> " China and Ind, Hellas or France
> Each hath its own inheritance ;
> And each to Truth's rich market brings
> Its bright divine imaginings.
> In rival tribute to surprise
> The world with native merchandise."

CHAPTER V.

WHEREIN ARE CONSIDERED SOME OF THE PROBLEMS RAISED BY COMMERCE AND INDUSTRY.

I.

THE names given to stretches of the West Coast of Africa—"Gum Coast," "Grain Coast,"[1] "Ivory Coast," "Slave Coast," "Gold Coast"—indicate the kind of commodity that was drawn from those regions in early modern times. During four hundred years the principal export consisted of black men and women. Slavery has existed in Africa from a remote period. Copper bangles, which appear to have been slave-fetters in use ten thousand years ago, have been unearthed in Rhodesia. Negro slaves were possessed in Ancient Egypt, and were exported to Crete and Greece. In more modern times they were, as they still are, taken across the Red Sea into Arabia and other countries of the Near East. But it was not until after the discovery of America that the slave-traffic arose in its most loathsome form. The problem became acute of finding labour to cultivate the

[1] "Grain" stands for a kind of pepper which was called "Grains of Paradise"—malaguetta pepper (*amomum melegueta.*)

rich soil of the West Indies and mainland, and it seemed that Providence had created the brawny, docile Negroes of Africa for the purpose of supplying this need.

British merchants did not begin the traffic, but of course they soon succeeded in out-trading their rivals. From the day that John Hawkins, in 1562, discovered that "Negros were very good merchandise in Hispaniola and that store of Negros might easily be had upon the coast of Guinea," British capital and enterprise were increasingly engaged in trafficking flesh and blood in order that English ladies might enjoy sugar in their tea, that English gentlemen might indulge in their pipe of tobacco and glass of rum, and that English looms might be fed with cotton. There has probably never been a more lucrative trade in the world. "A great part of the wealth which went to build up the immense prosperity of Lancashire in the second half of the [eighteenth] century, and to make the Industrial Revolution possible, was derived from the slave trade and the trade with the West Indies which was linked with it."[1]

The slave trade brought wealth to Europe and America; for Africa it was the greatest of calamities. It is estimated that from 1680 to 1786, 2,130,000 negroes were imported into British colonies alone. But such figures tell only a small part of the cruel tale. To procure victims for the eastern and western markets, bands of marauders raided the

[1] Ramsay Muir, *A Short History of the British Commonwealth* (1920), Vol. 1, p. 683.

interior, provoking quarrels and intestine wars, burning, killing, destroying. Livingstone wrote in 1871: "It is awful, but I cannot speak of the slaving for fear of appearing guilty of exaggerating. It is not trading: it is murdering for captives to be made into slaves." The descriptions penned by him and other travellers read to us to-day like the record of some horrible nightmare. The slave-routes were marked by whitened skeletons; twelve per cent. of the slaves who were put on board perished at sea; they were packed between decks like herrings in a barrel, or like volumes on book-shelves; and a large number died overseas before the sale and during the period of seasoning necessary before commencing their labours under new conditions. Out of every hundred captives shipped from Africa only fifty lived to be effective labourers on the plantations. The mortality among the slaves was enormous: between 1690 and 1820, 800,000 were landed in Jamaica, yet in the latter year only 340,000 Negroes were counted on the island. Taking everything into consideration, and including the operations of Europeans and Arabs, it does not seem an exaggeration for Du Bois to say that the slave trade cost Negro Africa 100,000,000 souls.[1]

The traffic went far to destroy the man-power of the continent. What an asset those hundred million and their progeny would be to Africa to-day when the deficiency in the population is causing

[1] Du Bois, *The Negro*, pp. 155-159.

so much anxiety! The slave trade is thus proved to have been not only an appallingly cruel business, but also an economic disaster.

Before any nation took steps to prohibit the traffic, Adam Smith had demonstrated in *The Wealth of Nations* that slave-labour was uneconomic.[1] But, as Wilberforce in one of his speeches said: "Interest can draw a film over the eyes so thick that blindness itself could do no more." Upholders of the trade were so obsessed by the immediate profits to be made that they were indifferent not only to the sufferings of the Negro but to the future and permanent welfare of mankind. Such inhuman folly has been perpetrated again and again. No fable is more pertinent to the history of Africa than the fable of the man who killed the goose that laid golden eggs.

Seventeen years elapsed between William Wilberforce's first denunciation of the traffic in Parliament (1789) and the final passing of the act (1806) which made it illegal for British subjects. A further period of twenty-seven years passed before slavery, as distinct from the slave-traffic, was abolished in British dominions. Vast political events, such as

[1] "The experience of all ages and nations, I believe, demonstrates that the work done by slaves, though it appears to cost only their maintenance, is in the end the dearest of any. A person who can acquire no property, can have no other interest but to eat as much and to labour as little as possible. Whatever work he does beyond what is sufficient to purchase his own maintenance can be squeezed out of him by violence only, and not by any interest of his own."—Vol. I, page 345 (Everyman Edition). *The Wealth of Nations* was published in 1776; Denmark took the first step in 1792 toward abolition of the slave trade.

the French Revolution and the struggle against Napoleon, undoubtedly accounted in part for this delay, but vested interests were even more potent in hindering the Abolitionists at every turn. Many people, who were not unsympathetic, sincerely believed that cessation of the trade would mean the commercial ruin of the mother-country and the downfall of the Empire. The sea-power of Britain seemed to be involved in maintenance of the traffic. Appeals were made unblushingly to the electors' pockets. Harrowing pictures were drawn of the calamitous effects of abolition. Charles James Fox, however, in a speech delivered in the House of Commons, pronounced the final condemnation of the trade: "I believe it to be impolitic. I know it to be inhuman. I am certain it is unjust. I find it so inhuman and unjust that, if the Colonies cannot be cultivated without it, they ought not to be cultivated at all."[1]

Then as later, men cloaked their selfishness under the insufferable cant that slavery was really an excellent thing for the slaves. They anticipated the old Portuguese official who, in our own day, with a glow of noble enthusiasm, expatiated to Mr. Nevinson on the philanthropy of slavery: "Both in our own service and at San Thomé," he said, "the slave enjoys a comfort and well-being which would have been forever beyond his reach if he had not become a slave."[2] Sadder still, professedly Christian men found arguments for

[1] R. Coupland, *Wilberforce* (1920), p. 166.

[2] H. W. Nevinson, *A Modern Slavery* (1906), p. 54.

slavery, and persuaded themselves that to hold slaves, and even to traffic in them, was not contrary to Christianity. John Newton, the author of the hymn "How sweet the name of Jesus sounds," engaged actively in the trade both before and after his conversion. "I never knew sweeter or more frequent hours of divine communion than in my last two voyages to Guinea," he said. Twice every Sunday as captain he conducted public worship on board the slave-ship—a thin plank separating the worshippers from the weltering crowd of helpless black captives fettered in the noisome cavities below deck.[1]

The emancipation (in 1834) of 800,000 slaves on British territory was "more than a great event in African or in British history. It was one of the greatest events in the history of the world."[2] Even that did not mean the end. It was not enough for one country, even though that country was Great Britain, to decree abolition of the traffic and freedom of the slave. It only meant that the traders of other lands benefited by the withdrawal of a powerful competitor, for slaves were still in demand. Great Britain gave money lavishly to induce Spain and Portugal to follow her example. International agreements were drawn up. And then for many years it was thought that at last the iniquitous thing was dead.

That this was not so is known to-day. Neither

[1] *The Works of the Rev. John Newton* (1835), p. 31, etc. R. COUPLAND, *op. cit.*, p. 37.

[2] R. COUPLAND, *op. cit.*, p. 517.

slavery nor the slave trade is extinct—though the traffic is diminished to very small proportions. Slavery—"the assumption of property rights in another person," as the Convention proposed by the League of Nations in 1925 defines it—still prevails in many parts of the world, even under the British flag in Sierra Leone and the Sudan.[1] The Temporary Slavery Commission reported in 1925 that there were no fewer than nineteen areas in Europe, Asia and Africa where slave-raiding, slave-trading and slave-markets exist to a certain extent. Notwithstanding the efforts of France and Italy, slave-raiding is still carried on in countries bordering the Sahara desert. As for slave-dealing in Abyssinia: "There is reliable evidence of recent date that many thousands of slaves (an estimate which appears to be trustworthy says 10,000) are brought by Abyssinian traders to the north-western districts, where slaves are purchasable at any time in the markets." Ras Tafari, the Regent, has issued edicts abolishing slave-dealing, but he has met with strenuous opposition, for many of his people abide by the Mosaic Law which in their opinion sanctions the practice.[2] From the coast of the Red Sea, slave-dhows still succeed in escaping

[1] Sir A. R. Slater, the Governor of Sierra Leone, stated when opening the 1925-6 session of the Legislative Council, that a bill would be introduced to remove the last vestige of recognition by local law of the status of slavery. As for the Sudan, the Government has decided that no person born after the reoccupation in 1898 is otherwise than free, so that in due course slavery will come to a natural end.

[2] A very distressing account of the slave-raiding by Abyssinians is given by an eye-witness, Major Henry Darley, *Slaves and Ivory* (1926).

the vigilance of British and other cruisers, and find a ready market for all the slaves they can land in Arabia. It is devoutly to be hoped that the nations who are members of the League will sign and vigorously enforce the Draft Convention of 1925[1] which pledges them "to prevent and suppress the slave trade" and "to bring about progressively and as soon as possible the disappearance of slavery in every form." Some of these nations have already agreed by the Convention of St. Germains "to secure the complete suppression of slavery in all its forms and of the slave trade by land and sea."[2]

The enlightened conscience of mankind will no longer tolerate what our forefathers supported. But vigilance is always necessary. For the circumstances that made slavery and the slave trade possible continue to exist. White men still need the black to cultivate the ground for them. Now as ever helplessness breeds tyranny. Some people talk about "superior germ-plasm," others of shifting many of the burdens hitherto borne by the working classes in civilized countries, to the backs of other races, in order that we may "still maintain the richness and colourfulness of our culture."[3]

[1] This Convention, which will come up for discussion in June, 1926, has been described by Sir Frederick Lugard in *The Nineteenth Century and After*, January, 1926. He points out its faults, especially in that it embodies a sanction for forced labour for private profit. It is to be hoped that this clause will be satisfactorily amended.

[2] The statements in this paragraph are based upon the Minutes and Report of the Temporary Slave Commission (A.18.1924.VI; C.426. M.157. 1925. VI; A.19, 1925, VI.) and debate in House of Lords, 16th December, 1925 (*Hansard*, Vol. 62, No. 97). [3] C. C. JOSEY, *Race and National Solidarity*.

Practically this is Aristotle's argument for slavery. If slavery and the slave trade, naked and unashamed, stand condemned, we must beware lest they creep back in disguise.

II.

In 1876 Stanley found these market-prices prevailing at Ujiji on Lake Tanganyika, one of the principal centres of the Arab slave trade: Ivory, per lb. one cloth of four yards of sheeting; a bullock, 10 cloths; a girl (10-13), 50 to 80 cloths; a girl (13-18), 80 to 200 cloths; a woman (18-30), 80 to 130 cloths; a woman (30-50), 10 to 40 cloths; a boy (13-18), 16 to 50 cloths; a man (18-50), 10 to 50 cloths.[1] The sheeting thus used for buying slaves was the product of British, European and Indian looms.[2] Then, as earlier and later, there was a demand in Central Africa for such things as the factories of Europe could supply. While the Abolitionists appealed primarily to the religious and humanitarian sentiments of their fellow-countrymen, they were not above appealing also to their business instincts. Why not, said they, establish real

[1] H. M. STANLEY, *Through the Dark Continent* (1878), Vol. II, p. 5.

[2] "During the continuation of the slave trade Great Britain exported manufactures to Africa to the extent of £1,000,000 annually, entirely for the purpose of barter in that trade. It is not too much to say that all the other European nations sent an equal amount for the same purpose."—J. M'QUEEN, *Geographical and Commercial View of N.C. Africa* (1821), p. 254.

commerce in Africa, based upon free labour, to displace this wicked traffic?—it would be more profitable in the long run. They knew that in the best sense, philanthropy pays. This was, however, no mere *argumentum ad crumenam.* Wilberforce and his colleagues were profoundly convinced that commerce may be a humanizing agency; that one sure way of delivering the Africans from slavery and a servile mentality, and of elevating the race, was to promote free industries.

As early as 1821 that prescient geographer, James M'Queen,[1] was saying that the slave trade would never be abolished by force—that a navy stationed off the coast of Africa could only lop off branches, but that commerce established in the interior would attack the roots of the evil tree, dry up its juices and supplies. He used the same language then as we are using now about the need for new markets and the advantages of growing cotton in Africa rather than relying upon America.[2] While the greater part of Africa was still unexplored he was proclaiming her ability of producing every kind of tropical produce that the world needs. "It is by her agriculture alone, the cultivation of

[1] JAMES M'QUEEN, *A Geographical and Commercial View of Northern Central Africa* (1821); *A Geographical Survey of Africa* (1840), *passim.*

[2] "In the present depressed state of our manufactures and commerce, no permanent relief can be hoped for, if new markets for our trade be not discovered and established. . . It must be of the first importance to our cotton manufacturers to be independent of America for a supply of fine cottons. Africa . . . can furnish that supply."—This was not written in 1926 but in 1821. (M'Queen, pp. 212, 218.)

her soil, that Africa can be regenerated, or produce that permanent and useful commerce which will tend to extend her knowledge, tend to make her and her people independent members of the general human society, and remove the present bitter evils that afflict her."

The leaders of the anti-slavery movement needed no conversion to such views. One of Wilberforce's earliest resolutions in Parliament had recorded the need of substituting for slaves the export of "those special products of the African soil which were required for the manufactures of this country." Early one morning in 1837 Thomas Fowell Buxton, after lying awake all night thinking about slavery, said to his son: "The deliverance of Africa is to be effected by calling out her own resources." Another maxim of his ran, "It is the Bible and the plough that must regenerate Africa."[1]

In 1840, Whigs, Tories and Radicals, Free Churchmen and Anglicans, inaugurated a scheme for a settlement on the Niger which should embody the ideas of Wilberforce, M'Queen and Buxton.[2] The expedition was defeated by the mosquito, for out of 150 white men who sailed, 42 died within two months. This venture is remembered to-day chiefly through Charles Dickens' caricature in *Bleak House* —Mr. Quale and Mrs. Jellyby; Borrioboola-Gha; and the scheme for teaching the natives to plant

[1] EUGENE STOCK, *History of the Church Missionary Society*, Vol. I, pp. 451-2; *Memoirs of Sir T. Fowell Buxton* (Everyman Edition), p. 193.

[2] *Proceedings at the first public meeting of the Society for the extinction of the slave trade and for the civilization of Africa* (1840).

coffee and turn pianoforte legs for export. The project failed calamitously, but it pointed in the right direction. The conviction was dominant in the mind of David Livingstone (who, it is interesting to remember, attended that meeting in 1840) that a righteous commerce was a necessity in Africa: "an open path for commerce and Christianity," he declared it to be his purpose to discover. In 1859, writing from Nyasaland, he said: "If our countrymen were here they would soon render slave-buying unprofitable." In this region, he declared, Englishmen "might enjoy good health, and also be of signal benefit, by leading the multitude of industrious inhabitants to cultivate cotton, maize, sugar and other valuable produce, to exchange for goods of European manufacture, at the same time teaching them, by precept and example, the great truths of our holy religion."[1]

Words such as these fell on fruitful soil, as readers of Mr. Moir's "trade romance"[2] will know. His company—The African Lakes Company—was founded in 1878 for the express purpose of cutting the tap-root of the slave trade by introducing commerce into the region of Lake Nyasa.

A righteous commerce enriches both him that gives and him that takes. It remains the conviction of the truest friends of Africa that trade and industry may be of the greatest benefit to the Africans.

[1] W. G. Blaikie, *Personal Life of David Livingstone* (1917 ed.). pp. 216, 220.

[2] F. L. M. Moir, *After Livingstone, an African Trade Romance* (1923).

Honest exchange of the products of their labour confers blessings, not material only but spiritual, upon both black men and white.

III.

If the development of the resources of Africa is beneficial, or might be rendered beneficial, to the Africans, it is absolutely indispensable so far as the well-being of Europeans is concerned. "At no remote date," wrote Benjamin Kidd in 1898, "with the means at the disposal of our civilization, the development of these resources must become one of the most pressing and vital questions engaging the attention of the Western races."[1] That no remote date has already arrived. The factories, not of Europe and the United States only, but also of India and Japan, are demanding raw materials in ever increasing quantities, and new markets for their products.

No country has greater needs in these respects than Great Britain. Its inability to produce within its borders either the food it requires or the raw materials for its factories, makes it absolutely dependent on foreign trade: if goods could not be exported, food could not be imported and starvation would follow. In 1924 this country imported from the tropics, or semi-tropics, 1,462,184 centals of rubber; 7,649,000 centals of wool; 585,175 cwt. of coffee; 296,000 tons of palm kernels; 86,019 tons of copra; 99,226 tons of ground nuts;

[1] BENJAMIN KIDD, *The Control of the Tropics* (1898), pp. 96, 97.

182,673,483 lbs. of unmanufactured tobacco; 512,348,600 lbs. of tea; 35,218,700 cwt. of sugar; 37,781,600 cwt. of maize; and many other commodities in greater or less quantities. Customers are needed to purchase our manufactured goods. Fresh markets are required. Countries that once bought from us are now manufacturing their own stuffs. The higher standard of living makes British goods so expensive that some peoples who once purchased them can no longer afford to do so. Everybody who knows anything about it is aware that British trade is in a very unsatisfactory position and that there is no possible remedy for unemployment unless somehow foreign trade can be vastly extended. What would it not mean to the forty-four million inhabitants of Great Britain if the forty-nine million British Africans had a spending power equal to theirs? At present, the great majority have practically no spending power at all. The development of Africa's resources, and the education of the African masses, would not, it is true, solve all our commercial problems, but they would go a long way towards solving them. As a people we simply cannot afford to neglect Africa. That is why Parliament has guaranteed a loan of £10,000,000 for the building of new railways and roads and for the improvement of harbours in British East Africa.

Certain writers, with whose desire for the well-being of Africans and with whose protests against their unjust exploitation all sympathy is due, are strangely blind to the value of the continent.

Mr. Leonard Wolf, for example, speaks as if only European capitalists benefit by the development of Africa and as if, even so, the worth of African lands were negligible. He instances Uganda. "It is clear that the incorporation of Uganda [into the British Empire] has had no more and no less effect upon British trade, industry and employment, than if it had been sunk in the Indian Ocean and blotted off the map of the world."[1] He wrote this in 1919. In 1925 Uganda produced 80,000,000 lbs. of cotton and 600,000 lbs. of rubber, and while some of the cotton went to Japan and other countries much of it came to England. The Lancashire cotton-mills are now using over a million pounds of African cotton a week, a large proportion of it being Uganda cotton. Uganda imported goods to the value of about £4,250,000 in 1925, more than half being the produce of the United Kingdom and of other parts of the Empire; the balance came from other countries and the profit made by them adds to the power of purchasing other British goods for themselves. Uganda is not so negligible as Mr. Wolf believed. The fact is that in this, as in other instances, he omits the time element from his calculations. The value of the aggregate imports and exports of British East Africa was under £1,000,000 in 1905; in 1925 the figure stood at £16,000,000. The Royal Commission which in 1890 examined the project of a railway to Uganda estimated that the line might secure a

[1] LEONARD WOLF, *Empire and Commerce in Africa* (1919), p. 334.

freight of produce and trade goods amounting to as much as £80,000 per annum. Actually in 1925 the freight was valued at £8,000,000. Cotton piece goods to the value of nearly a million sterling were imported from the United Kingdom into British East Africa in 1925. These African countries, both East and West, are only at the beginning of their development. Their value to British trade—if only they are wisely managed—is bound to grow tremendously.

Mr. Wolf argues that if these territories were not part of the British Empire there is no reason why they should cease to supply raw materials and markets—negligible as he thinks these to be.[1] But Uganda, and Nigeria (whose trade is now worth £23,000,000 a year) would not have remained independent had they not come under the British flag; they might well have formed part of the French African Empire, and the French do not provide in their colonies an open market for the world. Had they remained independent (which is inconceivable), they could not have developed as they have done. Who would have built the railways? And would any one really wish for all kinds of traders and industrialists to be let loose in Central Africa beyond the control of European governments?

In espousing the cause of the Africans it is folly to minimise the value of Africa. That rich continent cannot be allowed to remain undeveloped. It is blindness not to see its importance in the economic

[1] Leonard Wolf, *Economic Imperialism* (1921), p. 57.

life of the world. The soil has as yet been barely scratched, but its pre-eminent wealth has been amply demonstrated.

The gold won from the bowels of the earth in the Transvaal (mainly by black hands, directed and financed by Europeans) has sustained the industrial prosperity of Europe during forty years.[1] The labour of Africans in the mines of Katanga (again directed and financed by Europeans) helped the allies to win the war, for while the Germans were raking in the copper utensils from every household to make munitions, hundreds of thousands of tons of copper came to Britain from these mines—£10,000,000 worth, at least. During the war the happy discovery of a mountain of manganese (used in smelting high grades of steel) in Gold Coast Colony contributed largely to the efficiency of our aeroplanes—to say nothing of the chlorine gas made from it. Fifty-five per cent. of the world's total supply of cocoa is grown in the Gold Coast Colony. The rubber of Africa, the fibres, the hides, the coffee, the sugar, the vegetable fats, the fruits, the wool, and a hundred other products, enter our factories and homes daily, and make an enormous difference to our well-being and comfort. More and more we depend upon Africa.

Cotton has been referred to, but the subject is so important that the lesson it teaches must be emphasised. British cotton-mills give employment

[1] LORD BURNHAM: "I do not believe it would have been possible to carry on the industries of Europe without the gold from South Africa."

to 630,000 people—directly or indirectly about eight millions depend upon the industry. Four million bales of cotton a year came into England before the war; in 1924 the figure dropped to 2,700,000 bales. This material cost about £100,000,000 and worked up into cotton goods was worth £250,000,000—the difference between the figures representing wages for the most part. Four-fifths of the manufactured article were exported.

The bulk of our raw cotton comes at present from the United States. For various reasons that need not be stated in detail, their crop diminished from 16,000,000 bales in 1911-12 to 11,290,000 bales in 1923-4: in 1925-6 it rose to over 15,000,000. The Americans are using more and more of their own cotton (32 per cent. in 1905, 64 per cent. in 1925); their spindles have increased nearly 30 per cent. in twelve years. It is estimated that by the year 1942 they will be using the whole of their crop and no part of it will be available for our mills, nor for those of Italy, France and Germany. The prospect for our cotton industry is a gloomy one—comparable only to the condition realised during the American Civil War when all supplies ceased—unless in the meantime other sources become available.

India grows much cotton, but of a low-grade; she uses most of what she grows, and exports the remainder chiefly to Japan and China: in 1924-5 only 60,909 bales, out of the total crop of 6,450,000 came to Great Britain. In the rest of the British

Empire, 343,142 bales[1] were produced in the season 1924-5 and of these Uganda is to be credited with 170,000 bales—nearly one-half. At present the African output is only about one-tenth of what Great Britain uses in a bad year and less than a hundredth part of the world's consumption. Strenuous efforts are now being made to increase this output. At no distant date Uganda may produce 500,000 bales of first-class cotton suitable for Lancashire's needs. The immense irrigation works[2] constructed in the Sudan will ultimately, it is said, bring a million acres under cultivation, and of these, about 100,000 acres are now producing cotton. Nor does this exhaust the possibilities. It is calculated[3] that in the countries ranging from Abyssinia to Bechuanaland (excluding Belgian Congo and Angola) the cultivable area is about equal to that in the United States and that 90,000,000 acres are suitable for cotton-growing. The U.S.A. produced its 1923-4 crop of 11,290,000 bales on 38,700,000 acres. At the same average rate of 144 lbs. of lint to the acre, this African area

[1] American bales weigh 500 lbs ; British, 400. The facts and figures given above are derived in part from an article by ROBERT L. LOWY in the *English Review* (February, 1925) ; in part from a speech made by Mr. Sandeman in the House of Commons (*Hansard*, July 27, 1925) ; and in part from information supplied by Mr. H. Worsley, of the British Cotton Growing Association.

[2] The reservoir created by the Sennar Dam on the Nile, officially opened in January, 1926, holds sufficient water to supply the needs of Greater London for about two years. The dam is nearly two miles long and contains a million tons of masonry.

[3] By H. L. SHANTZ (of the Bureau of Plant Industry U.S. Department of Agriculture) in *Education in East Africa* (1925), p. 353, sqq.

should be able to produce 28,510,000 bales (of 500 lbs.), which is nearly 7,000,000 in excess of the world's total consumption in 1924. Whether this can be done depends almost entirely upon population—a subject to be considered in the next chapter.

So far as can be seen at present, the future of the British cotton industry depends upon the cultivation of some of these vast areas. In other words, the destiny of Lancashire lies in the lands of Africa.

IV.

At one time I thought of entitling this book, "The Nigger Question Up to Date." I had in mind that terrific "occasional discourse" which the humour of Thomas Carlyle ascribed, whether as orator or reporter, to one Phelim M'Quirk.[1] How very modern some of the language is! The West Indian Negroes are pictured "sitting yonder with their beautiful muzzles up to the ears in pumpkins, imbibing sweet pulps and juices." Let them be worked! cries our M'Quirk.

> "No black man who will not work according to what ability the gods have given him for working, has the smallest right to eat pumpkin, or to any fraction of land that will grow pumpkin, however plentiful such land may be; but has an indisputable and perpetual *right* to be compelled, by the real proprietors of said land, to do competent work for his living. This is the everlasting duty of all men, black or white, who are born into this world. . . Induce him, if you can . . . but if your Nigger will not be induced? In that case, it is full certain, he must be compelled."

[1] First printed 1849. *Latter-Day Pamphlets*, pp. 1 sqq.

To the M'Quirks of Carlyle's generation and our own, the Nigger Question is a matter of getting the black man to work for the M'Quirks' advantage. Any "work" that the black man may do for himself is not work. They preach to-day as eloquently as ever the duty and nobility of labour—not always, however, as the duty of black *and* white. In this respect, our M'Quirks sometimes fall behind their prototype.

The M'Quirks' oratory may amuse us, or it may arouse indignation. But the facts must be squarely faced. The development of the resources of Africa, which has become a serious and pressing question, can only be accomplished by the collaboration of capital and labour. Under present conditions in tropical Africa, European labour is out of the question. Chinese or Indians might be imported, but previous experiments have shown that this creates more problems than it solves. Co-operation between Europeans and Africans seems to be the only practicable plan. It is idle to suppose that if left entirely to themselves the Africans would in the future, any more than in the past, make the best of their land from our point of view: not because they are unintelligent and incapable of labour, but because they need training and supervision and because apart from railways and ships built by Europeans they have no means of exporting their produce. Co-operation is the word. The goods are wanted, but our conscience demands consideration of the conditions under which they are produced. We are no longer content that all the advantages shall be reaped by ourselves—that the Africans shall pay with their blood and tears for our prosperity. And the question now takes this form : How, in conformity with the respect that is due to the manhood of the Africans, can these be induced to co-operate effectively with Europeans in developing the resources of the continent for their mutual advantage?

The solution of the problem is attended by many difficulties. The African is capable of working and does work. It is high time that the notion of his incurable idleness was abandoned.[1] Even to produce "pumpkins," Dr. Phelim M'Quirk, entails some work! Not all African soil and climatic conditions are such that food stuffs will grow without strenuous cultivation. The African in his natural state does work; he does not leave it all to his women. The demand now made by the Europeans upon them is that in addition to growing their own food, building their own houses and tending their own cattle as heretofore, the Natives shall grow crops for export, undertake all the navvy-work on roads and railways, excavate mines, till and harvest plantations and act generally as the hired servants of the whites. It is a considerable

[1] See for example the irrefutable statements made by W. H. DAWSON (*South Africa*, p. 161): "The truth is that he (the Native) does not need one-half of the apologies which benevolently disposed defenders are in the habit of advancing on his behalf. A general accusation of indolence is absolutely unjustifiable—so much so as to be ludicrous . . . the Native confutes his critics by his daily life. . . He carries the entire mining industry upon his shoulders. He works the 85,000 European farms of the country besides his own," etc.

demand to make upon people who, before the Europeans came, knew nothing of earning wages, nothing of leaving home to seek employment; who, while they worked diligently on their own lands and in their own villages, during periods when it was necessary, were never accustomed to labouring on contract, without intervals for rest and recreation, for six months or longer; and whose wants were few and simple. It is not sufficiently realised what a revolution such a demand causes in the African's manner of life.

There are two methods by which the desired co-operation may be attained: first, by persuading the Native to cultivate economic crops on his own land in addition to his own food-stuffs; and second by employing him as a wage-earner. Both methods are actually in operation.

The first method is generally adopted in British West Africa, and it is being used in Uganda and elsewhere with gratifying results. Since the first cocoa-plant was brought into the Gold Coast Colony by a Native and the first eighty pounds of cocoa were exported in 1891, the industry has expanded till in 1924 the out-put rose to 223, 329 tons and the Colony has become the premier producer in the world. Neither this cocoa industry, nor the groundnut and palm-oil industry of Nigeria is dependent on European capital so far as actual production is concerned, though a great deal of it is employed in collecting, shipping and marketing the produce. A missionary of the C.M.S. (Mr. Burrup) introduced cotton-seed into Uganda and the crop, entirely grown by Natives, has grown from eight bales in 1904 to about 200,000 in 1926. In Tanganyika Territory the more recent encouragement by the Administration of Native production has been vindicated by the output and by the increased prosperity and contentment of the Natives: in 1924, rather more than 50 per cent. of the coffee and about 75 per cent. of the cotton was grown by Natives.[1] The European Governments co-operate by means of the encouragement and expert advice given by officials of the Agricultural Department, and by providing transport; the traders by collecting and exporting the crops.

Various dangers attend this system. The sudden acquisition of wealth is apt to unbalance the native mind. In favour of crops which bring him money, the Native may neglect to grow sufficient food for himself and his family, or may throw the entire burden of this upon his wife, or wives. The inexperienced and careless African farmer may easily be worsted in the incessant struggle against insect pests and plant-disease—whence the need for agricultural education and for sedulous supervision by European experts. The palm-oil and kernel trade, the biggest trade of the West Coast, is, so far as cultivation and preparation are concerned, in the hands of Africans, but its supremacy is threatened by the competition of the Dutch East Indies where large areas are worked on scientific lines: and unless the Africans can learn better methods the industry is doomed. These are some

[1] Government Report for 1924 (Colonial No. 11, 1925).

of the evident drawbacks which require the attention of their European guides. But, on the other hand, the system has its advantages, of which cheapness of production is perhaps the least. As Sir Frederick Lugard says, "The native holder occupies a higher status, and working in his own sole interests and at his own time will produce more than if working for another."[1] Booker Washington was right in saying: "There is all the difference in the world between working and being worked."

"Native production," says the East Africa Commission, "should be encouraged, trained, and supervised . . . by training the native to become a better and more progressive agriculturist on his own land we shall be adopting one of the best means to his economic, moral, and social advancement."[2]

Admirable as this system is, it does not preclude the necessity for the employment of wage-earners. Railways and roads must be constructed if the native-holdings are to be successful; mines have to be worked; and there are certain kinds of crops which must be grown somehow, somewhere, and which cannot be grown except on plantations owned and managed by Europeans: for all these and other things labourers are needed. To attract this labour is not always easy, especially where the population is scant and the Natives are encouraged to grow economic crops for export. The two systems then become rivals: and East African

[1] *The Dual Mandate*, p. 419. [2] *Report*, p. 36.

settlers at their wits' end for labour are provoked to denounce the growing of cotton by Natives as "Manchester slavery."

To induce Natives to work various methods are used, which may be classified thus: 1. Force; 2. Persuasion; 3. Forceful persuasion—"the benevolent whip" of Dr. Phelim M'Quirk.

The method of enslavement, pure and simple, has become for ever impossible so far as Christian Europeans are concerned. But the needs are so urgent, and some men in their hurry to be rich are still so blind to the well-being of future generations and, it must be said, so inadequately alive to the claims of humanity where their own immediate interests are in conflict therewith, that they may, and at times do, succumb to the temptation of adopting methods that are in reality scarcely, if at all, distinguishable from slavery.

Happily a League of Nations is in being. Those Powers which administer African territories as Mandatories of the League must submit annual reports and undergo cross-examination by an international Commission, whose minutes are published. No doubt it is strange that Great Britain, whose standard of administration is so high, should have to submit to questioning by a national of Portugal, whose standard is so deplorably low; but even the best administration is not immaculate, and the critics, if their criticisms are not to sound ridiculous to the world, must feel compelled to labour hard to bring their own country's policy and practice at least as high as the standard of those upon whom they sit in judgment. For these to attend meetings of the Mandates Commission is like going to school. The Mandates, with their insistence that territories shall be administered not solely in the interests of the mother-country but also in the interests of the Natives, will become a model for governments other than mandatories. The trouble is that resolutions adopted in Geneva depend for their efficacy upon people in Africa, some of whom regard the idea of Trusteeship as mere sentimental bosh. The International Labour Office is also concerning itself with African conditions of labour. It may be confidently expected that certain practices which have prevailed will be abandoned.

Forced labour, which in one form or another is sanctioned by every Government in Africa, is of two kinds which must be clearly distinguished: 1. Forced labour for purposes of State; 2. Forced labour for private gain. These are again to be classified according as the labourers are remunerated or not. Unpaid compulsory labour is commonly employed for the repair and maintenance of roads in the vicinity of native villages. Remunerated compulsory labour is resorted to for the building of railways and for the porterage of government stores when voluntary workmen cannot be obtained. The French, Portuguese and Belgian governments would seem to use this method freely in the public service; the British government sanctions it reluctantly and imposes stringent safeguards.

This system, which is liable to obvious abuses,[1] is defended on the grounds that every State has the right to the services of its citizens; in the debate on the subject in the House of Lords Viscount Cecil instanced the compulsion a man is under to clear the snow from before his doorstep, and Lord Raglan asked, in reply to criticism, What about jury service? I believe that a democracy has the right of calling up all citizens for military service in time of need, and if this be conceded it cannot be denied that the State has in the abstract the right to conscript citizens for necessary and urgent civil work in time of peace. But the justice of selecting particular classes for this compulsory service is open to doubt—it should be imposed upon all, if upon any; and the justice of forcing the Africans alone to construct railways which are for the benefit of the entire community, white and black, can be called in question. "If," says Sir Harry Johnston, "the public needs require that labour should be forced for public works or public emergencies, the resident White man must obey the call as much as the Native."[2] If white men

[1] It was stated, on good authority, in 1925, that on the Midland Railway in French Cameroons men had worked seven months without pay and it was admitted by the authorities that the death-rate was about 80 per 1,000. Doctors were employed in the proportion of one to 6,000 workmen. (Minutes of Permanent Mandates Commission, C.386, M.132. 1925. VI, pp. 41, 42.) In July, 1925, the Supreme Court of Kenya quashed the conviction by a magistrate of certain natives who were alleged to have refused a call to compulsory labour on a railway. The Court found that the authority of the Secretary of State had not been proved for this work. (*The Times*, July 31, 1925.)

[2] SIR H. H. JOHNSTON, *The Backward peoples and our relations with them* (1920), p. 60.

cannot do this work, they should pay an equivalent in cash and their land, whose value is enhanced by the passing of a railway through it, should be taxed to meet part of the cost of the line. At present, Natives are compelled both to work and to pay taxes. On the average a Native of Kenya pays for himself and his dependents thirty shillings a year in direct taxation, while a European may own a hundred thousand acres of land traversed by a railway, and pay no more than thirty shillings a year in direct taxation, irrespective of the line. It would be more in accordance with equity to abolish compulsory labour entirely. This, however, goes beyond the recommendations of the Temporary Slavery Commission, the provisions of the Mandates, the draft Convention on Slavery, and the principles of the Anti-Slavery and Aborigines Protection Society, all of which consent to compulsory or forced labour on the part of the Blacks for essential public works and services if paid.

On the other hand, no argument can be sustained in favour of forced labour for private profit. Lord Cromer stigmatized it as "wholly unjustifiable and as synonymous with slavery." It is no longer permitted in British territory but prevails elsewhere.[1]

[1] When he was requested, in 1925, to supply labourers for the farmers, Sir John Chancellor, Governor of Southern Rhodesia, replied: "All I can say is that that will never do. . . Every subject of the King is free to enter into a contract or to abstain from entering into a contract for the disposal of his labour. Any measures taken by Government to apply compulsion to natives to secure an adequate supply of labour for private employers would be opposed to the traditional policy of His Majesty's Government and would be altogether repugnant to the sentiment of the Imperial Parliament."—*Anti-Slavery Reporter*, January 1926.

According to the investigations of an American sociologist, Dr. Ross,[1] both in Mozambique and Angola the Portuguese compel men and women to labour on the roads without payment and, moreover, supply private individuals with this forced labour. In Mozambique "the standard term of compulsory labour is six months of 30 working days each." Dr. Ross saw children as young as twelve years, and women nearing the time of their delivery and women carrying infants on their backs, all working on road-making. The labourers are recruited by native policemen, men of the most brutal character, who make full use of their opportunities to extort money, to beat and rape. The planters, traders and hotel-keepers to whom forced labourers are assigned, cheat them of their wages in a most despicable fashion. After serving six months they may receive sufficient to pay the head-tax, and return home having gained nothing more than bitter experience. If only ten per cent. of the statements made in Dr. Ross's report are true, such treatment is an infamous scandal. No wonder that the Natives cannot cultivate sufficient food for themselves and that many thousands have migrated across the border into British territory.[2] The Portuguese, by their inhuman

[1] EDWARD ALSWORTH ROSS, *Report on Employment of Native Labour in Portuguese Africa*, New York, 1925. I understand, it is only right to say, that the Portuguese deny the accuracy of Dr. Ross's statements.

[2] The Nyasaland Census of 1921 reckoned that of one tribe inhabiting Portuguese East Africa 108,204 persons had crossed the border. No statistics relating to other territories are available.

folly, are ruining some of the fairest lands of the continent.

In French West Africa a fiscal labour levy (*prestation*) is imposed. Adult males between the ages of 15 and 60 are obliged by law to work for the State for a term not exceeding 15 days a year. The Mandate given to France for part of Togoland and of the Cameroons provided that all forced or compulsory labour should be prohibited except for essential public works and services and then only in return for adequate remuneration. The French deny that the *prestation* constitutes a violation of this rule, because, though the Togoland natives are expected to work four days, and the Cameroons natives for ten days, without pay, the levy is commutable for a money payment of one franc a day—the natives are not rendering a service, but paying a tax. Sir Frederick Lugard rightly contended at the meeting of the Mandates Commission that you cannot legitimize forced labour by labelling it "fiscal."

The old iniquitous system in Belgian Congo, under which the natives were brutally compelled to gather rubber in lieu of taxes, has happily passed away, but the record remains to point the danger of forced labour.

The second method of inducing Natives to work is that of persuasion. How effectual this may be depends upon the needs felt by the Native of earning money and on the inducements held out to him in the way of good wages and proper treatment. It is almost universally admitted that some settlers never have difficulty in securing all the labour they need, while others are always in trouble. The former know how to handle the men ; the latter do not.

It is a widespread custom to gather labour by means of agents of a recruiting organization, who enter into contracts, supervised by a magistrate, with the Natives. Many men prefer to seek work for themselves, but where these organizations are skilfully and humanely run they offer many advantages to the natives, especially when these are to work at great distances from their homes. They are looked after on the road, receive medical attention and at the close of the contract are repatriated with their wages.

Even the best system on paper may, in the absence of stringent supervision, become the means of oppression. The so-called indentured-labour which obtained in Portuguese West Africa, and which has been exposed and to some extent, at any rate, reformed, looked very well on paper, but in reality was nothing but slavery : all the pretence of signing contracts was, as Mr. Nevinson said, nothing but "a dodge to delude the anti-slavery people." He described it as "one of the blackest crimes which even Africa can show."[1]

The third method of obtaining labour is that of "forceful persuasion." Under this term may be included all such things as depriving the Natives of their land, the enactment of vagrancy laws, and the imposition of direct taxes, with a view to

[1] HENRY W. NEVINSON, *A Modern Slavery* (1906), p. 58.

inducing the people to work for wages. The highest authorities, such as Sir Frederick Lugard,[1] agree that while taxation of the Africans by European Governments is legitimate and has an excellent educative effect, the primary object of the tax should not be to compel them to labour or to provide revenue. But the Governments have frequently acted against this principle and rather on the lines enunciated by a former Governor of British East Africa who said, "We consider that taxation is the only possible method of compelling the native to leave his reserve for the purpose of seeking work,"[2] They have imposed a tax of say four shillings with the alternative of a month's labour; or have allowed a rebate of 50 per cent. if the man could prove that he had worked for a European for a period; or have remitted the tax altogether in case of continuous employment. Taxes vary in amount, but they are often the equivalent of a month's wages or more.

Lack of space forbids my entering more fully into the subject of taxation, whether direct, by means of hut or poll tax, or indirect by means of customs duties, railway rates, and so on. Its incidence is often unfair. The Native is in some colonies made to contribute more than his share to the public revenue, and in effect subsidizes the European settlements. A more equitable system

[1] *The Dual Mandate*, p. 235. Chapters XII and XIX should be carefully studied.

[2] Sir Percy Girouard in 1913. Quoted by NORMAN LEYS, *Kenya*, p. 186.

would be to return a large part of the money to the natives in direct ways that he could appreciate —in educational and medical facilities, for example, which, as is generally admitted, are inadequate at present.

Other indirect methods are for the magistrates and Native Commissioners to instruct, or advise, or encourage, Native chiefs to send men out to work. This, it is now recognized, may be liable to abuse, for the Natives and their chiefs take official advice and encouragement as commands. Sometimes the latter make it a means of petty tyranny. Sir Frederick Lugard tells of a headman who was also a butcher and who took the opportunity of getting rid of his competitors in the village by compelling all the butchers to go out to work! The British Government has disallowed the practice.

These various forms of compulsory or semi-compulsory labour have often been defended on the ground that, while in themselves objectionable, they are permissible as temporary measures to accustom the Natives to work for the European. There may be something in this, but it is generally recognized that forced labour is uneconomic: it is certainly attended by many grave abuses. After all, it is hard to justify the white man's presumption that he has a natural right to enter Africa, dominate the people, take their land and compel them in some way to labour for his benefit. My own faith in the virtue of hard work is as fervent as Dr. Phelim M'Quirk's. While in Africa I preached the Gospel of Labour by precept and example. Industrious habits are the foundation of all strong character. The words that Robert Louis Stevenson addressed to the Samoans who built for him, "The Road of the Loving Heart" should be displayed in every schoolhouse in Africa (with the alteration of "Samoa" into "Africa"): "Who is the true champion of Africa? . . . It is the man who makes roads, who plants fruit trees, who gathers harvests, and is a profitable servant before the Lord, using and improving that great talent that has been given him in trust . . . because all things in a country hang together like the links of the anchor cable, one by another; but the anchor itself is industry." But the only legitimate method of inducing the African to work harder is to raise his standard of living, creating new ambitions and needs by a rational system of education.

CHAPTER VI.

WHEREIN ARE CONSIDERED THE FUNDAMENTAL QUESTIONS OF POPULATION AND LAND.

I.

THE area of Africa, including Madagascar, is estimated to be 11,660,000 square miles. In other words, it occupies a space nearly three times the size of Europe, nearly four times that of the United States of America, and ten times that of British India. The whole of Europe, India, China and the United States could be comfortably tucked within its borders. Yet the population of Africa does not exceed 130,000,000[1]—much less than half that of British India, a tenth of its area. Spread over the whole continent, the population averages about eleven persons to the square mile. Even when every allowance is made on account of deserts, lakes and mountainous regions, the density compares very unfavourably with that of other countries. The main island of Japan carries 649 persons to the square mile—as do England and Wales; Bengal, 608; and parts of Belgium, over 1,200. Outside

[1] SIR LEO CHIOZZA MONEY'S figure is 129,414,700. (*The Peril of the White*, p. 189.)

the Delta of the Nile, where 939 persons are crowded to the square mile, the densest rural population in Africa would seem to be in Southern Nigeria, where some districts number over 300 to the square mile, and in parts of Kavirondo bordering on Lake Victoria, where, it is said, eleven hundred persons are crowded to the square mile. The province of Kano in Northern Nigeria carries an average of 116; Gold Coast Colony, 50; Basutoland, 42; Kenya and Tanganyika, 11; Northern Rhodesia, 3. Some areas are inhabited by less than one person to the square mile.

Why is the population of Africa so scanty?

The slave trade, as we have seen, cost perhaps 100,000,000 lives. The inter-tribal wars, except for such sanguinary conflicts as that associated with the Zulus, in which it is said two millions of people were destroyed, may not in particular instances have been attended by a great mortality, but in the aggregate they must have diminished the population considerably. The customs of the people—the human sacrifices and the slaying of men, women and children on the death of a chief, the smelling-out of witches, the infanticide, the widespread practice of abortion—have been important factors in the case. The long lactation period, extending over two or three years, may limit the size of families. Whether this is balanced by the effect of polygamy is doubtful. Unquestionably, polygamists occasionally produce large families; the last South African Census reports one Native who had 55 wives, 51 sons and 42 daughters; but no wife had more than three children, and the question must be asked, How many young men were prevented from marrying by this monopolist? Mr. Strachan investigated the affairs of 393 South African women, wives or widows of monogamists, and 591 wives and widows of polygamists; the former had borne an average of 5.65 children, the latter an average of 5.58. Mr. J. H. Harris and other writers have recorded similarly inconclusive figures. My own impression is that polygamy is not generally conducive to a high population.

Life is not easy for Central African peoples: deaths by starvation and by misadventure are numerous. It is quite a mistake to suppose that they are relatively immune from disease. Apart from venereal and tubercular diseases introduced by foreigners, severe epidemics of measles, plague, influenza and smallpox have periodically swept off great numbers, while endemic diseases (malaria, dysentery, yaws, sleeping-sickness, bilharzia, pneumonia, leprosy, hookworm, cancer,[1] and others) has had almost unchecked sway. There are areas where hookworm affects 70 or 80 per cent. of the population. Vast regions in the tropical zone, aggregating almost a third of the continent, are infested with the tsetse-fly, the various species of which are responsible for sleeping-sickness among human beings and the no less deadly nagana-disease among domestic cattle. In the areas dominated by

[1] It is supposed sometimes that cancer is confined to highly civilized nations, but 622 persons died of it in Uganda during 1923.

this pest, no cows can be kept, and lack of milk is detrimental to the stamina of the inhabitants, to that of the children especially. A native chief told Mr. Ormsby-Gore that his tribe had decreased from 10,000 to 4,000 in four years owing to the death of the cattle through the invasion of tsetse.

Generally speaking the birth-rate is low and the rate of infant mortality is appallingly high. The low birth-rate is due to disease (chiefly venereal), to deliberate restriction in some instances, to the precocity and promiscuity of sexual relationship in others. The high death-rate of children is due to mal-nutrition, ignorance of child-nurture, disease and the practice of infanticide. In European countries the deaths of children up to five years of age vary from 40 to 120 per mille: in England during 1925 out of every thousand children born seventy-five died before they were a year old. Even in relatively civilized African towns such as Lagos and Accra the infant mortality varies from 350 to 483 per thousand. In the Kingdom of Uganda an official report shows it to have been 226 per thousand in 1923. In Kenya it is estimated at over 400 per thousand. Among the Baila we reckoned that from 50 to 70 per cent. of the infants died. In one district of Belgian Congo, Dr. Schwetz[1] found, by actual count, that for every 1,000 adult women, 2,685 children were born; and of these, 1,466, i.e., 550 per mille, were living, and 1,219, i.e., 450 per mille, were dead. A considerable proportion of the women had borne no children.

[1] J. SCHWETZ, in *Congo*, March, 1924, p. 350.

This was a sleeping-sickness area. In another district Dr. Schwetz counted 12,356 mothers and 4,429 childless wives.

> "Do you wonder," asks a medical missionary, "that even the healthy-born kiddies of Africa die in such large numbers? Exposure with its *sequelæ* of bronchitis and pneumonia, and mad feeding, with its stomach diseases and its dysenteries, kills them off like flies in the first two years."

He tells of a woman who one night bore a child in a shanty out in the fields; at dawn she slung the naked child on her back, under a ragged old skin, and walked through the long sodden grass to the village. They arrived drenched with water and shivering. Next day he saw her cramming down the child's throat a porridge made of manioc tubers. He adds:

> "She is a first-class mother and was following the best traditions of mothercraft."[1]

Every missionary in Central Africa is familiar with such sights as this.

When one considers the conditions of life that have prevailed in Africa, one is not surprised that the population is so small. The wonder is rather that there are any people at all.

There can be no doubt that the European invasion has, directly and indirectly, brought about a diminution of the population in some parts of Africa. Here, however, caution must be exercised. It is only within recent years that anything like an accurate enumeration of the people has been made: and even now the figures are, in most cases,

[1] G. E. TILSLEY in *World Dominion*, September, 1925.

admittedly only approximate. Even where recent estimates are fairly reliable, we rarely possess statistics of any value made thirty years ago, and it is therefore impossible to arrive at an accurate judgment in the matter. An example of the doubts thus caused is offered by the Census of Northern Nigeria, taken in 1921. An estimate made soon after the British occupation put the population at twenty millions, but this was soon discovered to be far too high. For the first "Census," of 1911, we have three sets of figures: the Residents calculated the population to be 8,115,981, but the Acting Governor added about a million on his own account, and the Blue Book gave a rather less figure than his. The "Census" of 1921, though substantially accurate, is not claimed to be faultless. For a small staff of Europeans to count these millions on a single day was out of the question; the work was spread over a period and was conducted largely by careless and untrained native officials who were not above omitting their friends, "with a view" says the Commissioner "to the concealment (as they thought) of their taxable capacity." Many villages being still beyond the control of Government, their inhabitants had to be guessed.[1] In other countries, the total figures are based upon the numbers of hut-tax payers and are only approximate. We therefore have to work upon estimates, not upon precise enumerations. And for a comparison with ten, twenty, or fifty years ago,

[1] C. K. Meek, *The Northern Tribes of Nigeria* (1925), Vol. II, pp. 169 sqq.

we have in most cases to rely upon impressions formed by authoritative observers.

Such facts as we possess do not substantiate any reckless statement that everywhere the population has diminished since Europeans assumed control. The North Nigerian figures show, for example, that between 1911 and 1921 the people increased from 8,115,981 to 9,998,314 In South Africa, where the Census is more reliable, the non-European population increased by 2,630,000 in thirty years, notwithstanding the high rate of mortality at the mines and the ravages of influenza and tuberculosis. Under the Mahdist régime the people of the Anglo-Egyptian Sudan decreased from over 8,500,000 to less than 2,000,000;[1] under British rule they now number 5,500,000:—thus they have more than doubled in twenty-five years.

On the other hand, our authorities agree that (apart from the slave trade) in some parts of Africa the population has decreased since the Europeans came. The virtual extinction of the Bushmen and Hottentots of the Cape needs no comment. Nor is it necessary to dwell upon the decimation caused by war. The Germans were ruthless in putting down rebellion in Tanganyika and South-West Africa. According to their own figures, they reduced the Hereros from 65,000 to 21,600. Between 1904 and 1911 the Hottentots decreased

[1] This was Sir R. Wingate's estimate, quoted by Earl Cromer who saw "no reason to doubt its approximate accuracy" (*Ancient and Modern Imperialism*, p. 112, note). Nearly 3,500,000 are said to have died of disease (largely smallpox), and 2,200,000 were killed in war.

from 20,000 to 10,000; and the Berg-Damaras from 30,000 to 13,000.[1] How many Africans died in the Great War nobody knows but God. The industrial innovations cause a heavy death-rate: on the railway which the French are building in the Cameroons it is reported as 80 per 1,000; in the mines of South-West Africa it is 110 a thousand. And these figures do not include the men who creep home to die, away from doctors and statistical officers.

M. Allégret describes as "positively appalling" the depopulation of French West Africa as a result of porterage, the heavy labour on roads and railways, the exactions of the native troops and the spread of disease following on the opening up of the country.[2] Madame Vassal speaks of the French Congo as "depopulated." This is no matter for wonder in view of some of her descriptions—the following, for example:

> "The manioc for the natives of Brazzaville frequently comes from a distance of 100 kilometres, and in this depopulated Congo it is the child-bearing women who undertake one of the most painful tasks. These groups of carriers generally arrive at midday, panting, exhausted, blinded by the glare of the sun and perspiration, which streams down their faces. It would be a pitiful sight if the carriers were men, but when they are women with babies it is harrowing."[3]

[1] G. L. Beer, *African Questions at the Paris Peace Conference* (1923), p. 14.

[2] Dr. Elie Allégret in *The International Review of Missions*, Vol. XII, No. 46, p. 162 (April, 1923).

[3] Gabrielle M. Vassal: *Life in French Congo* (1925), pp. 96, 97.

Here is an incident, related without a shudder :—

> "It was at Crampel, too, that Governors Gand and Toqué lived. . . A huge hole is shown containing thousands of skeletons. On the slightest pretext or provocation natives were thrown into it alive, and the executions by blowing up the victims with dynamite have to this day left a most vivid impression on the minds of the populace."[1]

One is not surprised to learn that, according to official figures, the population of French Equatorial Africa has diminished from 4,280,000 to 1,250,000 since 1911.[2]

The ruthless Leopoldian régime in the Congo, to which Belgians look back with disgust and shame, has been replaced by a humane system. But its effects are still felt. On altogether insufficient grounds the population was at one time estimated as high as forty millions. At present with greater knowledge it is reckoned as 7,152,779. It seems unquestionable that there has been a great decrease. Missionaries speak of "this appalling and shaming spectre of depopulation" as "an indisputable fact."[3] M. Wauters, the ex-minister of Labour, has no hesitation in ascribing this state of affairs to economic policy: "The danger comes to-day," he says, "no more from the rubber collectors, but from those impatient folk who would like to advance too rapidly in exploiting the depths of the earth or industrial cultures."[4]

The Belgians asked themselves, "Are we not on

[1] *Ibid*, pp. 188, 189.
[2] *L'Afrique Francaise*, January, 1926, p. 10.
[3] *Congo Mission News*, July, 1924 (Published in Belgian Congo).
[4] JOSEPH WAUTERS, *Le Congo au travail* (1924), p. 43.

the way to kill, slowly or quickly, according to circumstances, but surely, the goose that lays the golden eggs?" None too soon they appointed commissions of inquiry and sent out a band of doctors who in four years visited 3,272 villages, examined 534,323 Natives and administered 847,000 injections to patients suspected of sleeping-sickness. Dr. Schwetz, the head of one commission, has published some of the results of his investigations in frank, courageous papers, written without passion, as scientific documents should be written. One chief cause of depopulation, he says in regard to his district, is epidemic disease, especially sleeping-sickness, and, he adds, "everybody knows that sleeping-sickness has been spread through European penetration." The principal cause is the coming of civilization. Porterage, permanent labour, sudden changes of diet, transplantation into other districts, all these things inherent in the employment of natives on a large scale, kill off the people. In the form that civilization is presented to the Congo natives, he says, they cannot stand it. He tells his fellow-countrymen that they are impaled on the horns of a dilemma *peu enviable*: they must choose between having a stagnant, populous colony, and a temporarily progressive colony with a rapidly disappearing population.[1] The Belgians are putting forth strenuous efforts to remedy this state of affairs.

Turning now to British East Africa, we find a Commission reporting "there is no conclusive

[1] J. Schwetz, in *Congo*, March, 1923.

evidence that the population is increasing or declining in any part of East Africa." But on a later page they say, "There is only one territory which we visited, namely Uganda, where the native population is certainly increasing, and it is only for the year 1923 that this increase has been noted. In all other parts of East Africa there seems some ground for believing that deaths still exceed births."[1] According to figures quoted by Mr. F. C. Linfield in his supplementary memorandum, the population of Northern Rhodesia increased by over 150,000 between 1911 and 1921. In Nyasaland there was a larger apparent growth, but it was due to immigration. Actually the local tribesmen are decreasing. The last Census Report states the causes of decline in the following order of importance: 1. Venereal disease; 2. long absence of males from home; 3. the decline of the powers of hereditary chiefs; 4. wilful restriction of size of families; 5. contact with European civilization. Tanganyika Territory reports a decrease owing to losses from famine and the war, and to the spread of venereal disease during the war. As for Kenya, "The Chief Native Commissioner considers that, when every allowance has been made for defects in the estimates, it is difficult to avoid the conclusion that the population has lately shown a tendency to decline."[2]

The East Africa Commission was definitely of opinion that employment of male adults away

[1] *Report of the East Africa Commission*, 1925, pp. 46, 54.

[2] Mr. Linfield's memo. *E. A. C. Report*, p. 185.

from their homes in the reserves had no serious effect on the birth-rate. In the absence of statistics it is impossible to controvert this—or to substantiate it. The opinions we have quoted regarding other African territories testify that the new industrial system is a *vera causa* of a declining population. In Great Britain during the war we had experience of what the absence of a large part of the adult males means in domestic disturbances and a diminished birth-rate. In Africa the same effects are produced when large numbers of men are taken from home to work for a long period. Moreover, the social upheaval has, without question, produced among many Africans a listlessness, a lack of will to live, which with fatigue and malnutrition renders them an easy prey to disease.

II.

Leaving aside all considerations of sentiment for the moment, it is obvious that a declining or stationary population is a very serious drawback to the economic prospects of some African territories[1] Almost everywhere the complaint heard from European miners and planters is that labour is

[1] The East African Commission reported : " We are convinced that the Governments now fully realize that the future of the country is dependent upon the care of the native population, the increase in its effective birth-rate, and, above all, the prevention and cure of disease. We found that every section of the community in East Africa is unanimous in demanding an increase in the provision made for medical services. Irrespective of motive the demand is sound and it must be satisfied."—*Report*, 1925, p. 53.

scarce. If that is so to-day when the industries are still in their infancy, what is the outlook for them in the future? The potential cotton area of East Africa, for example—how is it to be cultivated? The Negro population of the U.S.A. cotton states is over 7,000,000, "more or less occupied in cotton-growing,"[1] the area worked in 1923-4 being 38,700,000 acres. On the same proportion the 90,000,000 acres in East Africa, said to be suitable for cotton,[2] would require 18,000,000 people. Where are these to be found in addition to all workers on railways, etc.? Mr. Linfield puts the matter in a common-sense way: "It is futile to press forward schemes, whether of European settlement, or of large scale native production, if the natives, who in either case must supply the labour, simply are not there."

Some people say: "Press on with your schemes of development; even though the present generation suffers, the future will reap the advantage!" This sounds like a cynical disregard for the well-being of posterity.

Happily the actual state of affairs is not irremediable. As South Africa and large parts of West Africa prove, the Africans are capable of increasing prodigiously under propitious circumstances. The causes of decline, if they have been correctly diagnosed, can be removed. Many of the diseases can be eradicated to a large extent, or entirely, if the resources of modern science are applied on

[1] *Encyclopædia Britannica*, 11th Edition, Vol. 7, p. 259.

[2] See *ante*, p. 116.

a large scale and with determination. What is being done in Uganda can be done elsewhere. The decline in population had set in before Europeans arrived—Sir Harry Johnston has said that Christianity saved the Baganda from extinction. Sleeping-sickness, introduced through European invasion and the cause of 200,000 deaths, has been successfully dealt with by missionary and Government doctors: in the kingdom of Buganda, 8,003 persons died of the disease in 1905; in 1915, three; and since 1917, none.[1] Now they are combating the even greater scourge of venereal disease—the outstanding hygienic problem of Uganda.[2] That success is attending their efforts is shown by the fact that the population is now beginning to increase.[3] More doctors, hospitals, maternity centres and dispensaries; instruction in hygiene and mothercraft; training of African medical assistants and doctors; a vigorous campaign against the tsetse: these are some of the things most needed in tropical Africa to-day and they must be provided if the population is to be saved from decay and enabled to increase. In so far as deaths are caused by customs founded upon African religious belief, the extension of Christian missions will avail.

Moreover, some review of economic policy is

[1] DR. J. HOWARD COOK in *Medical Practice in Africa and the East* (1923), p. 37.

[2] Dr. A. R. Cook found that 84 per cent. of the population of Bunyoro gave a history of venereal infection.

[3] The official Medical Report for 1923 says: "It is believed the tide has now definitely set in the direction of a steady increase in population."

called for. Careful investigation must be made, and statistics must be compiled, as to the effects of European industrialism in any area, and economic development must there be regulated in accordance with the facts thus obtained.

To their credit be it said, the Belgians have taken the lead in this matter. The report[1] of a very influential Commission, appointed in 1924, goes to the heart of the question by asking what proportion of workers can be taken away without injuring a native community and lowering the birth-rate. They reply that five per cent. of the men may be recruited, if these are to work a long distance from home for a lengthy period; ten per cent. if they work within two days' journey; fifteen per cent. if they work for Europeans without ceasing to live their family life. By education and other means the safe proportion might be increased to 25 per cent., but this must be regarded as the absolute maximum. There is no need to repeat the other findings of the Commission which emphasize the importance of conserving the population and of proportioning the economic development of the country strictly to the number of workmen available within such limits.

The principles they lay down should be applied in all territories where the demand for labour is heard. Whether the ratios they decided upon for the Congo are applicable to Kenya and elsewhere is a matter for investigation. It is difficult to avoid

[1] The Report is published in *L'Essor Colonial et Maritime*, April 11, 18, 25, May 2 and 9, 1925.

the temptation of discussing the problem, as it occurs in the other colonies, in the light of these findings, but the statistics available are so scanty and where they exist are so confused that discussion would be unprofitable. The subject cannot be left, however, without pointing out the startling difference between the Belgian maximum figure of 25 per cent. and the 50 per cent. contemplated by the East Africa Commission as the limit beyond which " it is neither desirable nor to be expected " that the men should be absent from home. This Commission saw that, if economic success is to be assured in East Africa, two things are absolutely necessary, (1) an increased native population, and (2) a greater economy in the use of labour. And Viscount Cobham, Chairman of East African Estates, Ltd., says very sensibly, " Planters and land companies would be ill-advised to embark upon any considerable development requiring a large supply of Native labour."[1]

III.

" The native question is the land question." All our authorities are agreed upon this point. Here the irritation caused by the contact of cultures reaches its culmination. The views of modern Europeans have diverged so considerably from the views of Africans as to proprietorship in land that mutual understanding becomes extremely difficult.

[1] *East Africa*, Wembley Souvenir number, July 2, 1925.

Europeans disregard views so different from their own and generally fail to appreciate the intense attachment of the Africans to the soil. There is only too much truth in the dictum: White men at one time robbed Africa of Africans, now they rob the Africans of Africa. No other single transaction has resulted in so much injustice on the part of Europeans and in so much resentment on the part of Africans.

According to high legal authority, there is no such thing as absolute ownership in the soil of England for any subject of the King. The ultimate landowner is the sovereign acting on behalf of the State, that is to say, the whole body of the people. What in England is a legal theory is actual practice in Africa, except where foreigners have introduced new conceptions. The African admits no individual ownership in the soil. All land within the tribal boundary, whether cultivated ground, pasturage, waste ground or forest, belongs to the community as a whole, and not to the present occupiers only but to the community in perpetuity. The individual acquires certain rights by reason of his being a member of the community, but no right of proprietorship. Where the chief is said to be the owner, he is nothing more than a representative and trustee of the tribe. It follows that no man, not even the chief, can alienate the land. Purchase and selling of land are inconceivable to an African.

Here and there may be found some modification of this theory and practice; for example, in Uganda where a feudal system was introduced by invaders of Galla origin.[1] On the West Coast and in South Africa ideas of individual ownership have come in with the Europeans. But all who have studied the question would I believe accept as correct the exposition I have given of the purely African system.

When Europeans entered Africa they naturally presumed that land could be bought and sold as in their own countries. They struck bargains with the native chiefs, bargains which they interpreted in one way and the chiefs in another, since each started from his own preconception and they knew neither the language nor the views of each other. The chief granted (or thought he was granting) permission to occupy a parcel of ground ; the white man was convinced that he was purchasing the ground in the sense that he would purchase freehold land at home. Naturally troubles followed. The white man, by reason of superior force, got his own way, and a sense of injustice was left to rankle in the minds of the people.[2] In this way Europeans have acquired immense areas for the proverbial old song—for hats and rum and pots and knives. The land around the Bay of Natal was "purchased" by the British for goods of the nominal value of £1,650 ; actually the goods were worth £50. But it was no real sale ; for nobody had a right to sell the land.

[1] JOHN ROSCOE, *The Baganda* (1911), p. 268 ; *Twenty-five years in East Africa* (1921), p. 83.

[2] An illuminating instance of what has happened many times is given by ESU BIYI in his article on Temne Land Tenure (*Journal of the African Society*, July, 1913. No. XLVIII, Vol. XII, p. 407, sqq.)

This land question must be studied also from the standpoint of the broad interest of humanity. "The earth is the Lord's and the fullness thereof," and He has granted it to men: the whole of the earth belongs to the whole of mankind, for the use of all, and it is man's duty to make the most of his patrimony. From this point of view, any individual, or any community, that allows the land to lie undeveloped betrays the common good. Mr. George Edwards (National Union of Agricultural Workers) declared at the Trades Union Congress of 1925: "I would make it a criminal offence for a man to own land and refuse to cultivate it."[1] If it is a crime against humanity for a British landowner to "refuse" to cultivate his estate, is it a virtue for Africans to "refuse" to cultivate the vast areas which they hold? East African settlers have been quick to draw the parallel.[2] On the African's own collectivistic principles, if a man does not use his share of the tribal land it may be allotted to another tribesman; and this rule must surely be extended to any community, white or black. It was Carlyle's view that the true owner

[1] *The Daily Herald*, September 14, 1925. It is interesting to note this in connection with the anti-imperialistic resolution adopted the same day. See p. 67.

[2] See e.g., "Our Kenya Letter" in *East Africa*, December 31, 1925, and its comments on the Chief Native Commissioner's statement that the settlers covet the land of the Lumbwa tribe. "They [the Natives] graze their goats and cattle over one of the richest and best watered areas in East Africa which, put to its best uses, is capable of producing enormous revenues from tea, coffee or other crops and dairying, and of which they have no knowledge whatever." The correspondent calls it "wasted land."

is he that can the best educe from the soil the beneficent gifts with which the Maker endued it.

Where does this argument lead us? Does it warrant Europeans in arrogating to themselves a mandate from humanity to assume possession of the uncultivated areas of Africa? The facts already given as to the paucity of the population prove that much of the continent is not fully occupied, and the right of Europeans, or of other peoples, to occupy and cultivate the areas that are not occupied by aborigines cannot be contested. But an intolerable injustice is done when, supported by such arguments, Europeans oust the Natives, by force or by legal fictions, from land which the Natives occupy—even though the native standard of occupation is not higher than that of Europeans who hold huge estates of 100,000 acres and more.

Has such injustice been committed?

This question might be answered by reference to South Africa, where the unwise and unjust handling of the land problem in the past is causing an acute problem to-day The Natives have been compelled to live on about one-fifth of the land which they held when they were much less numerous; the existing native reserves are inadequate and sometimes dangerously congested; while some of the European areas are becoming depopulated owing to the monopolization of land by big landowners, often for purely speculative purposes.[1] South African

[1] See the pamphlet by PROFESSOR W. M. MACMILLAN (of the Witwatersrand University): *The Land, the Native and Unemployment* (1924). In the Transvaal, 543,485 Europeans hold 110,450 square miles; 1,544,151 non-Europeans hold 3,837 square miles.

experience has much to teach East Africa in regard to land.

To East Africa we now turn, and the position will be appreciated better if comparison is made with Nigeria and other West African territories.

In 1861, the British Government, reluctantly and solely with a view to suppressing the slave trade, took possession of Lagos in virtue of a treaty with the Chief. In subsequent years a Protectorate was extended over various Native States near the coast, and in 1886 a charter was granted to a Company which induced many inland chiefs to place their territories under British protection. From the treaties published in Hertslet[1] it is quite clear that no general rights over the land were conveyed by the Natives to the Company, which was given powers of administration over foreigners and the right to work mines. It was in this way that Southern Nigeria came into the Empire, for when the Company's charter was revoked in 1899 the British Government assumed direct administration. A large part of Northern Nigeria was conquered by the British, who assumed the rights of property held by the Fulani chiefs and claimed the right to dispose of unoccupied lands. The British Administration held the land as a trustee for the people, with due respect to private and communal rights. No interference was made with native occupation or title, but no alienation of the land to foreigners was permitted. No freehold

[1] SIR E. HERTSLET, *The Map of Africa by Treaty* (3rd Edition, 1909), Vol. I, pp. 89 seqq.

grants are made in Nigeria. "The grant of large blocks of land to 'concessionaires,' unless uninhabited, is," Sir F. Lugard declares, "altogether opposed to the principle of trusteeship."[1] The system which has prevailed to a large extent in French and Belgian territory, is not allowed in British West Africa.

> "The Government fully recognizes," said Sir Hugh Clifford, then Governor of Nigeria, to the Legislative Council in 1925, "that the land in the Southern Provinces is the inalienable communal property of the various Native communities whose rights to it are based upon effective occupation or upon immemorial usage. . . . . To dispossess any such tribe of any extensive area, no matter what the admirable uses to which the land thus taken from them might be put, would therefore be an act of the greatest imprudence; and the final result of any such action would probably be the establishment of European-owned estates among African communities which were outgrowing the areas available to them. It is my very earnest hope that the land policy of the Government which, in my judgment, is the corner-stone upon which the entire edifice of Native prosperity and well-being in this country depends, will never be suffered to be altered or abandoned, no matter how strongly it may be urged that such action is demanded in the name of economic expediency."[2]

Referring in another speech to Lord Leverhulme's grievance that white men are not allowed to purchase land in Nigeria, Sir Hugh Clifford said:

> "We have a sacred trust to discharge and if we did what Lord Leverhulme advocates, I say we should be

[1] *Op. cit.*, p. 298. Sir F. Lugard discusses with his usual lucidity and fulness, the question of Land Tenure and Transfer in Chapters XIV and XV.

[2] *West Africa*, April 11, 1925.

> betraying that trust; and on the day the Englishman forgets his duty to the Native and tries to exploit him for his own advantage, that day Nigeria goes down the hill to her ruin. God forbid that any such day should ever dawn."[1]

This is perfectly plain. In Nigeria the Government disregards any pleas of economic expediency that tend to weaken the principle of trusteeship by removing the African from his land.

The British dependency now known as Kenya was acquired, not by conquest, but, like much of Nigeria, by virtue of treaties. First of all, the Sultan of Zanzibar conceded to Sir W. Mackinnon and other "prominent capitalists" the administration of his territories on the African mainland, and these gentlemen formed the Imperial East Africa Company which received a royal charter in 1888. This coastal region, in part, forms the Kenya Protectorate, which is separate from Kenya Colony. Between 1887 and 1891 the Company concluded a great many treaties[2] with the native chiefs in the interior, who had no right to surrender their tribes' rights in the land and did not in fact surrender them, but ceded all sovereign rights over their territories, peoples and subjects. The Company having surrendered its charter, the country lying between the coast and Uganda became a British Protectorate in 1895. Our right to govern the country rests upon the cessions previously made; so far as I am aware, no further agreements were

[1] *West Africa*, July 11, 1925.

[2] Details in HERTSLET, *op. cit.*, Vol. I, pp. 297, seqq.

made with the Natives,[1] who in virtue of those treaties should to-day be enjoying possession of the lands as the Nigerians enjoy theirs.

When the railway to Uganda was being built it was discovered that much of the land through which it passed was very rich and suitable for European settlement,—"a white man's country." "This being so, I think it is mere hypocrisy," said the Commissioner, "not to admit that white interests must be paramount and that the main object of our policy and legislation should be to found a white colony."[2] From 1902 onwards the British authorities made grants of the land, the first being of 500 square miles, to European syndicates and individuals.

How stands the matter to-day? I quote from the Report of the East Africa Commission:

> "At every meeting we had with the natives of Kenya Colony there was evidence of a feeling of insecurity as regards the tenure of their lands. The legal position appears to be that no individual native and no native tribe has any right to land in the colony which can be recognized by the Courts."

They quote a decision of the Kenya High Court in a land case in 1921, to the effect that all native rights had disappeared and that the Natives had become tenants at will of the Crown.

[1] A treaty was made with the Masai in 1904 recognizing their right in part of the land they had occupied, and another in 1911. How these agreements were kept has been told by Dr. Norman Leys, *Kenya*, Chapter IV.

[2] Sir C. Eliot, *The East African Protectorate* (1905), pp. 105, 310.

"This judgment," the Commission go on to say, "is now widely known to Africans in Kenya, and it has become clear to them that, without their being previously informed, or consulted, their rights in their tribal land whether communal or individual, have 'disappeared' in law and have been superseded by the rights of the Crown."

In the House of Lords, Lord Buckmaster (formerly the Lord Chancellor) thus commented upon this situation: "How the Crown asserted and obtained the rights of ownership over the whole of the soil is due to a series of legal fictions which is not always easy to follow."[1] On the same occasion the Earl of Balfour said: "Legally I have no doubt that the Crown is the technical owner of these lands, but . . . their [the Natives'] rights, their moral rights, have always been recognized." How they have been recognized has been laid before the British public by Dr. Norman Leys in his thought-provoking book, *Kenya*. He has been plentifully abused, but his statements about the allotment of land have never been controverted. He tells that some 2,000 square miles in freehold and some 5,500 square miles in leasehold have been granted to Europeans; to Indians 22 square miles, either freehold or leasehold; to Africans no land at all.[2] Certain lands have been proclaimed as "reserves," i.e., as native areas, but the Government is free to dispose of them without notice and without compensation to the occupiers. Dr. Leys is confident

[1] *Parliamentary Debates*, House of Lords, Vol. 61, No. 44 (May 20, 1925), p. 402.

[2] *Kenya*, p. 79.

that 5,000 square miles would be an over-estimate of the arable land in these "reserves." "So we get the extraordinary contrast of 10,000 square miles alienated to Europeans and populated by 1893 occupied Europeans, with 5,000 square miles, reserved, somewhat precariously, to nearly 2,000,000 Africans. And this, be it remembered, in a country never conquered, as most of India was conquered, but which we occupied with the professed object of protecting its inhabitants."[1] And, we may add, in a country of which His Majesty's Government declared they regard themselves as exercising a trust on behalf of the African population.[2]

It is not contended that Europeans should never have been invited to form a settlement in Kenya: there was room for them. But it certainly is not right that individuals and Companies should have been allowed to acquire practically for nothing huge areas for speculative purposes. Nor is it right that the Natives should have been ousted from much of the land they were occupying. The most liberal estimate I have seen of the Native Reserves is 30,400,000 acres (47,500 sq. miles).

[1] *Kenya*, p. 144.

[2] Dr. Leys, it will be noticed, gives two sets of figures for the alienated lands, 7,500 and 10,000 square miles. The Kenya Agricultural Report for 1924 puts the land, allotted and available for Europeans, at 7,000,000 acres (10,937 square miles) and the number of European occupiers in June, 1924 at 1,715. A map prepared by the Statistical Officer of the Kenya Agricultural Department shows 7,589,760 acres (11,859 square miles) as "surveyed into farms." This map indicates Native Reserves as 30,400,000 acres (47,500 square miles). The East African Commission states these to be 46,837 square miles. The figures, of course, vary from time to time.

This includes stretches of arid soil that no European would accept as a gift, and, according to Dr. Leys, only one-ninth of the total area is arable. A Land Commission in Rhodesia reserved 24 acres for each man, woman and child for exclusive and permanent native occupation.[1] On this basis, the arable and pastoral land needed by the Natives of Kenya would be about 48,000,000 acres (75,000 square miles).

Justice and the fulfilment of our duty as Trustees demand that sufficient land,[2] allowing for some growth of the population, should be allotted to the Natives, and that their title to it should be absolutely secured, so that no more of it should be alienable, except with the assent of the Natives and of the Imperial Government. The East Africa Commission proposed the setting up of a Trust Board, in which all native lands should be vested, and upon which representatives of the Natives should be appointed. By the time this book is published, the Government will, it is to be hoped, have given effect to this recommendation.

Whether the figures here given are strictly

[1] *The Dual Mandate*, p. 328.

[2] It is not in Kenya only that large areas have been alienated to Europeans. In Northern Rhodesia the North Charterland Company holds 6,400,000 acres, and various individuals and syndicates nearly 3,000,000 acres more. The British South Africa Co. (which no longer has administrative powers) owns over 10,000,000 acres—2,758,000 of which are in Northern Rhodesia—valued at about £5,000,000 in the Company's Balance Sheet. Outside Barotseland, no land in Northern Rhodesia has as yet been definitely reserved for Natives, but measures to this end are in progress. In Tanganyika Territory Europeans and Indians hold 1,769,000 acres.

accurate or not—and it is a very difficult matter to determine—the main differences between what is called "Westcoastism" and "Kenyaism" are not in dispute. The difference is noted and welcomed by some colonists in Kenya who look upon West Africa as "a paradise of the bureaucrat" and say, "Kenya is the antithesis of West Africa. We want it so and are proud of the contrast."[1] For justification of the divergent policies it is not sufficient to point to the fact that West Africa is deadly for Europeans while much of East Africa is "a white man's country"; nor to the fact that the West African dependencies have an average density of population six times greater than that of the East African dependencies.[2] The two systems, "Westcoastism" and "Kenyaism" represent two ideals which are in conflict throughout Africa. This fact may be obscured because the former obtains, not only on the West Coast but in parts of East Africa also: the Colonial Office has adopted in Kenya the dual policy of promoting development of the Natives and of encouraging European settlement. But the two ideals persist. According to one system, the aim is to build up an African community, economically independent, holding and cultivating its own land, and advancing in a civilization, which while absorbing the best of the European remains African, under the active

[1] "Our own correspondent, Kenya," *East Africa*, August 6, 1925.

[2] *The Dual Mandate*, p. 332. The table given by SIR F. LUGARD on p. 45 shows: Western Group, 44.6 persons to the square mile; Eastern Group, 7.5.

encouragement and advice of a few sympathetic Europeans; while according to the other system, the aim is to establish an aristocratic, land-owning European class which looks to the Africans to supply labour and whose intention is, while improving the African as a worker, to keep him in a permanent position of inferiority. The professed belief of these settlers is that the African advances, and can only advance, in contact with European enterprise. The future will determine which system is the more in accordance with the highest interests of humanity at large. For the present, it may be noted that in the former case, the Natives are loyal, industrious, progressive, on the increase, and are producing enormous crops (as of cocoa and cotton); while in the latter case, they are restless and dissatisfied, and (in some countries) tending to decrease in numbers.

CHAPTER VII.

Wherein the Questions are asked, How are the Africans Governed? How should they be Governed?

I.

On returning to Africa in 1898, I spent the greater part of the first twelve months as the guest and pupil of missionaries of the Paris Evangelical Society in Basutoland—the Switzerland of South Africa. The greatest figure in the history of that little country—it is about half as large again as Wales—is that of Moshesh, the Chief who, out of the chaos that reigned in South Africa subsequent to the rise of the Zulu power under Chaka, gathered around him numerous Bantu clans and welded them into a nation. It was he who in 1833 invited the French missionaries to settle in his country. With remarkable prescience he foresaw that the tide of European civilization which at that time was rising in South Africa would ultimately beat around his frontiers, and he expected, not vainly, that the presence of the missionaries would not only elevate his people but would help them to retain possession of their land. Moreover, he appealed again and again to be taken under British protection. When at last in 1868 his prayer was granted, this was only just in time to save the remainder of his territory from the Boers, who had already taken possession of a large part of it.

In 1862 Moshesh used what Sir Godfrey Lagden rightly calls "remarkable words"[1] in his appeal to the British authorities:

> "I will be under the Queen as her subject, and my people will be her subjects but under me. . . I wish to govern my own people by native law, by our own laws; but if the Queen wish after this to introduce other laws into my country, I would be willing; but I should wish such laws to be submitted to the Council of the Basuto; and when they are accepted by my Council, I will send to the Queen and inform her that they have become law."

Here in 1862 we find an African chief laying down the principles of Indirect Rule which to-day are so widely adopted in the administration of African territories. When in 1884, after a somewhat stormy interval of annexation to Cape Colony (1871-1884), Basutoland came under the Imperial Government, these were the lines upon which it was governed, and the system has continued to the present day.

The British power is represented by a Resident Commissioner, with a staff of British magistrates and other officials, and he is responsible to the High Commissioner of South Africa, who alone possesses legislative authority. The customary Native law is administered in the courts. The

[1] SIR GODFREY LAGDEN, *The Basutos* (1909), Vol. I, pp. 314, 315.

Chiefs settle cases between Natives which are brought before them (except cases of manslaughter and other grave crimes), while, as a protection against possible oppression, right is given to appeal to the British magistrates.

Native institutions have in this way been recognized and fostered. The most remarkable of these is the Pitso, or National Assembly, which reminded Lord Bryce of the Agora, the assembly of freemen described in the Homeric poems, and the primary assemblies of the early peoples of Europe.[1] At this annual gathering all Basuto men enjoyed the rights of attendance and free utterance. The way in which not only the principal chiefs, but commoners expressed themselves was most impressive. Their eloquence, frankness, and dignity would be creditable at Westminster. Both the Chiefs and the British Government, whose officials were present at the Pitso I attended, were freely criticized. It is an admirable feature of the customary law of the Basuto that no man may suffer in consequence of anything he says in the Assembly.

In 1903 a Council, or House of Representatives, was established, the members, about a hundred in number, being in part selected by the chiefs and in part nominated by the British Government. This Council discusses the expenditure of money raised by taxation, ventilates opinions and grievances, and considers legislative proposals which

[1] James (Lord) Bryce, *Impressions of South Africa* (1899). p. 424.

with the High Commissioner's sanction become laws. In this way, the Basuto are being helped to govern themselves. It is a matter of regret, which many Basuto share, that the people no longer have the opportunity of expressing themselves at an annual Pitso. This Assembly is now only summoned on very special occasions, such as when the Prince of Wales visited Basutoland.

It is alleged against the African tribal system that it spells stagnation, since the customary law remains unaltered and unalterable from generation to generation. The history of the Basuto proves that this is not necessarily so, for, even prior to the establishment of the Protectorate, the Paramount Chief, in consultation and by general agreement with his people, had introduced many changes. Moshesh, for example, abolished the smelling-out of witches. He also prohibited the importation of alcoholic liquors. British rule involves the abolition of customs that are repugnant to civilized minds. But there is a vast difference between changing traditional customs by the arbitrary decree of the foreigner, and bringing about changes through native channels. The system in Basutoland makes it possible to introduce reforms gradually, in accord with the growing enlightenment of the people.

No land troubles exist in Basutoland such as those which emerge elsewhere when Whites and Blacks come into contact. The rights of the Basuto in the soil have been frankly recognized and enforced. Traders are allowed to carry on their business, but they cannot own a particle of land, and there are no European farmers. The French mission occupies its sites on the same conditions as Natives occupy theirs—no freehold rights are claimed.

The Basuto enjoy considerable material prosperity, though the dryness of the soil, which in an increasing degree afflicts South Africa generally, affects them also. No extensive area of South Africa has been more effectively cultivated than the western plain of Basutoland. Wheat and other cereals, wool, hides and skins and live stock are exported to the value of nearly a million pounds a year. "No white population," says Sir Godfrey Lagden, "would produce as much in the space available."[1] The country pays its own way and has a considerable balance in the bank. The revenue, derived from taxation, customs, fees, etc., is spent for the benefit of the people. Good roads, hospitals, dispensaries, a leper settlement, have been built. Wealth also comes into the country through the earnings of men who leave home for a period to work on the mines and farms: in 1924, 88,627 passes were given to such men leaving the territory.

In Basutoland, the British Government and the Christian Church, represented by French, Anglican and Roman Catholic missions, have co-operated in raising the standard of life. Sir H. Sloley, formerly the Resident Commissioner, said in 1896, "If one influence more than another has helped the Basuto it is the missionary influence which began seventy-five years ago. The results achieved are such as to

[1] *Op. cit.*. Vol. II. p. 642.

encourage missionaries and laymen alike to do their plain duty and to trust the future of the native people." Over 40,000 pupils are enrolled in the elementary schools, all conducted by the Missions, and 600 pupils in normal and industrial institutions. Grants amounting to £35,000 a year are voted by the Council for the support of these schools, besides a large sum for agricultural training.

It is not pretended that everything is ideal in this highly favoured land. Reference will be made presently to some of the criticisms that may fairly be urged against the system. But here, it can be claimed, is an object lesson in the art of governing an African people. Basutoland (in Sir Godfrey Lagden's words)[1] "furnishes the unique opportunity for the experiment, not so easily possible in any other country, of testing the intellectual altitude to which these native people as a mass can rise on their own lines under paternal government and guidance, without being compelled by the presence of a European population to adopt a spurious form of civilization." Under this system, an African tribe is given the opportunity of developing sanely and securely along the lines of its own ethos, while gradually absorbing the best elements of our European civilization. On the whole, the result is encouraging. One criterion of African happiness is increase in population. In 1875 Basutoland contained 127,707 people ; in 1924, 540,000. That is to say, in fifty years the population has grown more than fourfold.

[1] In *The Native Races of the Empire* (1925), p. 48.

II.

When Europeans took possession of African territories the problem arose as to the best method of governing the people. Various methods have been tried but they may be reduced in principle to two, which have been described in the following terms by Mr. Amery, the Secretary of State for the Colonies.[1] The first method begins by destroying the institutions, traditions and habits of the people and then superimposes upon the ruins whatever the governing power considers to be a better administrative system. The other method, while checking the worst abuses, tries to graft our higher civilization on the soundly-rooted native stock, bringing out the best of what is in the native tradition and moulding it into a form consonant with modern ideas and higher standards, and yet all the time enlisting on our side the real force of the spirit of the people.

The latter of these two methods, commonly known as Indirect Rule,[2] is the method adopted in Basutoland. It is also applied in Uganda, Nigeria (partly at least) and other British territories.

An extreme example of the other method, Direct Rule, is afforded by the system established by the Germans in their East and West African territories. In the Cameroons they deliberately broke down, as far as possible, all the native

[1] Speech at the Nigerian Dinner Club, December 17, 1924.

[2] The two methods have been ably discussed by Mr. C. L. TEMPLE (late Lieut.-Governor, Northern Provinces, Nigeria) in his *Native Races and their Rulers* (1918). He unhesitatingly supports Indirect Rule.

machinery of government. They nullified the powers of the Chiefs and set up European officials, who were ignorant of the local languages, unversed in native law and custom, and all too few in numbers to cope with the work of governing, though sufficient and powerful enough to break down the native system and to dishearten the true leaders of the people. Since the British took over part of the German colonies, under a Mandate of the League of Nations, they have made strenuous and largely successful endeavours to resuscitate the indigenous form of government. The British officials now act as advisers of the native authorities, educating and controlling them, keeping their fingers on the pulses of native life, and guiding the people, along their own channels, into the paths of progress.[1]

The degree of success attainable by Indirect Rule and the extent to which it can be applied depend largely upon the character of the pre-existing native government. Where, as in Basutoland, Barotseland, Northern Nigeria, Uganda, the system was highly organized under strong Chiefs, the foundation was already laid, but in other districts where small headmen ruled village communities and paid no allegiance to a superior Chief, the establishment of Indirect Rule is a much more difficult task. In this case it is the aim of the British authorities to draw scattered units together under one head, or to form Native Councils to which a large measure of self-government may be entrusted.

[1] Report on the British sphere of the Cameroons, 1922, pp. 13 sqq.

These Native Councils were first established by Mr. Cecil Rhodes in the South African district of Glen Grey in 1894 and were set up subsequently in the Transkei. In 1924 the Native Authority Amendment Ordinance bestowed a considerable measure of local self-government upon the already existing indigenous Councils in Kenya Colony where the chiefs ruled, not as autocrats but with the advice of the elders. The native system has proved capable of development. In Kenya the elective principle has been introduced with the object of giving a voice in tribal affairs to the more educated and progressive tribesmen. "In one district," says Mr. Denham, the acting-governor,[1] "the candidates were all lined up in a row, each candidate being given a number: there were over 2,000 Natives present, each of whom was given in turn a wand with which he tapped on the shoulder the candidates for whom he wished to vote, up to the number for which there were vacancies. District Commissioners and Assistant District Commissioners then recorded the votes against the number of each candidate." The management of communal matters such as land, forests and veterinary services are entrusted to these councils, as well as health, education, agriculture, trade and labour recruitment. They are empowered to levy a rate, the proceeds of which are devoted to these objects. In time it is hoped to bring together representatives of the separate

[1] Cmd 2573, 1926: Report by Mr. Denham on his tours in native reserves. Report on Kenya for 1924, Colonial Reports, No. 1282.

councils and thus form a kind of native Parliament. This is an excellent system for training the people.

The system of Indirect Rule has been adversely criticized by competent observers. Mr. F. W. H. Migeod, an official of long experience in West Africa, has frankly expressed his preference for the direct and autocratic government of the Germans in the Cameroons. He believes that it makes for progress, while Indirect Rule spells stagnancy. Speaking of Northern Nigeria, he says: "Until indirect administration is replaced by direct British administration, as in the southern provinces of Nigeria, it will never be possible to eradicate slavery."[1] "Every native," he declares, "prefers to be under a British officer instead of under a native chief." And again: "The trouble with indirect rule is that it can only work as it were in a glass case. When subjected to the jolts and jars of economic progress it shows signs of weakness."[2] Captain J. F. J. Fitzpatrick, an official of seventeen years' experience, has trenchantly criticized Indirect Rule in Northern Nigeria, which he roundly describes as "Nigeria's Curse," expensive, inefficient, and oppressive.[3] The system as it exists in Basutoland has also its critics. The Chiefs are said to withhold justice and to be open to bribes; extortionate in their demands, tyrannical,

[1] F. W. H. Migeod, *Through British Cameroons* (1925), p. 206.

[2] In *Journal of the African Society*, Vol. XXIV, No. xcvi, July, 1925, p. 378.

[3] J. F. J. Fitzpatrick in *National Review*, December, 1924.

and opposed to the progressive and educated elements of their people.

Indirect Rule unquestionably is liable to such abuses as these. It demands unceasing vigilance on the part of strong European administrators, who, while in sympathy with the principle involved of trusting the native rulers, must insist upon justice being done to the people. Much has been said about the tyranny of European rulers in Africa, but there is no more cruel tyranny than that which African rulers are capable of inflicting upon their own people. The alternative to Indirect Rule is to multiply the number of highly trained and competent white officials and to bring the Natives under their direct supervision. No doubt this would result immediately in a more incorruptible and humane, and, in many respects, a more efficient government; but besides being impracticably expensive, such a system would be alien and exotic. Indirect Rule is founded upon the belief that "all races prefer local self-rule, relatively inefficient though it may be, to direct alien rule however just and benevolent."[1] This belief is well-grounded in fact, though here and there dissatisfied subjects may wish for the antithetical system without realising its implications. The strongest justification for Indirect Rule is that it is educative. It rests upon a conviction that every system of government, if it is to be permanent and progressive, must have its roots imbedded

[1] Report on the Administration under Mandate of British Cameroons for the year 1924 (Colonial No. 16), p. 48.

deeply in the framework of indigenous society; that native systems contain elements of high value and are capable of development in an upward direction under the stimulus of sympathetic European administrators. The policy enables the people to keep their self-respect. It is preparing them, as Direct Rule does not, for complete self-government in the days when they will be capable of standing alone. Progress must be slow, and in the meantime deficiencies are inevitable. Native public opinion must be trained to demand and accept reform. It is needless to insist that this implies the moral elevation of the community and especially of the ruling class.[1]

III.

Behind all systems of administration lies the fundamental question of what we intend to make of the African. This question has, whether in explicit terms or not, been answered in several ways. One possible and largely practised policy is that of Repression, which means keeping the Native in a subject and inferior position ("keep him in his own place") as a mere serf of the dominant race. This is an impracticable policy: the African refuses to be repressed; and if the Whites continue to attempt doing this, they will either provoke hatred

[1] An excellent description of Indirect Rule, and of the good results achieved, is given by A. C. G. HASTINGS in his *Nigerian Days* (1925).

and wars of extermination, or they will suffer by the decay of the Natives.

The French have, in the past, been the protagonists of the policy of Assimilation, which means that the same government, laws, political and social rights, are to be given to the Natives as to the citizens of the controlling Power. The French ideal is the creation of a Greater France in Africa. They have seized upon General Mangin's aphorism: "France is a country of a hundred million inhabitants," and to make this vision an actuality have striven to bring their African subjects into the great French family (*"de faire entrer l'indigène dans la grande famille française"*). Since a civilization is the expression of the mind of a people, the capacity to acquire an alien form is dependent upon the preliminary acquisition of certain definite mental characteristics: in other words, the African must first be endowed with a European mind if he is to be civilized in the European manner. The French have therefore persisted in teaching their language to their North and West African subjects—this is the principal reason of their schools. They pride themselves on the fact that in a few years there will not be a single village, however distant and isolated, where the Natives will not understand and speak French. The policy has been most fully developed in Algeria, where by the introduction of French laws and institutions, individual tenure of land, and the naturalising of Algerians as French citizens, the utmost has been done to assimilate the people.

This policy of Assimilation has been very severely criticized by French writers.[1] For one thing, they say, it cannot be carried out consistently. If the five millions of Muslims in Algeria became French citizens, they would swamp the French colonists at all elections, and make it impossible for the French to remain in the country. For it has been proved that participation in French culture does not make Frenchmen of the Algerians. An acute American observer tells us that beneath a placid surface, there persists the "silent, hidden bitterness of a conquered people,"[2] and French writers themselves admit that the Algerians are "our mortal enemies." Students of colonial policy like M. Louis Vignon unhesitatingly commend the system of Indirect Rule, as it has been adopted by the British and as the French are themselves carrying out in Morocco. Statesmen like M. Albert Sarraut, the French Colonial Minister, who refuse to subscribe to any creed that sets forth the permanent inferiority of the Africans, and declare that the traditional government of the Natives must not be substituted by bad copies of our constitutions, will allow only a very gradual assimilation—a slow infiltration by little doses of civilization.[3]

In times past the Belgians aimed at breaking

[1] For example, LOUIS VIGNON, *Un programme de Politique Coloniale* (1919).

[2] W. M. SLOANE, *Greater France in Africa* (1924).

[3] In *Etudes de colonisation comparée* (1924), pp. 4, seqq.

down native society and their agents on the Congo were expected every year to answer the question, "What progress have our ideas and principles made among the native peoples?" Now their leaders have pronounced decidedly against assimilation. "Any policy," declares the ex-Colonial Minister, M. Louis Franck, "which, under the pretext that native institutions will inevitably weaken, tends to neglect them and not to sustain them, and to substitute for them the direct administration of the White, will lead to anarchy . . . . We wish to make better Africans . . . we have no wish to make copies of Europeans who will never be more than humans of a third category." And M. Franck asserts the ideal of the Belgian rule to be, "By gradual action and by an education appropriate to the mentality and character of the people to develop in the Congo an African civilization."[1]

The French often speak of themselves as the true heirs of the Roman civilization and as continuing the work of Rome in Africa. We ourselves look back upon the Romans as we hope the Africans will look back upon Europeans in centuries to come—with gratitude. Our land was an integral part of the Roman Empire for a period as long as from the Reformation until the present day. "It was not for nothing that Western Europe was forged on the anvil of Rome, and who can say how much we owe to those long years of Roman law, Roman discipline, Roman faith and partnership

[1] *Ibid*, pp. 85, 129.

in a common Empire?"[1] We have much to learn from that period of history in relation to our dealings with the African peoples. As Earl Cromer has pointed out,[2] the central political conception of Rome was not to autonomize, but to Romanize, or at least Hellenize the world. Her difficulties in the West were much less than those which confront modern Europeans in Africa. There seems to have been no colour question and no racial aversion in the Roman Empire,—little prejudice against intermarriage between Romans and barbarians. Every office, even that of Emperor, lay open to every man of every sort of blood. Of the great poets who adorned the literary ages of Rome only one was Roman born.[3] There was indeed but a narrow ethnical gulf separating the Romans from their western subjects. Linguistic barriers were soon overcome, because there was some close kinship between the languages (much closer than between any European and African language), and Gauls and Italians and Iberians rapidly acquired Latin, which remains the basis of their vernaculars to-day. Religion presented little difficulty, for Rome was tolerant. Where the native religion was intransigent, as was the religion of the Jews, Rome failed most conspicuously to assimilate the people.

Rome failed to maintain her empire, as any Empire must fail that pursues a policy of assimilation.

[1] Mr. Stanley Baldwin, Presidential Address to the Classical Association, January 8, 1926.

[2] *Ancient and Modern Imperialism* (1910), p. 117.

[3] JAMES (VISCOUNT) BRYCE, *Race Sentiment as a Factor in History* (Creighton Lecture, 1915), pp. 11, 12.

Sooner or later the insurgent national spirit rebels. There comes a time when a people realise that they too are somebody and have their own contribution to make to the wealth of humanity. The language of the dominant race does not permanently bind the subject peoples to the conqueror. They may drink deep of his spring, but the day comes when they resent the imposition of an alien culture. The Romans ruled Britain four hundred years, but while the Britons took much from them, as a people they never became Romans. Deeply as the Romans influenced their ancestors, the Welsh remain characteristically Celtic.

At first sight it appears more consonant with our professed duties as Trustees to bestow upon the Africans all our culture, in place of their own. Do we not believe this to be the very best in the world—our language, our literature, our educational system, our democratic institutions? Can it be that we are acting rightly towards our adopted children if we withhold any of these things from them? Some people, like M. Louis Vignon, oppose assimilation on the ground that Africans do not think, and constitutionally are incapable of thinking, as Europeans think. But others adopt a totally different attitude. They do not despise the African. On the contrary they believe that to deprive him of his own tongue and social institutions is to inflict an intolerable wrong upon him—a wrong which, if in his ignorance he does not resent now, he certainly will most energetically and rightfully resent in time to come. His culture is, it must be admitted, not equal in value to the European's by a very long way; but poor as it may be it is the African's own—the expression of his ethos. It is capable of development, and it is the Trustee's duty and privilege to help him to conserve it, to breathe a new spirit into it, to mould and shape it in harmony with the lessons we teach him.

IV.

This is comparatively easy where the Native is living on his own land, and removed from all but occasional intercourse with Europeans. It becomes a matter of very considerable difficulty when Europeans colonize and insist upon a complete revolution in the African's life, as in Kenya, Southern Rhodesia, South Africa and elsewhere. The native problem in South Africa—i.e., the problem arising from the contact of White and Black—is one of the most difficult in the world to-day.

Here are some of the elements of the problem: A relatively diminishing white population placed in the midst of an overwhelming and rapidly increasing majority of Africans. A section of the Whites deteriorating, while a section of the Blacks is advancing in efficiency. The Whites supremely anxious to maintain a high standard of European civilization, yet conscious that wherever White and Black meet miscegenation is proceeding. The Whites have participated in educating the Blacks, but now shrink from giving political and economic equality to those who are fitted for it, fearing that once they did this the black voters, being in the immense majority, would rule the country, and that black skilled workers would drive the Whites off the labour market. The few Whites own most of the land and generally speaking populate it sparsely, while the Blacks are overcrowded in the areas now assigned to them and large numbers are compelled to become squatters and slum-dwellers ;—half the native population lives on land owned by Europeans, or in urban and mining areas. A large section of the Whites is anxious to do justice to the Blacks, but a larger section still maintains a policy of repression ; while the educated Blacks are losing their respect for the Whites, and clamour for a removal of all disabilities.

The problem that South African statesmen have to solve is in brief this : How to secure the realisation of European ideals while satisfying the aspirations of the Africans ?

The obvious solution is to devise some plan by which the two races can live side by side in the same country, each following its own ethnical path, co-operating where possible but competing against each other as little as may be in the economic sphere. In a word, some measure of segregation is necessary.

This policy has been advocated by some of the best friends of the South African Natives. Dr. John Philip, the eminent superintendent of the London Missionary Society, strongly urged the partition of the country into white and black areas. He was in his time the best-hated man in South Africa and it is only now becoming clear, thanks largely to the studies of Professor W. M. Macmillan of the Witwatersrand University,[1] that if his prescient advice had been followed in this matter the problem would be nearer solution. Segregation was the policy deliberately framed and put into practice in Natal by Sir Theophilus Shepstone, perhaps the greatest administrator of native affairs Africa has ever known. It is the policy that has maintained the Bechuanaland and Basutoland Protectorates as native territories. It was advocated in one of the best books published on the Native problem—Sir Maurice Evans's *White and Black in South-East Africa*, and has since received the support of such friends of the African as Mr. E. J. C. Stevens[2] and Professor Brookes.[3] The central doctrine underlying the policy is that set forth in an earlier section of this book, viz., that the Africans have an ethos of their own which is of value to humanity, and that to destroy this and to insist upon making them into black Europeans is to inflict a wrong upon them, and to rob mankind of a valuable asset. No doubt there are Europeans who advocate the policy from a less worthy motive: they would gladly segregate (or profess that they would segregate) the lot "by driving them into the Sahara or into the sea"[4]—anywhere, so as to get

[1] See for example his paper read at the Conference on Native Affairs held under the auspices of the Dutch Reformed Churches at Johannesburg, September, 1923.

[2] *White and Black* (n.d.).

[3] *History of Native Policy in South Africa* (1924).

[4] Quoted from a South African paper by Stevens, *op. cit.*, p. 144.

rid of the hated race. But such hostile views must not hinder us from supporting on higher grounds the better course both in the African's and the European's interest.

The policy of Segregation is distrusted by many white men. They fear that if the natives possess their own land they will not go out to work. The example of Basutoland should relieve their minds on this matter. And even if territorial segregation in the full sense of the term could be carried out, it is certain that at no distant date sufficient arable land could not be found to allow every native to have his small plot: there would always be a surplus of labour available for the Europeans. Another argument against segregation also fails to convince those who are acquainted with Basutoland. For segregation does not mean "to hedge the African into a garden, however pretty and safe and sufficient in itself, and tell him to be a good little boy." Basutoland proves that segregation may spell sane and orderly progress.

Some measure of segregation—or differential development, as Professor Brookes prefers to call it—has become the accepted policy of South African statesmen. It was embodied in Cecil Rhodes' Glen Grey Act of 1894 which set up the admirable Council system of local self-government among the natives; in the Natives' Land Act of 1913 ("an unsatisfactory measure in all conscience"[1]); the Native Affairs Act, No. 23, of 1920 (providing for separate administration) and the

[1] Brookes, *op. cit.*, p. 336.

Act of 1923 which applied it to urban areas. The principle has been accepted by Generals Botha, Smuts and Hertzog. The Johannesburg Conference of missionaries and others, British, Dutch and Africans,—"the largest and most important unofficial Conference on Native Affairs ever held in South Africa"—expressed itself "in favour of the principle of the differential development of the Bantu so far as such differentiation is based on Bantu traditions and requirements, and is not used as a means of repression"; and approved of segregation "so far as this general differential development can be described as 'segregation.'"[1]

To accept a principle is one thing, to put it into practice is another. General Hertzog, the Prime Minister of the Union, has promised to bring in a Bill during the 1926 Session of Parliament, and by the time this book is published his scheme may be known in full. At present we have only the outline of it as set forth in his speech at Smithfield in November, 1925.[2] According to this he proposes to extend to all native areas the Native Councils already at work in the Transkei, with General Provincial Councils and a Union Council of fifty members, the majority to be elected by the Natives and a minority nominated by Government. This Union Council would have advisory powers at first, but ultimately would legislate on purely Native affairs. The existing Parliamentary

[1] *European and Bantu, being Papers and Addresses read at the Conference on Native Affairs* (1923), p. 44.

[2] Reported verbatim in *The Friend, Bloemfontein*, November 14, 1925.

franchise is to be taken from Natives in the Cape Province (the only province where they can now vote), and Natives throughout the Union are to elect seven members, who must be Europeans. General Hertzog refuses to admit Natives to the Union Parliament. The Coloured man (as distinct from the Native) is to be placed on an equal footing with the European, economically, industrially and politically.

This is a far-reaching, and even revolutionary, scheme and whatever may be its fate, General Hertzog merits praise for his courage in proposing it. The crux of the whole matter lies in the proportioning of land, and on this subject the Prime Minister has not unfolded his plan. Difficult as the question is, he believes it not to be insurmountable.

The ideal plan would be to demarcate areas which would be so many Basutolands where the Natives might develop naturally under the guidance of European administrators and missionaries. Mr. Stevens made such a proposal. In the book to which reference has been made, he suggested that in addition to the areas now held by them, part of the Transvaal and the whole of Natal should form part of a great native state under the control of the Union.[1] But this scheme is rendered impracticable by the opposition of the Natalians who have taken as their slogan, " Not another acre for the Natives." The Land Commission set up by the Act of 1913

[1] See the map in J. W. GREGORY, *The Menace of Colour*, p. 139.

recommended substantially the division of the land between White and Black, allocating about 232,000,000 acres for occupation by the million and a half of Whites, and about 27,000,000 acres to the four and a half millions of Africans: in other words, 11 per cent. of the land for the use of three-fourths of the population and 89 per cent. for the other one-fourth. A Native representative at the Johannesburg Conference[1] spoke of the injustice and unfairness of this allocation and asked that fifty per cent. of the land be given to the Natives and fifty per cent. to the Europeans. But even the areas allocated by the Land Commission, other than those already occupied by the Natives, have not been set apart for them, because it was impossible to induce Parliament to sanction the ear-marking, for exclusive native ownership, of land already occupied by Europeans. The Natives are therefore worse off than they were before the Land Act was passed: first, because restrictions have been put upon their purchasing land in areas allocated to the Whites; secondly, because inroads have been made by Whites upon areas theoretically allocated to the Natives; and thirdly, because in the economic sphere the principle of segregation has been carried out to the natives' detriment by employing white men on railways, etc., in their place. No wonder that many of the Natives believe that "Segregation" is only a camouflaged form of "Repression." If

[1] REV. Z. R. MAHABANE in his paper on Segregation, Report pp. 38, seqq.

now the principle is carried so far as to segregate the Natives still further economically by means of a Colour Bar Bill,[1] excluding them by law from performing skilled labour, while depriving them of the existing franchise in Cape Province and refusing them adequate land on which they can live their own lives and secure some measure of economic independence—then the state of the Native will be definitely worse than ever. The truth of the matter is that the solution of this most serious problem calls for self-sacrifice on the part of South Africans. Repression is a policy that is impracticable and unjust—the conscience of enlightened white men forbids it. Segregation, in the limited sense here indicated, can only be carried out if adequate land is provided for the Natives. If the Whites cannot brace themselves to making the surrender, then there is only one alternative that squares with justice. Economic segregation and political segregation must be dismissed, and the Natives must be allowed to work and vote according to their abilities. It would be preferable to make it possible for the Natives to develop their own civilization on their own land, but if this cannot be secured then let us go in for thorough, out-and-out Assimilation.

[1] Thrown out by the Senate in a previous session, the Bill was promptly reintroduced in 1926 and passed the third reading in the House of Assembly on February 4, by sixty-four votes, to forty-seven, in spite of General Smuts' warning, " The natives are seething with discontent all over South Africa." The Senate rejected it again, but a joint meeting of the two Houses gave a majority of 16 in favour of the Bill on May 12th.

CHAPTER VIII.

Wherein is Pictured the Disintegration of African Social Life and its Evil Consequences.

I.

PEOPLE cannot live together in a group unless they recognize some common principles which regulate their conduct towards each other. Their deep-seated instincts pull them in diverse directions. Social life becomes difficult, if not altogether impossible, where the passions are uncontrolled. Unless the altruistic tendencies are fostered and consecrated by a civic conscience society cannot exist. There must be some restraints, objective or subjective, upon the individual's impulses. Never since our primeval ancestors began to live in groups has freedom existed in the sense that every man could do as he liked. Rousseau began his *Social Contract* by saying *L'homme est né libre, et partout il est dans les fers.* In a sense he did not intend, the words are true. Men have forged fetters for themselves, in order that they might live together.

Neither in principle nor in practice are the Africans anarchists. Some of them are fierce in their love of independence and sensitive as a highly-trained race-horse to the touch of whip or spur, but even these have to submit to restraint, or they could not live together. The behaviour of Africans is not left to unchartered freedom, but is governed by a system of rules and regulations, so extensive, so complicated, that Europeans who study it stand amazed, and are tempted to declare the Africans to be the slaves of tribal custom. That the Africans rebel against such restrictions upon their liberty is only to say that they are human. The principles of conduct are there, however, and are known to all members of the community. Africans may be immoral; they are not unmoral.

The unsophisticated African lives at the collectivistic stage of human evolution. This is not to say that there is no recognition of individuality; personal property, for example, is held; but the individual is far less distinct from his group than he is in a European community. What M. E. Jacottet says of the Basuto is true of Africans generally: "the individual never really attains his majority, he must remain more or less in the tutelage of his family, clan and tribe." The African acts as part of a whole. His well-being depends upon his conforming rigidly to general practice. All through life he remains a unit in a group, and thinks of himself as such: he is a member of his clan, of his age-grade, of his tribe. A stringent etiquette regulates every relation with his fellow-men. He shapes his conduct according to the thinking and doing of his fellows and comes to fear and hate all change. Indeed it is dangerous to do anything contrary to the general practice. The community is always on guard to protect itself against any innovation. Inventors of new ways are liable to be charged with unholy compacts with the devil—or with what stands for the devil in African minds. On the Congo, we are told by the Rev. J. H. Weeks, the introduction of a new article of trade always brought upon the introducer a charge of witchcraft, and there is a legend that the man who discovered the way to tap palm trees for palm-wine was looked upon as a warlock and paid the penalty with his life. The blacksmith contrives the making of a new kind of knife, and instead of admiring his initiative his neighbours are alarmed by the disquieting novelty and react against him. All this, of course, is not peculiar to the Africans ; to a lesser extent the hatred of new ways has marked Englishmen in the past, if it does not mark them to-day. But Africans are more conservative than ourselves because they are so much less individualistic than we are. Pushed to extreme limits the misoneism of the Africans would stereotype everything and no change could ever take place. As a matter of fact, change does take place. But it must come through recognized channels ; an unauthorized individual may not strike out upon a fresh path.

When we succeed in getting behind the African's

stock answer that he does things because his fathers always did them so, what do we learn? We learn that he bases his practices upon his belief in "supernatural" agencies. The riotous instincts are restrained by forces that are not of this tangible sphere. In other words, the ethics of the Africans, their customary morality, is grounded in their religion. Their morality is not ours in all respects—from our point of view it sometimes appears, indeed, highly immoral. Nor is their religion ours: it differs so much from ours that some observers have denied that Africans have any religion at all. But such as their morality is, and such as their religion is, the two are inextricably fused together, are, indeed, but aspects of one whole.

The part that religion plays in the life of Africans has not always been recognized by Europeans. To many students a realization of it has come home with surprise. Mr. Hobley, for example, confesses that he lived for some years in close touch with the natives of Kenya without understanding this side of their life. "There is no doubt," he concludes, after a prolonged study, "these beliefs tend to check progress and development, as we understand them. Although this cannot be doubted, we must not lose sight of the fact that, on the whole, they undoubtedly act as moral restraints and perform in very much the same way the functions which a dogmatic religion fulfils among people of a higher culture."[1] To ignore the religious basis of African

[1] C. W. Hobley, C.M.G., *Bantu Beliefs and Magic* (1922), p. 282.

social life is a great error—the kind of error that was made when the Golden Stool of Ashanti was treated as a purely temporal object, without consideration of its deep spiritual significance. One is not surprised to find Captain Rattray beginning his chapter on Land Tenure in Ashanti with an examination of the religious aspect of the matter.[1] You cannot divorce religion from social custom and law in Africa. Religion, so far as the Africans are concerned, is, in M. Vignon's words, *un puissant appareil de contrainte.*

II.

To describe the diversified forms of religion found in Africa would be impossible here. It must suffice to mention a few relevant features. Amidst all the variations of belief, three articles may be said to be common to the African creed: viz., a belief in a Supreme Being; a belief in survival of the human personality after death; and a belief in *mana*—if we may transfer to Africa a Melanesian word. We are here concerned with the relation between these beliefs and the customary morality. Probably the recognition of a High God has the least effect upon conduct; but many of the Africans declare that their customs were established by Him and that any breach of them is a transgression of the divine will. Much more commonly the spirits of deceased ancestors are regarded as the guardians of the tribal morality. The customs have come

[1] R. S. Rattray, *Ashanti*, p. 214.

down from ancient times and it is natural to suppose that if not ordained by God they were established by great men in the past. These ancestors still live, though invisible. They are concerned in the well-being of their descendants, and any breach of traditional custom is an offence against them. They have the power of visiting their wrath upon transgressors. What Mr. Casalis said of the Basuto is true of Africans generally: "there could be no more direct provocation of the anger of the ancestors they worshipped than by departing from the precepts and examples they left behind them." The land where their bodies lie buried, and the forest which now harbours their spirits, are rendered sacred by their association with the ancestors. They form the strongest bond of union between the tribesmen. In a word, African society does not comprise the living only; the living and the dead compose a close interdependent community, and anything which disturbs the harmony between them is regarded as a crime.

Neither of the two articles of belief mentioned is sufficient to account for the permanence of all traditional custom. A still larger factor is what we commonly think of as "magic," but it is more properly described as a belief in that impersonal potency which the Melanesians call *mana*. It may be difficult to discover equivalent terms in African vocabularies, but unless we presuppose a belief in *mana* it is impossible rightly to appreciate many important elements of African life. As in Melanesia, so in Africa, religion consists largely in getting *mana* for oneself, or in getting it used for one's benefit. This is why "charms" play such an important part in the African's daily life—they are vehicles of *mana*. In the form of "mascots" these have of late been much in evidence among certain emancipated folk in our own land: but what is a mere silly superstition in England is a vital thing in Africa. Belief in them forms part of the faith by which Africans live. They have firmer trust in their charms than many of us repose in the providence of God.

The taboos which so largely regulate the black man's conduct also have their basis in a belief in *mana*. He must not do this, or that, say this thing or the other, eat this or that, because otherwise some evil consequence will follow. He will not necessarily be punished by the chief and council; but his deed will automatically and inevitably react upon him. The peculiarity of a true taboo lies in the fact that infringement brings its own punishment. If a man touches a live wire, contrary to official warning, there is no necessity for a magistrate's court to inflict a penalty upon him for a breach of regulation: the live wire does its own work. Certain deeds and words and even desires are charged with a kind of spiritual electricity which will at once give you a shock. A person may be taboo—there is something about him that jeopardises the well-being of others. Things may be taboo—they are a source of peril: there is a kind of malefic essence in them which makes them dangerous.

All this may seem fantastic to us, but here in the belief in all-pervasive mystic force we find one of the strongest sanctions of tribal morality. A few illustrations will bring home the force of this belief.

In books on Western Africa much can be read about Fetishism. It is a term that might well be eliminated from our vocabulary, for it has come to have an ambiguous meaning. Captain Rattray would confine the word to translate the Ashanti term *suman* which means "charm" (amulet or talisman). We may then say that Fetishism includes a belief in *mana* and the practices which grow out of that belief. Mr. Claridge has an interesting chapter on "Some useful applications of Fetishism."[1] He says:

> "There is scarcely anything in trade, sport, civic life, law administration, land rights, etc., but that the order which regulates them comes from and, in a large measure, is dependent upon fetishism. It supplies the law *civile* and the law *divinum*. It provides the standard by which one negro deals with his fellow negro. . . It stipulates what *ought* and what *ought not* to be done according to fetish standard. To take these away and to leave nothing in their place would be to reduce heathendom to the most hopeless pandemonium of lawlessness and self-destruction."

A fetish set up in a garden will invariably keep off all thieves and robbers. Fetishism therefore protects ownership and moreover staves off the sense of guilt which would result through acts of stealing. A specific charm tied on the garment of

[1] G. Cyril Claridge, *Wild Bush Tribes of Tropical Africa* (1922), pp. 126, sqq.

a girl will effectively protect her virginity if she wishes it to be protected. Charms sometimes regulate honesty in trade—for a sharper will not try tricks upon a man whom he believes to live under their protection.

In fact, here is the truth so eloquently expounded by Sir James Frazer in his *Psyche's Task*, namely that "among certain races and at certain stages of evolution some social institutions which we all, or most of us, believe to be beneficial have rested on a basis of superstition." Civilized folk defend these institutions by solid and weighty arguments; and these very institutions have, among peoples of lower culture, derived (says Sir James) much of their strength from beliefs which nowadays we should condemn unreservedly as superstitious and absurd. His book is devoted to establishing the fact that superstition has (1) strengthened the respect for government and has thereby contributed to the establishment and maintenance of civil order; (2) strengthened the respect for private property; (3) strengthened the respect for marriage and has thereby contributed to a stricter observance of the rules of sexual morality both among the married and unmarried; and (4) strengthened the respect for human life and thereby contributed to the security of its enjoyment. By doing these things superstition has rendered a great service to humanity. As a body of false opinions it is indeed a most dangerous guide in practice, "but vast as are these evils, they ought not to blind us to the benefit which superstition has conferred on society by furnishing the ignorant, the weak and the foolish with a motive, bad though it be, for good conduct."[1]

What then, it may be asked, will happen if the old theoretical basis of the African's tribal morality is shattered? Destroy the religion (or, as Sir James Frazer would say, the superstition) and the community is resolved into lawless, masterless individuals who recognize no tie, no restraint—unless a more solid foundation is built for the tribal morality to rest upon.

III.

Now, one seemingly inevitable consequence of the invasion of Africa by Europeans is the disintegration of African society as organised prior to their arrival. Even though no frontal attack be made upon the African's religion, so closely interfused are the religion and the system of society, anything that tends to destroy the one necessarily destroys the other.

Let us see how it works.

From what is here said the impression must not be gathered that it is only wicked white men who do the mischief, or that all who do the mischief are wicked. The argument is that white men *qua* white men, not because of their maliciousness, but simply because they represent a culture and have notions diverse from the African's, tend to destroy African social life.

I knew of one trader who at the time when

[1] Sir J. G. Frazer, *Psyche's Task* (1920), p. 155.

money was first coming into use in Northern Rhodesia brought in quantities of brand-new bright farthings and palmed them off as half-sovereigns among the natives, who did not then know the value of coins or the difference between copper and gold. He went off with a mob of cattle, having inflicted a heavy blow upon the white man's prestige. But nobody in his senses would represent that trader as a typical British merchant in Africa. Men like the brothers Moir[1] represent a host of like-minded men, who have conferred great benefits upon the Africans and have worthily sustained the reputation of Britons. But even if we take commerce at its best (forgetting such things as the trade in gin) and give every merchant the high character of the Moirs, commerce has not been an unmixed blessing to the African.

For one thing, the introduction of European goods has gone a long way towards destroying African arts and crafts.

The Ibibios of Southern Nigeria, Mr. Talbot says,[2] used to cover the face of a dead chief with a carved wooden mask—" conventionalised enough, but with a certain dignity, imitating however rudely, the golden burial masks of old Greece." The carving of this mask was a work of great skill, reverently and sorrowfully carried out by one of the chief's own retainers. But, nowadays, Mr. Talbot tells us, the chief often sits in state and is laid to his last

[1] F. L. M. Moir, *After Livingstone : an African Trade Romance* (1924).

[2] P. Amaury Talbot, *Life in Southern Nigeria* (1923), p. 147.

long rest, his features covered with a flimsy fifth of November caricature introduced by some enterprising trader.

The Ba-ila chiefs in old days wore two kinds of ornaments which marked their dignity. On their arms they carried ivory bracelets cleverly turned on a lathe by native craftsmen; and upon their forehead, or upon their breast, they wore the *impande*—the base of a shell imported from an unknown source. Traders have introduced clever celluloid and porcelain imitations of these things. I remember the disgust showed by a chief whose newly-acquired *impande* fell into the fire and vanished in a gust of flame. Nowadays any Tom, Dick or Harry can purchase these things at a trader's store. The ivory-turner's skill is no longer in demand.

These are examples of the substitution of flimsy things for genuine pieces of native art. In other cases the trader induces the natives to abandon their own more flimsy articles for substantial things from his store of imported goods. Many Africans used to manufacture cloth from cotton or the bark of trees; now they purchase stuffs woven in Lancashire and elsewhere. They smelted iron ore and fabricated hoes and knives and axes, showing no little skill and taste; nowadays they get them from the traders. In the old days native Nigerians smelted tin and made various articles of it; now Europeans employ natives to mine tin for export; the native industry is suppressed; the furnaces are broken down; the native smelters have been pensioned off.[1] Natives of the Katanga district of the Congo used to make handsome articles out of the copper they smelted: to-day the industry is dead, because Europeans control the mines and export the copper. Thus mining companies conspire with traders to destroy African industries.

It may readily be granted that the Natives can buy a better axe than any they could make out of iron or copper, and better cloth produced by Lancashire looms than any they could produce on their own primitive hand-looms. They can purchase crocks which are superior perhaps to their own earthenware. But it is no gain to native character when infant (infantile, if the word is preferred) industries are thus supplanted. That the Africans have skill and taste in their craftsmanship a visit to the British Museum proves abundantly. These arts and crafts gave them an outlet for their creative power, which should be developed rather than suppressed. Even the despised Negro has something to teach the world in art.[2]

[1] See *The Geological Survey of Nigeria*, bulletin No. 4.

[2] See a paragraph in *The Negro Year Book* (published in U.S.A.), headed "Primitive African Art Continues to Attract Attention of Art World." It is claimed that "all the interesting developments in art have drawn inspiration from African creations." Referring to an exhibition at Brooklyn it is said, "Visiting painters and sculptors as well as people of the industrial world are stirred by the new and inspiring art of the natives of the Belgian Congo."—"There are sufficient indications not to prove, but certainly to make not ridiculous, a theory which might attribute to the ancient negroid penetration of Europe and Asia a love of music and a desire to reproduce in painting, engraving, or sculpture the striking aspects of beasts and birds or of human life."—SIR H. H. JOHNSTON in *Interracial Problems* (1911), p. 333.

The evil does not consist merely in discouraging and destroying African arts and crafts. A blow is given to the religious sentiment of the craftsmen. Blacksmiths, for example, depend for their skill upon what they regard as supernatural aid; to take away their craft is to inflict a wound in the body of religious feeling which is the cement of society.

We need not wonder then that here and there some far-seeing African leader has opposed the entry of European traders. Mr. Torday tells of a chief who forbade the use of European goods under the penalty of death.

> "From his point of view it was a very wise though drastic measure: peaceful penetration is best achieved by creating a want and then making its supply dependent on the admission of the trader; after the trader comes the missionary, after him the state official, and they bring in their suite tax-collectors, judges, soldiers and other troublesome, meddling people, whose activities bring about without fail the collapse of the native's whole social fabric, as it happened with the Bushongo."[1]

IV.

A new era has opened in Africa wherever under European influence the land has assumed great value. It is not only where natives have been dispossessed of their lands that social changes have taken place. On the Gold Coast the British Government has encouraged cultivation of cocoa by Natives on their own lands. The growing of

[1] EMILE TORDAY, *On the Trail of the Bushongo* (1924), p. 235.

cocoa trees means a revolution in methods of agriculture, seeing that it involves abandonment of the old system of hoeing a plot of land and then moving on to fresh soil after two or three years. Land is taken up with the more permanent crop and there remains less land to be cultivated on the old extensive plan. Instead of allowing the soil to remain fallow, the native farmer must adopt intensive methods, with manuring and rotation of crops, if he is to grow his own food. The cultivation of land for many years in succession and the planting of trees inevitably affect his ideas of land tenure. He becomes discontented with the old system under which the land belongs to the tribe; he wants his right acknowledged to the plot with which he has taken so much trouble. "The extension of plantations and the intensive cultivation of native food-stuffs are slowly but surely cracking the common law of communal holding of land and the rootlets of private ownership are appearing in the cracks."[1] Here again is the conflict between the old culture founded upon immemorial custom, and the new which introduces unwonted personal interests in its train.

When, on the other hand, the Africans are dispossessed of their lands, a still greater wound is inflicted upon society.

[1] W. H. Barker (Reader in Geography, University of Manchester) in *Journal of the African Society*, Vol. XXIV, p. 380. See his valuable papers: *The Gold Coast Colony and Protectorate*, in the Journal of the Manchester Geographical Society, Vols. XXXVII-XXXVIII, Parts I-IV, 1921-22; *Historical Geography of West Africa* and *Economic Geography in West Africa*, in *The Geographical Teacher*.

Other land may be given them in place of that taken by the farmer or mining company. Conceivably it may be better land, but it has not the same value to them. On the old site stood the sacred groves, rich in association with the venerated ancestors. There too lay the graves in which their ancestors were buried and to which they were accustomed to repair periodically with their offerings. A new site can never be the same to the people, for African religion is rooted in the soil and bound to the parcel of ground hallowed by the presence of the dead. To understand the firm attachment of the people to their land, one needs to hear the pagan African's lament for the piteous condition to which the spirits of the dead have been reduced by the enforced emigration of their subjects and children. Separation from their land means a severance between the corporeal and incorporeal members of the community, with the inevitable slackening of the moral obligations which that communion entails.

A government official once expressed surprise when I represented to him in this way the wrong done to the Natives' deepest sentiments by enforced removal from their land. "As a missionary," he said, "you should rather welcome anything that breaks their attachment to old superstitions." But this is surely to take a short-sighted view of the matter. As a missionary it would have given me joy to see the Natives, of their own accord, and in response to my teaching, renounce their old faith, cut down or neglect their sacred groves in favour of the truth; but it is not to the interest of Christianity, any more than it is to the interest of the Government or of the Natives themselves, that the Natives should be shocked out of the old faith and lose their sense of obligation to powers supernatural before they are ready to receive Christianity with its new obligations. I would much rather deal with people who are zealous for the old faith than with people who are shorn of all faith.

V.

In the old days the Native rarely travelled far from his own village. In this secluded existence fresh conceptions rarely if ever invaded his mind. Now under new conditions thousands of men leave their homes for long periods in order to work for wages on mines and plantations, where they are brought into contact not only with white men but with black men of other tribes. For the first time in their lives, they find themselves free from the control of tribal public opinion. In some directions—namely, in regard to material wealth—there may be some gain, but little to compensate for the disastrous effect upon character. Liberated for a time from moral restraint, the detached African can do much as he likes so long as he does not come into conflict with European law. It is a common complaint in Africa that whereas the Native under old conditions was courteous, dignified, and disciplined, the "civilized" Native is impudent, sullen, jaunty—in fact, "spoilt." It is the new economic conditions that more than anything else "spoil" him. It is unreasonable to break down the system of tribal control and then to expect the Native to retain the tribal virtues.

How does it work? As it has been urged again and again, his religion does rule the African's conduct. But it is weak in the degree that it is not portable by the individual. It is a tribal faith, anchored to the ancestral soil. It is true that the African has a belief in God who is not localized, but this part of his creed which might give him support while he is living away from home is the part which exerts least influence upon conduct. The ancestral gods do not travel: they have great power over the members of the tribe while they live on their own land; they have none upon the solitary individual living away from home. When men of various tribes congregate at a mine or on a plantation they soon manage to converse, but they do not all observe the same taboos. A newcomer may, for example, be laughed into eating something he has always been taught to avoid. The danger is that he may go on to disregard obligations which are more ethical than food-regulations. After six months' absence men return home with morals loosened. They re-enter the tribal circle and the old constraints should once more exert their power, but these men have discovered that they can live very comfortably without their gods, and, while they will join with their fellows in the religious observances, they no longer have the respect for the gods that they once had. They do not show the same regard for the chief and other authority. They look with scorn upon the ancient restraints exercised upon stay-at-home folk. In the old days a charm placed upon a pumpkin-patch kept robbers away; these men have learnt from sophisticated companions to pooh-pooh such silly things, and now thieve with an easy conscience.

Is it to be wondered at that the Chiefs, who are the custodians of the tribal traditions, lament the growing anarchy of their young men?

The evil is intensified by the attitude too often taken up by those European employers who regard the Native as a being destitute of finer sentiments than a love for sensual gratification, for beer-drinking, feasting and sexual indulgence; who label all native religious observances as "superstition" which it is to the advantage of the native to have knocked out of him. The native is in a worse position than a young man in England who has been brought up in a pious home and is suddenly thrust out into the wicked world, friendless and alone. As with him, so with the Native, the case calls for sympathy and help. Generally the Native gets no assistance from his master, who if he has fed him and paid him eight shillings a month reckons that he has done his duty. It is, perhaps, too much to urge that a man should have a care for his servants' moral welfare. Yet it is really to the advantage of the master to do so.

Certain religious duties are impossible to observe

when a Native is absent from home. He may fall under the necessity of obtaining ceremonial purification from either what East Africans call a *thahu*, the impurity caused by breach of a taboo, or from the impurity left by a death in the family. If a chief or relative dies he is under obligation to take part in the obsequies. The man knows that the average employer would ridicule his request for leave of absence to attend to such religious duties, and he is faced with the alternative to run away without permission or to remain and fail in his duty. If he goes, he will be arrested and punished for breach of contract. If he remains it is with an uneasy mind, for he is sure that something evil will happen to his kindred or to himself. Then if after all nothing does happen, his religious susceptibilities receive a shock which cannot but have an effect upon his character. Mr. Hobley has well pointed out that it is to the interest of the employer to be sympathetic in such matters. Here lies one of the reasons why so many natives are reluctant to leave their homes to seek employment, and why their chiefs are reluctant to allow them to go. Europeans who understand these things and act accordingly do not have difficulty in getting labourers.[1]

Many of the natives who leave their homes to seek employment do not return—some settle as squatters upon some European farm, others drift into the towns. The last-named create the greatest problem of all. In South Africa the far-reaching

[1] C. W. Hobley, *Bantu Beliefs and Magic* (1922), pp. 283, 284.

industrial revolution has, since about 1885, transformed 35 per cent. of the native population into town-dwellers. "In Johannesburg itself the result of one generation's 'progress' has been the creation of slums where white and black live in a porcine juxtaposition—slums so disgraceful and immoral that the thought of them murders sleep."[1] The conditions under which natives live in the "locations" outside South African towns are awful beyond description. The same evils are cropping up in the new townships built in other parts of Africa. At Nairobi, the capital of Kenya, about 12,000 Africans are crowded together and all but a few of them, Dr. Leys tells us, "live in shelters that are inferior to village huts and are quite unfit for human habitation. The fact is widely recognized and bewailed in the colony."[2]

No pretence is here made that life in a pagan African village is sweet and clean, but it is wholesome compared to life in these slums. It is true that the European Governments provide policemen and magistrates' courts to preserve order, but, after all, these take cognisance only of breaches of the law. They cannot supply the moral restraints that are needed. Even where drink is excluded, the evils of prostitution (in some places the prostitutes are white women) and other things remain. There is no need to speak of the unholy influence of the Cinema upon the minds of Africans.

[1] Dr. E. B. Brookes, paper read before the South African Association for the advancement of Science. Reported in *The South African Outlook*, March 2, 1925.

[2] *Kenya*, p. 273. The figures quoted from Dr. Leys are old.

It may be said that such Natives as are here described should be congratulated upon their emancipation from tyrannous custom, that they have learnt manliness and the worthlessness of superstition. But if they have learnt to cast away old restraints upon natural desires and have not acquired new moral sanctions, how much the better are they? Are they not worse?

VI.

The methods of governing the African have already been referred to. I shall not be suspected of minimising the good work done by various administrations in Africa—I have seen it, and no man can have a greater admiration for it than I. But however anxious the British or any other Government may be to rule justly and well, and however much by a system of indirect rule they seek to conserve tribal institutions, they inevitably produce some amount of disintegration.

They rule according to native law except where this is repugnant to European morality. White men in Africa find it impossible to live cheek by jowl with human sacrifices, cannibalism and other barbarous practices, without attempting intervention. They do intervene, and rightly so, often with great sternness. Sir Hugh Clifford has stated that between the beginning of August, 1919, and the end of December, 1922, no fewer than 675 persons were condemned for murder in Nigeria (only 373 were actually executed), and that "approximately one-third of the murders on this list were committed owing to the perpetrators' belief in witchcraft, magic, or in some analogous superstition." All who are conversant with the facts know that, as Sir Hugh Clifford states, "in West Africa, at any rate, our primary *raison d'être* is to protect the simple African from merciless exploitation and spoliation at the hands, not of the unscrupulous European, but of his own more sophisticated fellows."[1]

It is true, and not of West Africa only. I do not think the African is by nature any more cruel than other people; but, with all our sympathy with his stumbling efforts in matters of faith, we cannot but admit that his religion (what Sir Hugh calls "superstition") leads him into many ruthless practices. Nobody with the slightest knowledge of the voluminous literature on the subject can doubt that fact.

I will content myself with one illustration out of hundreds that might be given. Mr. Amaury Talbot, a Government official in Nigeria, describes the doings of a native society devoted to Ekong, the War God, and the sacrifice offered to him.

> "Once arrived in the sacred enclosure, the unfortunate victim was given over into the hands of the priest. So soon as she saw the place, she knew that there was no hope for her. The apathy of despair, which is so peculiarly the heritage of black races, descended and enveloped her. Tearless, or with silent tears slow-falling, she moved toward the priest, unresisting always, since of what use to struggle when relentless Fate has seized and holds one fast? About her round throat—for only young and beautiful women

[1] *Blackwood's Magazine*, June, 1923.

> might be offered—a cord was flung and tightly drawn, so that she died by strangulation. No blood might flow, for this was a warriors' society and the victim was offered to the war god that he might rejoice in her agony and accept it as the price of his aid to the youth who to-day entered the ranks of fighters, so that no drop of the latter's blood need be shed to appease the thirst of the deity."[1]

What humane government could do other than stop such abominations? But to intervene is to aim a blow at native religion which is the cement and foundation of native society. Such are the horns of the dilemma upon which the Government is impaled!

Governments set forth proclamations for the suppression of witchcraft, and, strange as it may seem, hardly anything they do causes greater resentment among the Natives. A prominent native chief said to me one day: "You white men are destroying the community. The warlocks and witches are exultant and doing just as they please, because they know we can no longer kill them as we used to do." Out of our ignorance we have legislated against witch-doctors (or diviners) thinking them to be the people who bewitch their fellows, whereas it is they who seek out and denounce the warlocks and witches. In the native mind this is as if we legislated against detectives with the aim of stopping murder![2] We Europeans no longer believe in witchcraft, but Africans do most sincerely believe in it—and there is something to

[1] P. Amaury Talbot, *Life in Southern Nigeria* (1923), p. 179.

[2] See the sensible remarks made on this subject by Frank H. Melland, a magistrate of Northern Rhodesia, in his *In Witch-bound Africa* (1923), p. 198. Captain Dale and I pointed out this fallacy in *The Ila-Speaking Peoples* (1920), Vol. II, p. 90.

be said in support of their belief. We count as "murder" what they regard as ridding the community of dangerous criminals. The English law holds that if a person commits a crime under a delusion, the question to be decided is whether, if the delusion were true, it would justify the crime. If there is such a thing as witchcraft, then the Africans cannot be blamed for finding out and destroying the warlock and witch—though they may be rightly blamed for the cruel ways of detecting and killing them. They do not understand our British law which brands this act as murder, any more than we should understand the arraignment of the Lord Chief Justice and the police for murdering a Bill Sykes who was hanged by the neck till he was dead. As Sir Hugh Clifford says in the course of his article in *Blackwood's*, already quoted, the intensity and the sincerity of the unsophisticated Nigerian's (let us say, African's) belief "in the constant intrusion of the supernatural into the affairs of everyday life has to be taken into consideration when we are attempting to assess the guilt of persons who, while they have wilfully caused the death of one or more of their fellows, regard themselves as having acted in the most commonsense or even in the most exemplary manner." This remark applies not only to cases of witchcraft but also to the killing of infants that are regarded as ill-omens. To abolish such criminal practices proclamations are not enough—it is necessary to go to the root of the matter and replace by better beliefs the belief which prompts them.

When the power of capital punishment is transferred from the African Chief-in-council to the European judge, the prestige of the chief inevitably suffers. There is necessity for this, but the consequences to the chief in the eyes of the people are patent. Then, again, the chief is held responsible for the good conduct of the community over which he rules. It may happen that this man, who is so sacrosanct in the estimation of the people, is arrested and committed to prison—perhaps he is flogged—and this, to say the very least, does not augment his prestige. In some parts of Africa it is not unknown that the Natives elect a secondary chief, to act the part of whipping-boy when one is required; they keep the real chief secret, so as to avoid any offence against his sacred person. Even when the government fully respects the chief's person, and rules the people through him, appeal is allowed from his court to that of the magistrate, or cases may be taken direct to this official. This is necessary in order to guard against cruel, despotic acts on the chief's part, but the dignity of the chief in the eyes of his people cannot but be lowered thereby. We Britons rightly pride ourselves upon our just administration of the law, yet it cannot be doubted that greater justice is sometimes done by the Chief sitting in council, who is fully acquainted with the wiles of native suitors, than by the magistrate who is hampered by the rules of evidence.

Where Governments use the chiefs as a medium for calling out compulsory labour, which is hated by the men, their prestige is lowered further.

Governments introduce another innovation when they compel the people individually to pay taxes. For Africans to give tribute to their chiefs is one thing—for them to pay tax to a higher and alien authority is another. The taxpayer regards himself as a somebody and in proportion as he looks beyond his chief to others his estimation for the head of his community diminishes. It is not surprising to learn that some chiefs object to the poll-tax on the ground that it leads to the insubordination of their people. It would be better to levy a corporate tax on the community, paid through the chief.

Other illustrations might be given to show that when European government is introduced, native society cannot remain where it was—some disintegration always follows. Native society being founded on religious belief, any interference with its outward structure reacts upon the inward sentiment, and any injury to religious belief and the traditional custom has deleterious effects upon morals. The whole structure hangs together as one piece; one part cannot be touched without disturbing the whole.[1]

VII.

In short, what we are witnessing in Africa under the pressure of the European invaders is the rapid break-up of society. The African is being hurried out of his old collectivistic society into individualism.

[1] I shall show in Chapter XI that Christianity, as hitherto taught, has often co-operated in these disintegrative activities.

All peoples have to pass that way. The British peoples have not been exempt from this law. The pendulum swings to the tune of the Hegelian logic: *thesis*, collectivism: *antithesis*, individualism. The synthesis has not yet been found in a system which does equal justice to the social and self-regarding instincts of man. The Africans have hitherto lived in the collectivistic stage: the community has been the unit; every individual interest has been subordinate to the general welfare. In many directions this excites our admiration—even envy. There is a solidarity that civilized communities find it hard to attain. The corporate sentiment that trades unions create among their members is but a faint reflection of the brotherhood found within the African's clan. The Africans have, it is true, to pay heavily for their collectivism, in the injustice done to personal strivings and aspirations; just as we pay heavily for our individualism, in selfishness and greed.

The invasion of Africa by Europeans means the inoculation of the Africans with the germs of our individualism, and not in such minute doses as are administered with the hypodermic syringe: we are administering them with the hose-pipe whose stream carries everything before it with a rush. Taxes are levied upon and paid by individuals. Wages are paid to individuals. When crime is committed it is the single person and not the clan that expiates it. The missionary seeks the conversion of individuals and teaches that every man and woman is personally responsible to God. In more advanced communities Africans are led by European example to demand the electoral franchise and individual tenure of land.

Some acute observers, such as Dr. Leys[1], believe it futile and mischievous to attempt to revive the African's tribalism where it has decayed. Yet where it exists it should be jealously safeguarded in the moral interests of the natives. Every care should be taken to strengthen the tribal bond and to avoid breaking down the collectivistic structure prematurely. It may be that the Africans must pass out of the stage where the individual counts for little or nothing, into the stage where he is master of his own fate and captain of his own soul. Certainly the change may remove many fetters upon his intellect. We would fain hope that he might attain the synthesis wherein his present tribal virtues would be united to personal initiative and responsibility. At present all is confusion. The danger is that in the process of social revolution he should lose his old moral restraints and gain no others. The old restraints came, if you wish, of superstition; but they did control him from within; it will be no real gain to substitute dread of the gallows in the place of fear of the wrath of his ancestors. Dread of the gallows is a much feebler control than the old beliefs in ghosts and *mana*. A man may hope by sheer cunning to escape hanging: the old sanction of the curse was ineluctable. Individualism depends for its success upon a high standard of righteousness personally accepted; a

[1] *Kenya*, p. 299.

man must feel he is responsible to something or somebody. To depart from such control as the tribe exerts and not to find a higher control spells disaster.

This chapter may be summed up in the words of a highly placed and experienced administrator :—

> "We are undeniably introducing profound changes and tearing up deep-rooted ideas, at a most precipitate rate ; and with such far-reaching changes must come a new orientation for the native outlook. As Gustav le Bon says : 'When a faith ends, a revolution begins'[1] ; it is a dangerous thing to destroy one belief without substituting another for it."[2]

"What aileth thee ?" asked the children of Dan when Micah, from whose house they had taken the teraphim, overtook them : "What aileth thee ?" And Micah replied, "Ye have taken away my gods which I made . . . and what have I more ? and how then say ye unto me, What aileth thee ?"

It is a sorry business to strip a poor man of his gods, if we do not give him God in exchange.

[1] "Les révolutions qui commencent sont en réalité des croyances qui finissent."

[2] MAJOR G. ST. J. ORDE BROWNE, *The Vanishing Tribes of Kenya* (1925), p. 261.

CHAPTER IX.

WHEREIN AN ATTEMPT IS MADE TO ESTIMATE THE VALUE OF ISLAM TO THE AFRICAN.

I.

IF we do not give him God in exchange.

African paganism is doomed to decay and extinction. If they are to remain religious the only possible alternative open to the Africans is to choose between Islam and Christianity, both of which offer them a knowledge of God.

The two religions are alike in their claim to universality. Modern Muslims, at least Muslims of the Ahmadiya school, whose head-quarters in England are at Woking, are in no doubt as to the place Islam as based on the Qur'án should take in the world. "The Holy Qur'án was not meant for one people or one age, and accordingly the scope of its moral teachings is as wide as humanity itself. It is the Book which offers guidance to all men in all conditions of life, to the ignorant savage as well as to the wise philosopher, to the man of business as well as to the recluse, to the rich as well as to the poor."[1] While the first little band

[1] MUHAMMAD ALI, Preface to *The Holy Qur'án* (1917), p. xiv.

of his followers was suffering severe persecution, and there seemed little hope that the Faith would prove acceptable even to Arabians, Muhammad sustained the drooping spirits with the promise: "We will soon show them our signs in remote regions and among their own people, until it will become quite clear to them that it is the truth."[1] This is taken by Muslims to mean that Islam shall spread to the ends of the earth. They claim to have a Gospel for the African.

Within ten years of Muhammad's death his followers invaded Egypt (A.D. 640). Twenty years later, Ukba Ben Nafa spurred his horse into the Atlantic, crying: "By the great God, if I were not stopped by this raging sea I would go on to the nations of the West, preaching the Unity of Thy name and putting to the sword those that would not submit." By A.D. 708 North Africa was definitely (though not finally, we believe) won for Islam. The Christian Church in the coastlands—the Church of Tertullian and Augustine, which numbered its bishops by hundreds, but which was never a truly indigenous Church—was swept away. The superficially Christianized Berber population became Muslim. Only in Egypt did the Church survive. In the course of centuries Islam spread from the Mediterranean littoral southwards across the Sahara into the regions of the Senegal and Niger. It ascended the Nile and crossed the Sudan to Lake Chad. By the eleventh century it was

[1] *Qur'án*, XLI, 53. "remote regions," or extremities; "their own people," i.e., Arabians.

planted firmly within three hundred miles of the coast of Guinea. Its more southerly progress was stopped, in some degree, by the tsetse fly, which was inimical to the horses and cattle of the invaders; partly the arrest was due to the unhealthy climate of the coastal regions; and partly to the valiant opposition of some of the pagan tribes. In later years, the onward march was deliberately halted, lest the pagans should become converted and therefore immune, by Islamic principles, to slave-raiding.

The region of North Africa lying between the Mediterranean and the Sudan, the land of the blacks, was inhabited by various peoples of Caucasian type—Berbers (akin to the Iberians of Spain), and Hamites (allied to the Semites)—and by Negroids. These were to a large extent Islamized by the Arabs. The Muslims built up great states based upon pre-existing kingdoms founded by Negroes. For a thousand years empire succeeded empire, culminating in that of the Fulani, which was finally conquered by the British and French in our own days. A civilization was created of an astonishing type—at one time more advanced than anything then to be found in northern Europe. Firearms were in use while Englishmen were still fighting with the bow and arrow. The kings went on pilgrimage to Mecca—one of them, it is said, accompanied by a retinue of 60,000 persons and furnished with gold to the value of a million sterling. Immense caravans crossed the desert annually to and from Egypt—it is on record that one of these was made up of 12,000 camels, bearing

1,600 tons of merchandise. Important schools of learning were established, and extensive libraries. There was a time when black poets were welcomed at the court of Cordova, and the University of Timbuktu exchanged knowledge with the Universities of Spain.[1] This, of course, was when the Moors were in possession of Andalusia. Their expulsion and subsequent invasion of the Sudan had an important influence upon the Islamic culture in these regions. But the astonishing civilization created by Muslims was ultimately destroyed by Muslims, and when Europeans invaded the country it had fallen into irretrievable decay.

In East Africa there was never such an efflorescence of Islamic culture as in the north. Arab voyagers sailed down the coast and founded settlements at Mombasa, Zanzibar, and Sofala. It is said that they supplied the Portuguese with a map which revealed the possibility of doubling the Cape of Good Hope. From the coast they penetrated inland. The early European explorers found Arab traders settled on the shores of the great lakes. Stanley met them in Uganda, where they were endeavouring to convert the king and people.

In the southernmost part of Africa Islam was introduced originally through the action of the governments in importing Orientals. When in 1654 the Dutch East India Company established a penal

[1] LADY LUGARD, *A Tropical Dependency*, p. 345. This book contains the best account I know of the Islamic culture in North Africa.

settlement at the Cape, they sent thither convicts from East Indies who were Muslims. These men married coloured women who accepted Islam, and a community was formed that has grown steadily until there are now 24,513 Muslims in the Cape Province. Some of the original exiles were men of learning and sanctity—their graves are now centres of pilgrimage. In 1925 Dr. Zwemer found a school of 400 children studying Arabic in Cape Town. Islamic newspapers and literature in Afrikaans and native languages issue from the press and evidently form part of a determined propaganda to win the South African Bantu for Islam. Into Natal Islam entered when Indians were imported about 1860 to work on the sugar plantations. They have remained in considerable numbers and by marrying Bantu women have built up Islamic communities. In Natal the Muslims number 17,146. Labourers, small traders and skilled artisans have carried Islam from the coast into the Transvaal and Rhodesia. Even in Basutoland the last Census reported 102 Muslims. "With the Indian trader, who is found all over Southern Nyasaland and Portuguese territory, Islam is steadily gaining ground everywhere."[1]

Several attempts have been made to estimate the number of Muslims in Africa. Dr. Zwemer, in 1923, calculated that of 234,814,989 Muslims in the world, 59,444,397 were in Africa. As he puts the total population of Africa at 125,806,771, it is

[1] Dr. S. M. Zwemer, *Islam in South Africa*, I.R.M., October, 1925.

evident that he thinks nearly half the Africans have adopted Islam. Other authorities give a lower estimate. Captain André,[1] for example, reckons 3,875,073 Muslims in French West Africa out of a total population of 12,283,216, where Dr. Zwemer counts 6,716,000 Muslims. The Census of Northern Nigeria shows 67 per cent. Muslims, and 33 per cent. Animists.

It is difficult to say what progress Islam is now making. Among some West African tribes, undoubtedly, the progress is rapid, but there are many Negroes, principally in the forest regions, who have always opposed Islam and among these the Muslims make little or no headway. In other tribes advance is slow. Even among the Hausas in the French Niger colony, Captain André is inclined to compute a majority of pagans. In Dahomey he reckons less than 70,000 Muslims where Dr. Zwemer estimated 294,000. It is reported from British Cameroons that Islam is not gaining ground. Speaking of Islam in East Africa Dr. Norman Leys says: "The always feeble early missionary endeavours of its introducers have quite ceased. Its situation and character in East Africa suggest a last backwash of some already strongly ebbing tide." He says again: "In East Africa Islam shows no sign of growth—in knowledge or in zeal, or perhaps even in numbers. It will probably follow tribalism and much else beside into a past that men happily forget, as those new circumstances

[1] CAPITAINE P. J. ANDRÉ, *L'islam noir* (1924).

to which it once was so peculiarly fitted give place to newer."[1]

Islam has grown in Africa (1) by means of violent conquest, (2) by pacific propaganda, (3) by commercial influence, (4) by intermarriage. The opening up of the continent has in some ways helped it. In the old days communication between Mediterranean countries and the Sudan was by means of caravans, and entailed long journeys across the desert: now Muslim traders travel by steamship round the coast and pursue their way inland by railway. In consequence their power on the African coast has greatly augmented, but against this we must place the fact that the interior commercial centres have declined in a corresponding degree. Islam has also gained somewhat because of the support it has received from the British Government, which, while theoretically neutral to religion, yet follows Roman precedent in supporting the local cult as a means of preserving order. At the Gordon College in Khartum, for example, Islam is enthroned: the only Bible Dr. Zwemer could discover there was General Gordon's preserved in a glass case. Religious teachers from the indigenous village schools are trained in Government institutions.[2] At the same time, the extension of European rule has made it impossible for Muslims to carry on the time-honoured propaganda of the sword. The complete Islamic system is impracticable under European rule—its criminal law, e.g., must

[1] NORMAN LEYS, *Kenya*, pp. 263, 268.

[2] Report on the Sudan, 1923, Cmd. 2281, p. 40.

be modified. The prestige once enjoyed by Muslim conquerors is theirs no longer, and instances are known of tribes reverting to paganism since British rule has been established.

It must also be said that there is an almost unanimous opinion among qualified observers that Islam with the African is often only skin-deep. Mr. Ingrams, an Assistant District Commissioner in the Zanzibar Protectorate states—" . . . the veneer of Islam is but a flimsy veil for the simpler beliefs of the Africans . . . All that Islam does for the primitive African native, when it is so little understood as in Zanzibar, is to lend itself to the more efficient (in the native mind) practice of magic. Even receipts for killing one's enemy are headed 'In the Name of God the Merciful, the Compassionate.' "[1] Circumcision, the taboo on animal food containing blood, prayers, a more or less perfunctory observance of Ramadan, the adoption of Muslim names and dress—these may be the only marks of the African Muslim. The old dread of demons persists, together with the belief in the efficacy of charms,[2] and the morals remain as pagan as ever. Mr. Meek has recently portrayed the paganized Islam of Northern Nigeria. " Though there are many learned Muslims in Northern Nigeria inspired with the spirit of true religion, the general mass of the followers of the Prophet are like children imitating without comprehending, and believing

[1] Report of the Phelps-Stokes Commission: *Education in East Africa* (1925), p. 222.

[2] See Article on *Charms and Amulets* (*Muhammadan*) in Encyclopædia of Religion and Ethics, by Cana de Vaux, Vol. III.

that the public observance of prescribed formulæ raises them in the eyes of Allah, as it does in those of their fellow-men. Their religious outlook is little wider than that of the pagans they despise . . . Thus on the spiritual side Islam in Nigeria is but a poor imitation of the lofty religion of the Prophet."[1]

II.

I heard Dr. Aggrey declare passionately that no second-rate religion is good enough for Africans; they must have the best. The English people, at any rate, have no hesitation about what is best. Some few of them have embraced Islam, but the great majority, even though they may not practise the Christian ethic, would vote for Christianity rather than for Islam. But there are some who would say that while Christianity is best for Europeans, Islam is the best for Africans, for it is more suited to their nature than Christianity. What must be said about this? Let us start by saying all that can be said in favour of Islam.

It must be recognized that there is strength and a power of attraction in Islam. That so large a proportion of Africans have accepted this religion is sufficient proof. It is not satisfactory to account for this acceptance on the ground that Africans have been compelled to embrace Islam, for this is not true of the majority. Nor is it sufficient to

[1] C. K. Meek, *The Northern Tribes of Nigeria* (1925), Vol. II, pp. 4, 5.

say that Islam gains adherents by pandering to their sensual passions. Nor can we state that the Africans choose Islam because they have no other alternative to their unsatisfying pagan faith: in Zanzibar the Natives have had the opportunity of comparing Christianity and Islam during sixty years, and they remain Muslims for the most part.

The strength of Islam lies in the force of conviction it inspires. The Muslim believes in God. Day by day the impressive declaration of faith is sounded abroad in the call to prayer: *Allah-u Akbar. Ash-hadu al-la-ilaha ill-Allah . . . La ilaha ill-Allah.* "Allah is the greatest. I bear witness that nothing deserves to be worshipped but Allah. There is no god but Allah!" Christian theologians may point to deficiencies in the Islamic conception of God, but Africans are not theologians. The trend of their own thought is towards monotheism, and the confident assertion by Muslims that *they* worship the one God, makes a very strong appeal. The pagan African believes in and practises prayer. When he sees the Muslim break off from whatever he is doing when the hour for prayer arrives, and perform his devotions publicly with every mark of earnest conviction, he is deeply impressed. Moreover, as some one has said, the African seems to be so made as to worship a book. It comes as a new thing to him, but it is not strange to his mind that a material object can convey a message from the unseen world—he is familiar with the hucklebones and other implements used by his diviners.

And when the Muslim declares that his sacred book, the Qur'án, contains the actual words of God and is an infallible revelation of God's will, then again he is impressed and attracted. That the Qur'án is written in a language he cannot understand adds to its mystery and power over his untutored mind.

Moreover, Islam is propagated in Africa, not by strange white men who practice alien social customs, but by men of the African's own colour (or nearly so), and, if of manifestly higher grade of civilization, not removed to an impossible distance as the European is. There is not a gap between the Muslim missionary, be he trader or preacher, and the African, such as yawns between the Christian missionary and the African. The ordinary Muslim has the same implicit belief in magic as the African pagan; his jinns are not strange creatures—the African knows plenty of the same species. The rhythmic dancing and barbaric music of the corybantic Dervishes, who have done so much to spread Islam in Africa, are on the same plane as the African's own practices—it is no new thing to him that divine truth, messages from the unseen, are conveyed through trance.

On the social side, Islam appeals to the African through its offer of brotherhood—which again the African understands readily. Mr. E. D. Morel says that Islam "takes the Negro by the hand and gives him equality with all men. From the day the pagan adopts Islam, no Semite Muslim can claim racial superiority over him. Islam to the

Negro is the stepping stone to a higher conception of existence, inspiring in his breast confidence in his own destiny, imbuing his spirit with a robust faith in himself and in his race."[1] Muhammad Ali claims that Islam abolishes all invidious class distinctions. It lays down the basis of a vast brotherhood in which all men and women—to whatever tribe or nation or caste they may belong and whatever be their profession or rank in society, the wealthy and the poor,—have equal rights and in which no one can trample upon the right of his brother. He quotes a saying of the Prophet which lays down the strict rule of brotherhood: "No one of you is a believer in God unless he loves for his brother what he loves for himself."[2] No doubt certain reservations have to be made. Within the fold brotherliness may reign, but all without are Kafirs, the Muslim's legitimate prey. Love of the brotherhood accompanies and fosters hatred for others, and spiritual pride. As Sir Frederick Lugard says: "Islam as a militant creed which teaches contempt for those who are not its votaries, panders to the weakness of the African character—self-conceit and vanity."[3]

The fact that Muhammad allowed slavery and that Muslims have always practised slave-raiding and slave-trading, demonstrates the limitation in the Islamic conception of brotherhood. To this

[1] *Affairs of West Africa* (1902), p. 230.

[2] Preface to *The Holy Qur'án*, p. xv.

[3] *The Dual Mandate*, p. 77.

day the Mecca pilgrimage, sacred duty though it be, is made the occasion and means of traffic in slaves. Moreover, brotherhood has never prevented intestine warfare between rival Islamic sects. Yet when all these limitations are recognized, we cannot deny that the brotherhood of Muslims is a fact. When the Prince of Wales visited West Africa he received the Sacrament at the hands of a negro clergyman and the fact was distinctive enough to be reported in the newspapers. Numbers of Englishmen, who account themselves good Christians, would never dream of acknowledging in this way their fellowship with black-skinned Christians. Muslims make no such distinctions. Arab and Negro and Berber and Hindu are brothers in the faith and not only join in common worship, but in the affairs of everyday life freely help each other. "The ideal of a league of human races has indeed been approached by the Moslem community more nearly than by any other."[1]

Another thing to be said for Islam is that it is a theocracy. It draws no distinction between Church and State, between secular and religious.

[1] C. S. HURGRONJE, in *The Moslem World of To-day* (1925), p. 90.

"This solidarity was a great attraction for the conquered nations, and it was the desire to profit by it that brought over most of the recruits to Islam. Every convert at once enjoyed all the privileges of a Musulman: a foreigner and an enemy the day before, he became by simple conversion an equal and a brother. 'Know,' said Mahomet in his last sermon at Mecca, 'know that you are all equal among yourselves and that you form a family of brothers.'"—ANDRÉ SERVIER, *Islam and Psychology of the Musulman* (1924), pp. 71, 72.

The Qur'ān embodies both religious precepts and legal decrees. In Sir Frederick Lugard's opinion, the great strength of Islam, "lies in the fact that it combines a social code with simple religious forms and is thus interwoven with the daily life of its followers."[1] It is a great socio-religious system covering the whole life of the individual from birth to death. This kind of thing is alien to a modern European and may even appear to him to be an intolerable spiritual tyranny, but it appeals to the African because he too, in his pagan life, makes no distinction between the religious and the secular, and sometimes finds it difficult to understand why the functions of missionary and magistrate should be in the hands of separate individuals.

Islam has thus an integrative power. The African tribal life dissolves under the pressure of European civilization, but when the tribesmen embrace Islam they are introduced into a great system of religion and ethics, and are given new moral sanctions in the place of those which they have outgrown. In West Africa the Muslims bound scattered tribes into powerful kingdoms in which Negroes took high positions. Of islamized Africans, Mr. Morel states "their moral and spiritual well-being increased by leaps and bounds and their political and social life took an altogether higher level."[2] He concedes that in its relation to mankind as a whole, Islam may be sterile and make for

[1] *Op. cit.*, p. 77.

[2] *Affairs of West Africa*, p. 212.

stagnancy, but denies that it is so in West Africa. It gives the Negro (he declares) an energy, a dignity, a self-respect he has not known before. Mr. Meek confirms this so far as its political, social and economic aspects are concerned.

> "Islam has brought civilization to barbarous tribes. It has converted isolated pagan groups into nations; it has made commerce with the outside world possible . . . it has broadened the outlook, raised the standard of living by creating a higher social atmosphere, and has conferred on its followers dignity, self-respect, and respect for others. The intellectual and political superiority of the Muslim communities is due chiefly to their religion. Islam introduced the art of reading and writing, and by the prohibition of the use of alcohol, of cannibalism, blood revenge and other barbarous practices, it has enabled the Sudanese Negro to become a citizen of the world."[1]

It may be said that Christian observers have done ample justice to the rich fruits of personal character produced by Islam. Thus Dr. David M. Kay[2] speaks of the patience and diligence of the Muslim craftsman.

> "Kindness to animals, horses, donkeys, dogs, pigeons, is required by religion, and has become innate among Moslems.[3] . . . The ablutions prescribed before prayer have inspired cleanliness in the humblest houses and care in preparation of food. The theory of polygamy, which diverges so strongly from Christian feeling, provides all women with family protection; and the moral degradation of great European cities has no equivalent among Moslem

[1] *Op. cit.*, Vol. II, pp. 4, 5.

[2] *The Semitic Religions* (1923), pp. 168, 170. Dr. Kay resided in Constantinople for five years and spent four years with an army fighting against the Turks and their allies.

[3] I fancy the donkeys in Tangier might have something to say about this.—E. W. S.

women.[1] Judged by its fruits, Islam can claim a power over its adherents and a pervasive influence on their lives which contemporary systems attain only among their most zealous groups."

To this may be added what Canon W. H. T. Gairdner says:

> "A steady world-view, patience and resignation; respect for parents and the aged; love of children; benevolence to the poor and infirm and insane; kindness to domestic slaves and to beasts; fidelity to a rule of duty; these and other virtues when found may fairly be credited to Islam; and for their absence, if they are not found, Islam could not fairly be blamed."[2]

A word more must be said on two points. First, as regards intoxicating liquors. We know the havoc that has been wrought by the drink-traffic in Africa and the strenuous efforts made by international conferences and national governments to stop it. Adherents of Islam may well claim that if they, and not Christians, had dominated African commerce the Africans would have escaped this scourge at least. Muhammad laid down no law on the subject, but, as Dr. Kay states, by appealing in the name of Allah to the voluntary choice of his adherents, he succeeded where many zealous agencies have failed—he founded a society of total abstainers, numbered by scores of millions and lasting over a thousand years.[3]

[1] Equally and more experienced observers deny this.

[2] *The Rebuke of Islam* (1920), pp. 139, 140.

[3] *Op. cit.*, pp. 166, 167. Yet, according to statements made by Muslims to the Committee of Inquiry into the Liquor Trade in Southern Nigeria (1908) followers of Muhammad not only drank spirits, but traded in them. "An ordinary Muhammadan," said one Muslim, "may take spirits, but the headman is forbidden; they call him the high priest."—*Minutes*, p. 46.

The other subject that must be mentioned is polygamy. Of the four causes assigned by Mr. E. D. Morel for the rapid islamization of Africa, as contrasted with the "failure" of Christianity, one is that Islam recognizes, as Christianity refuses to recognize, that "the circumstances which regulate certain natural laws vary with climatic considerations and racial idiosyncrasies." In other words, Islam legalizes polygamy, while the Christian Church discountenances it, and European governments, by making taxation fall heavier on the polygamist than on the monogamist, discourage it. Mr. Morel is not alone in arguing that polygamy is a necessary institution on physical grounds for the Negro in Africa. Dr. Blyden goes so far as to say that "owing to the exhausting climatic conditions the life and perpetuity of the population depend upon polygamy." The question need not be discussed further at this point. But it must be said that experience warrants the statement that the monogamist Christian Africans rear as large or larger and more healthy families than the average polygamists. Unquestionably, however, the Africans, and particularly African women, cling to polygamy, and by recognizing it and sanctioning it by his own practice, Muhammad prepared unconsciously for an acceptance of his religion.

Neither Christianity nor Islam is indigenous to Africa. Islam is no more an African religion than Christianity is a European religion. They both had their origin among Semites. The Jews had undergone a long preparation for Christianity through the preaching of the prophets. The Arabs had no such training. They had to some extent come in contact with their more religiously advanced fellow-Semites and Muhammad drew much of his teaching from Jew and Christian. But the Arabs were idolaters and while Muhammad converted them to the worship of one God, both he and his converts retained much of the primitive Semitic animism. The ancient Meccan fetish—the black stone of the Ka'aba—remains enshrined to this day in the Islamic Holy of Holies and is kissed by the devout pilgrims. As Islam swept over other lands it absorbed something of existing religions—the confluence of Zoroastrianism and Islam, for example, formed the starting point of Sufism, the mystical sect of Islam.[1] When it entered Africa Islam was undoubtedly strongly influenced by the Christianity it swept away; it imbibed the Berber culture which was largely Christian. In contact with the Negro, Islam found itself more on a level with Arabian animism: it was perfectly easy and natural for it to amalgamate with the African religion and culture. It appealed then, as now, to the African because it was so near to them. It demanded no violent wrench from the past. It brought the African the surer knowledge of God which he had been groping for; it taught him new forms of prayer, it gave him a book (which he could not understand), and some simple ritual, added sundry taboos, brought him into a great brother-

[1] R. P. MASANI, *The Conference of the Birds, a Sufi Allegory* (1924), p. 46.

hood, clothed him, and left him his traditional customs and beliefs otherwise untouched. In doing this it undoubtedly conferred some benefit upon him.

III.

But the question remains, is Islam the best religion for the African? It may be good, but the good is sometimes the enemy of the best. The endeavour has been made to say everything possible in its favour. There is something to be said on the other side.

Here to begin with, is a statement made by one who knows Africa as few men know it, and who would not call himself an orthodox Christian. Sir Harry Johnston sums up a discussion in this way:

> "In short, judged by the test of output in the way of science and art, literature, material well-being, control of disease, sexual morality, public works, subdual of recalcitrant nature, can any comparison be sustained between the countries professing the Christian religion or governed by Christian nations, and the lands which still remain more or less independent under the sway of Muhammadan rulers? On these lines is there any sustainable plea of equality between Hungary and European Turkey, Spain and Morocco, Greece and Asia Minor, Italy and Tripoli, Afghanistan and British India, modern Persia and modern Caucasia? The language of Christian Magyars and that of the Muhammadan Turks are nearly related in origin, and the Magyars and Turks came from the same ethnic stock; but in the course of history one became Christian and the other Muhammadan. Can any impartial critic

maintain that the two peoples at the present day are on the same level of civilization, or place alongside Hungarian achievements in art, music, architecture, literature, biological science, engineering and political government similar achievements on the part of Turkey ? "[1]

In Africa a tribe, under the influence of Islam, may take a step forward, but it is the last they take and there they remain. "A striking unity marks the accounts of those who from Sierra Leone to Zanzibar describe to us the effect of Islam on the Negro. Everywhere one finds that a rise is spoken of to a certain level ; a dead stop at that level—a low one after all : a hardening ; and then the inner deterioration that comes to those who, contented with a low level, become the enemies of a higher one."[2]

In fact, the spiritual deterioration caused by Islam is paralleled by the physical ruin of countries invaded by the Arabs. It has been well said that they carried with them the desert into the fair Mediterranean lands of North Africa. An old Arabian writer declared that before the invasion

[1] SIR H. H. JOHNSTON, *Views and Reviews from the outlook of an anthropologist* (1912), pp. 191, 192.

[2] *The Rebuke of Islam*, p. 154. M. Servier is in agreement with these judgments. Islam, he declares, was not a torch, but an extinguisher, *op. cit.*, p. 153.

M. Vignon (*op. cit.*, p. 95) thus sums up his review of Islam in Africa : " Au resumé, l' impression dominante demeure celle-ci : les 'progrès' économiques ou sociaux que la religion musulmane fera réaliser à un peuple autrefois fétichiste, seront assez vite atteints. Pendant un temps court, il abandonnera l' état statique, passera à l' état dynamique, s' élevant ainsi d'un degré, mais bientôt . . . le 'progrès' cessera, l' état statique réapparaitra."

it was possible, so extended were the forests, to travel many days beneath the shade of trees. The land was, as Herodotus had described it eight centuries before, fertile, well-wooded, well-watered. The Romans planted vineyards and orchards, led out the water, and drove roads through the country. The Muslims cut down trees, burned the forests, neglected the roads. They ruined the country. When the French landed in North Africa they found famine to be frequent in what had once been a granary of Rome—a stagnant land, peopled by a stagnant people.

This stagnation of mind may be traced to the Islamic conception of God. Alike for individuals and for communities it does matter much, after all, what they believe God to be. "I *do* believe in God," Mark Rutherford protested to Mardon, and the atheist's answer was: "There is nothing in that statement. What do you believe about Him?—that is the point." The Muslim believes in God and in the Unity of God. He describes God as Merciful and Gracious, the Guardian over all, the Provider of daily bread. But it is as Power that the Muslim usually thinks of Him. He knows ninety and nine "most excellent names" for God, but not one that denotes God as Father. "In Islam the relation of man to God must ever be that of a slave, who lacks the freedom and dignity of a son."[1] The orthodox Muslim denies that God

[1] Dr. Edward Sell (of Madras), art., "God (Muslim)," *Encyclopædia of Religion and Ethics*, Vol. VI. M. Vignon (*op. cit.*, p. 70, etc.) has much to say of the narcotic character of Islam, particularly of its doctrine of predestination.

can be known, and stigmatizes all inquiries into His nature as impious. The All-Powerful is unrestrained by any law of holiness, and by the Muslim sin is regarded not so much as a breach of moral law as a violation of some arbitrary decree. The very evident lapses of Muhammad are not looked upon by his followers as sins, for he acted under the command of God. "God misleadeth whom He will, and whom He will He guideth," says the Qur'án. Such a conception of God does not tend to call forth the deep love of the human soul; "and, as it retards the growth of spiritual life in the individual, so also it hinders progress in the community and prevents the formation of a national life. A practical fatalism settles sooner or later on all Muslim communities."[1]

Another factor in the case is the rigidity of orthodox Islam leading to a petrification of doctrine and a stabilization of ethics to a standard set up in Arabia 1300 years ago. The Qur'án is regarded as uncreated and eternal; even the letters and words of the book as written, and the sounds of the uttered recitation or reading, are fixed by divine decree. Human freewill is denied, and the Will of God, which is the all-determining source of change and activity, has been revealed finally, once for all, in the Book which descended from heaven upon Muhammad. The orthodox Muslims—and it is these, the Sunnites and the more conservative schools, who prevail in Africa—are thus anchored in the past. Not the Qur'án only but the inter-

[1] Dr. Sell, *op. cit.*, p 302.

pretations of it by learned doctors are definitive and unchangeable. These men, André Servier declares, have killed any germ of progress in Islam. "The immutability of its institutions has ended in moulding individuals and the whole nation. It is this that explains how the Moslem nations have remained and still remain insensible and even hostile to Western civilization."[1] Of the commentators and interpretations he says again: "They have afflicted the brains of all believers with irremediable stagnation; and so long as they are in force, those believers will remain incapable of progress and civilization."[2]

The immobility of Islam is seen in education. There are thousands of Koranic schools in Africa, but what was said of the 700 such schools in Tanganyika may be said of them all: "The educational value of these schools is very slight, as pupils are rarely taught anything except the repetition of passages from the Koran and comparatively few ever learn to read and write in Arabic."[3] Mr. Meek states that only three per cent. of the Muslims in Northern Nigeria can read and write. Wherever more efficient education is provided, the Africans (Muslims included) owe it to Christian missions and Christian Governments. Muslims have never attempted to render their Scriptures intelligible to Africans—the only translation of the Qur'án into an African language has

[1] *Op. cit.*, p. 75. [2] *Op. cit.*, p. 201.

[3] Report on Tanganyika for 1924 (Colonial No. 11), issued by the Colonial Office, p. 60.

been made by a Christian missionary (Canon Godfrey Dale), in order that Christian Africans might be able to compare it with the New Testament. No Christian need ever shrink from placing the two books side by side and inviting a judgment. "If the question," Sir Harry Johnston has said, "could be submitted to the arbitration of an international court composed of impartial agnostics (many of them nominal Christians, nominal Muhammadans, or religionless Japanese), I do not hesitate to say that the verdict would be that there were very few sentences in the Koran which deserved quotation or which shone with that striking, convincing beauty of truth and practical application which characterizes—whether we wish to admit it or no—so much of the wording of the gospels and epistles on which the Christian faith is founded, or the Psalms and the prophetical and poetical utterances gathered together in the Hebrew Bible."[1] If Africans want the best, it is not the Qur'án they will choose. Christian missionaries give their people the Bible,—they make an appeal to the intelligence; they open schools where the pupils' minds are exercised on the greatest of Books, wherein is truth for every age and all conditions.

A further difference between Islam and Christianity is seen in their treatment of woman. Muhammad undoubtedly did much for the Arabian women of his time, but he put them—as Islam has kept them—on a very low level. "There is a tradition that Muhammad said he saw hell full of

[1] *Views and Reviews*, p. 188.

women."[1] The Qur'ān provides a Paradise for men, but none for women. Muhammad sanctioned polygamy, by precept and example. He allowed men to divorce their wives, by simply pronouncing the formula "I divorce thee" three times. In my judgment it is correct to say that in many pagan African tribes the women occupy a higher place than they do in Muslim society. Islam permits concubinage with female slaves. And when it is said that prostitution is absent and that the standard of sexual morality is high, it is well to recall the words of Dr. Norman Leys: "In one respect, indeed, Islam brings loss, not gain. The sex morality of coast people who introduced the faith into the interior is almost as low as it can be. . . . Unions for life are rare, and few Arab or Swahili husbands expect their wives to be faithful. So the fact is not surprising that the moral standard in matters of sex in Moslem villages is lower than in neighbouring pagan villages. Sexual perversions are also commoner in them than elsewhere, and ceremonial dances are more exclusively orgiastic."[2]

The easy morality of Islam may appeal to the pagan African and even act as an incentive to embrace the faith. But as his conscience becomes enlightened, he cannot rest there—he will rebel, and women will rebel, even as Muslim men and women are rebelling to-day in other Islamic communities.

One count that Africans have against Islam is

[1] GODFREY DALE, *The Contrast between Christianity and Muhammadanism* (1913), p. 59. [2] *Kenya*, p. 261.

its sanction of slavery. It is true that the hands of Christians—both nominal and practising—are not clean in this matter. But (whatever some Christians may have alleged to the contrary) slavery is repugnant and alien to the spirit of Christianity, while it is a concomitant of Islam, allowed by Muhammad who himself possessed slaves. The Muslim slave-traders have been one of the greatest curses of Africa—one has only to read the travels of Barth and Livingstone to realize that. "Were it not that human remains are destructible the caravan route from Tripoli to Hausaland would be paved deep with human bones."[1] Islam is still, in this year of grace 1926, a barrier to ridding Africa of the open sore of the world. In the Sahara slave-raids are still encouraged, if not organized, by Muhammadans. These statements are made on the authority of the Temporary Slavery Commission of the League of Nations, whose report[2] affirms:

> "Information from reliable sources enables the Commission to state that the slave trade is practised openly in several Mohammedan States in Asia and in particular in the Arabian Peninsula, especially the Hedjaz. It is known that the Hashimite Government received dues on slaves sold in the markets, which is equivalent to an official recognition of the legality of this trade. The Commission does not know whether the present Government of Mecca or the provisional Government established at Jedda have maintained or abolished this practice, but there can be no doubt that negroes from the African continent are imported and sold as slaves in several districts of Arabia."

[1] LADY LUGARD, *A Tropical Dependency*, p. 410.

[2] A. 19. 1925. vi.

What would be the condition of Africa to-day were the Muslims in uncontrolled possession? A slave-trading Emir, who was warned by Sir Frederick Lugard that the traffic must cease, replied: "Can a cat stop mousing? Will not a cat die with a mouse in her mouth? I will die with a slave in my mouth." If Islam ever perishes, it will die with a slave in its mouth.

"A religion which sanctions concubinage and slavery can never be accepted as final or perfect."[1]

Modern Muslim leaders extol Muhammad as the ideal character. Muhammad Ali speaks of him as "a great and noble Prophet whose varied earthly experiences furnish the best rules of conduct in all the different phases of human life." There is no wish on my part to be uncharitable and I am willing to admit that Muhammad possessed some traits of greatness, but a man who had thirteen wives (one of them, Zainab, the divorced wife of his own adopted son; another, Raihanah, a Jewess whom he took to his tent the night following the day when her husband had been slain in a massacre; and a third, Ayesha, betrothed when seven years old and married at ten), who ordered or connived at assassinations[2]—who commanded his followers "slay the idolaters wherever you find them"—such a man is not the exemplar for any people, least of all for the Africans.

[1] GODFREY DALE, *Islam and Africa*, p. 121.

[2] Canon Dale gives a list of seven, *op. cit.*, pp. 10, 11.

IV.

Remarkable changes are taking place in the World of Islam to-day.[1] Ever since Muslims came into touch with a higher civilization, there have been two parties—the Orthodox who keep rigidly to the doctrines of the Qur'án and the Traditions; and the Liberals who wish to modify the doctrines in accordance with a loftier ethic. With the opening of the Muslim world and with the increasing contact with Christians, the struggle between the parties has grown acute. In August, 1925, a learned Sheikh, Ali Abdel Razak, was sentenced by a superior Religious Council in Egypt to deprivation of his status as a professor of religious jurisprudence at Al-Azhar University, because in his book[2] he repudiated much of the Tradition and attempted to prove that Muhammad never cherished ambitions of earthly kingship and never revealed anything but matters related to religious faith and practice. The Sheikh claimed that there is nothing in Islam to prevent the most pious Muslim from adopting from unbelievers whatever he finds best in matters of government or in the affairs of daily life. In short, he attempted to demonstrate logically what the Turks have already put into practice. The Orthodox have repudiated this teaching as heretical. But Ali Abdel Razak has many followers. In

[1] See especially the Rev. W. W. Cash's book, *The Moslem World in Revolution*; and *The Moslem World of To-day* (1925), edited by J. R. Mott.

[2] *Islam and the bases of Government.* See review in *The Times Literary Supplement*, October 1, 1925.

India and also in England there are advocates of liberal ideas who believe that Islam is capable of reform. Were these to gain the ascendancy, the world might see a great change come over Islam.

Lord Cromer used to say, Islam reformed is Islam no longer. At present a radical transformation seems impossible. The Turks are not reforming Islam; they are breaking away from it. The great historic mistake of Turkish people, they say, was in embracing Islam, for it has kept them out of the stream of progress.[1] The danger for Muslims is that they should lapse into irreligion—thousands in North Africa have lost their old faith and gained no other. A theocratic system, which is itself undergoing disintegration and does not bear within itself the capacity of reform, is hardly likely to be a remedy for African disintegration.

But whether it is reformed, or remains unreformed, the nations of Europe, who hold so much of Africa, cannot look with equanimity upon an extension of Islamic influence and power. The French policy of arming and drilling hundreds of thousands of Muslims constitutes a great danger both to Africa and Europe. And the French are coming to see it. Influential writers among them are urging their countrymen to break up the mass of Islam in North Africa. The policy of France in regard to

[1] In proposing the acceptance of the new Civil Code, which treats the two sexes on a basis of equality, the Minister of Justice claimed that by its enactment, "the past thirteen centuries would be swept away, a new dawn would arrive, and a fruitful era of civilization begin." It was voted by the Assembly on February 18, 1926.

the Berbers of Morocco is, in the words of Marshal Lyautey, *de faire évoluer les Berberes hors du cadre de l'Islam.* The French are everywhere opening schools among these people and excluding everything Islamic; they teach French and discountenance Arabic because it is a *vehicule de l'Islam.*[1] It is their hope to make Frenchmen of these Africans. They need to bear in mind the words of Charles de Foucald, the soldier-monk of the Sahara. He hoped to see in Northern Africa *une France prolongée,* but believed this possible only on one condition. He wrote :

> "My thought is that if the Muslims of our Colonial Empire in the North of Africa are not gradually, gently, little by little, converted, there will be a national movement like that in Turkey: an intellectual *élite* will form itself in the big towns, trained in the French fashion, but French neither in mind nor heart, lacking all Muslim faith, but keeping the name of it to be able to influence the masses, who remain ignorant of us, alienated from us by their priests and by our contact with them, too often very unfit to create affection. In the long run the *élite* will use Islam as a lever to raise the masses against us. The population is now thirty millions: thanks to peace, it will double in fifty years. It will have railways, all the plant of civilization, and will have been trained by us to the use of our arms. If we have not made Frenchmen of these peoples, they will drive us out. The only way for them to become French is by becoming Christian."[2]

A warning of another kind comes from South Africa. After Dr. Zwemer had drawn public attention

[1] M. VIGNON (*op. cit.*, p. 501): "Il ne serait pas sage de favoriser dans nos possessions la propagande de la langue en laquelle s' écrit le Coran."

[2] See his life by M. RENÉ BAZIN.

to the growth of Islam, the *Rand Daily Mail* (July 30th, 1925) asked the question we have asked in this chapter: "What religion?" and concluded that white South Africans would not hesitate to declare for Christianity, and not for Islam, as the basis of civilization in that country. A native paper replied to this, that the Christianity which the whites wish to impose upon the blacks is not in fact Christianity—where is there Christian love in the laws which Christians have imposed upon Christian blacks? "Let the blacks put no faith in the affirmations, for their life is not in accordance with the teaching of Holy Scripture, where we are told forcibly that for those who follow Jesus Christ there is no longer any distinction of race,—no colour bar."[1]

V.

This chapter may close with the considered opinion of Bishop Hine, who spent twenty-five years in Africa, mostly among Muslims.

> "Is it to be a Mohammedan civilization or a Christian civilization to which we look? Islam may suffice in some of its outward forms and manifestations to raise those primitive races to a higher point, but it is Christianity alone which can purify the inner life; and it is, after all, the 'inner life which is the real life' of man, it is the 'inner life which is the working power.' Islam may teach the African to wash his clothes and keep himself clean. Christianity alone it is which gives him the secret of the clean heart

[1] I quote this from a letter of the Rev. Alfred Casalis in the *Journal des Missions Evangeliques*, October, 1925.

and the good will, and the love of all things that are pure and beautiful and just and of good report. . .

"Writers (like, apparently, the Dean of St. Paul's) who contemplate the spread of Mohammedanism among these many millions of people with equanimity, if not, indeed, with satisfaction, can hardly know what a mighty force they are encouraging, which one day may sweep the white man out of Africa. We who know; we who have lived and seen facts as they are, and man as he is in that country, feel that it is the teaching and witness of the Christian Church, and of the Christian life, which alone can befit these races for their rightful destiny in the world."

"A Mohammedan Africa might well be in time a great peril to the world. A Christian Africa, powerful for good, enlisted on the side of righteousness, may do much for the progress of mankind."[1]

[1] The Rt. Rev. J. E. Hine, *Days gone by* (1924), pp. 293, 307, ix.

CHAPTER X.

WHEREIN IS DISCUSSED THE CONTRIBUTION THAT CHRISTIANITY HAS TO MAKE TOWARDS THE SOLUTION OF OUR PROBLEMS IN AFRICA.

I.

I believe with all my heart that Bishop Hine is right: only Christianity can prepare the Africans for their rightful destiny in the world. It can give them all that Islam offers, and infinitely more. To us who are convinced that the religion of Christ conveys final truth concerning God and man, and concerning the relation of man to man; who are convinced, moreover, that the truth of Christianity is to be the light of all mankind, and that the minds of all men are capable of receiving it; to us it is inconceivable that the Africans can ultimately be satisfied with anything that even at its best is but partial truth.

Christianity aims at creating new personality in men and women—a dynamic motive, a renewed will, a higher sense of responsibility toward God and men. It aims at the conversion of individuals and the transformation of society, the building up of nations on the foundation of God's law. This is not to be accomplished in a day, nor in a century. The full achievement demands generations for the establishment of a new heredity and to capitalize the gains that are painfully made by individuals.

Many interesting and important questions that arise out of the evangelization of Africa, cannot be dealt with here. But an endeavour must be made to define the function of Christianity in the New Africa.

In previous chapters the view has been repeatedly expressed that there is a future for the African, and that to assure this it is necessary not to de-nationalize him, but to help him to develop according to his own ethos. This raises a problem of great importance for the Christian Church. Does such a principle exclude the endeavour to win the African for a more spiritual religion than any he has yet possessed? Can the African become a Christian and remain an African?

The question has been discussed in other terms by Mr. C. L. Temple, a very able British administrator, who is an enthusiastic exponent of Indirect Rule as established by Sir F. Lugard in Northern Nigeria. Christian missions have hitherto been partially excluded from some of the northern provinces of that territory, because "it is against the Government policy to permit Christian propaganda within areas which are predominantly Muslim."[1] This is not the place to argue for or

[1] C. K. Meek, *op. cit.*, Vol. II, p.247. The Church Missionary Society, however, has a missionary at Zaria, in a province which contains sixty-nine per cent. of Muslims.

against this policy, but it will be well to ask the reason for it. Mr. Temple is disposed to minimize the difficulties of a religious kind that might arise through attempts to convert Muslims, and does not think that the Muslims themselves would raise objections against a Mission on religious grounds, but he justifies the Government's action by pointing to the social disintegration, resulting in the ineffectiveness of the native administrations, that might follow the establishment of a Christian mission. For the same reason the Government might, he thinks, restrict missionary enterprise among pagan tribes which have emerged from a primitive stage, though allowing it among those peoples who were in a simpler and also among those who were in a more advanced and stable stage. He would gladly support Missions among Europeanized Africans, but, says he,

> "I venture to prophesy that if the policy of preserving the native institutions gains ground the missionary bodies will find that the Government will be forced, reluctantly enough but in the best interests of the natives, to restrict the sphere of their activities to an increasing extent, at all events for a time."[1]

Mr. Temple evidently regards religion from the point of view of its usefulness in maintaining law and order. He is not opposed to Missions as such. If they would recognize the necessity of the Natives being good citizens, patriotic and disciplined, and of their developing on their own racial and tribal

[1] C. L. TEMPLE, C.M.G., *Native Races and their Rulers* (1918), p. 217.

lines—then Muslim Emirs, pagan chiefs and Residents would, he says, clamour for the establishment of mission stations. He thus admits the possibility of Christianity being a bulwark and not a danger to native administrations.

Mr. Temple's observations have been quoted because they suggest some questions that are extremely pertinent to-day—not in Africa only, but in India and China. To win a people for Christ, is it necessary to Europeanize them? Can Christianity be so naturalized in a modern tribe or nation that it will foster steady development on natural lines without causing anarchy? Is it really necessary for Africans (or Indians or Chinese) to reject the religion of Christ, in order to retain the most valuable elements in their own culture? Does the acceptance of Christianity involve denationalization? And if in any particular instance Christianity, as presented, proves to be disintegrative, does the fault lie with Christianity, or with its presentation?

II.

In a previous chapter it has been pointed out that Governments also have a disintegrative effect upon the African social system, for they introduce many changes that are contrary to belief and custom on the ground that these are "repugnant to natural justice, equity and good government." This is true even where the principle of Indirect Rule is most scrupulously applied. The administration of the Muslim Emirs of Northern Nigeria has (in Sir Frederick Lugard's words) "been purged of its excesses." By putting down the slave trade and taking steps to abolish domestic slavery, a revolution has been caused in the economics of Islamic society. Mr. Temple concedes that "in almost every case the Government also must share a part of the responsibility" where in certain pagan districts the tribal organization is undermined. In Northern Rhodesia the Government, with the best intentions, interfered to prevent women from being married against their will, and the immediate result was, as Natives and District Officials complained, a disregard for marriage and an increasing drift of women to centres of population in search of irregular unions, money and excitement. A humane law thus appears to provide encouragement to immorality and prostitution. It is a question to what extent increased sexual licence has been caused by the putting down of intertribal wars which provided an outlet for the men's emotion. But it cannot be doubted that where the native penalty of death for adultery has been disallowed, adultery has become more common. These facts are not referred to in order to be able to say *tu quoque* to Mr. Temple, but only to show that both Governments and Missions are faced by the problem which their intervention causes.

"Native customs adopted and acted upon by our Courts," says the Acting Secretary for Native Affairs in Northern Rhodesia, "insensibly receive modification in the process;

> we have not pulled out any beam which is essential to the structure, but we have undoubtedly pulled out smaller supports, and the edifice must receive a shake every time we do this. At times we see the instability we have caused and are puzzled what prop to put in and where."[1]

There is always danger in legislating too far in advance of public opinion. What is needed is to raise the whole moral tone of the community—not merely the insertion of props from without, but the infusion of a new spirit into the social organism. Governments have their legitimate sphere of action, but some things lie beyond their powers. Laws and the administration of law can do much, but only religion can give the new moral basis to African society. There is therefore the best of reasons for a close co-operation between Governments and Missions.

But still we are confronted with the indubitable fact that the introduction of Christianity does provoke at least temporary social confusion.

Mr. Amaury Talbot, for example, records how a Christian Negro spoke to him, "not complainingly, but with the air of one who voices a misfortune for which there is no help," of the results of a decaying belief in the local tutelary spirit named Ndemm.

> "So strong," he said, "was the influence of this powerful Ndemm that in olden days hardly a woman of this town was known to prove unfaithful to her husband. Quietly they dwelt in their houses, and there were no divorces, save by mutual consent. Only nowadays, when women

[1] E. S. B. TAGART, *Native Customary Law* (Proceedings of General Missionary Conference of Northern Rhodesia, 1924), p. 60.

are beginning to lose faith in the Juju, because the school-boys have been taught that there is no real power in such things, are cases of unfaithfulness no longer rare in our town."[1]

There in Nigeria, as elsewhere in Africa, people lose faith in their old gods and have not yet accepted the new religion which would provide a more solid foundation for character. The result is confusion. Christianity appears in the false guise of a promoter of sexual vice. Sir Harry Johnston, after commenting upon the manner in which the Ba-ila are (in his own words) "governed, enslaved, by etiquette and custom," goes on to say, "This is not the case of the Ba-ila only, but of nearly all the savage tribes I have studied. One can easily understand how to most of them Christianity must come as Freedom and Reasonableness."[2] Christianity does so come to them, as Dr. Schweitzer has shown in a classical passage.[3] But the old fears and taboos were the sanctions of the tribal morality, and if the Africans surrender these, without accepting the new motives, the freshly-acquired freedom easily becomes anarchy.

This point must be more fully illustrated. The missionary comes among a people who for ages

[1] P. AMAURY TALBOT, *Life in Southern Nigeria* (1923), pp. 40, 41.

[2] In a review of *The Ila-speaking Peoples of Northern Rhodesia*, in *The Observer*, October 31, 1920.

[3] *On the edge of the Primeval Forest* (1922), p.154 : "Christianity is for him the light that shines amid the darkness of his fears ; it assures him that he is not in the power of nature spirits, ancestral spirits, or fetishes," etc.

have lived a group-life in which the individual scarcely counts. We who are accustomed to a very different state of things cannot realize what a revolutionary doctrine Christianity is: the idea, for example, that every man is responsible to God for his own actions. The missionary appeals to individuals—aims at securing personal conviction and conversion. For an African to respond means breaking in some degree from his group—an act which he has never before contemplated the possibility of doing. The stronger the cohesion of clan and tribe, the more difficult is the missionary's task of securing individual conversions. Some adventurous spirits make the plunge, asserting their right to stand alone as their fathers never did. When one thinks of what it means, it is a heroic thing to do. They find that some of the family, clan and tribal customs are incompatible with the new way of life. As others join their ranks, a deep schism is formed in the tribe: how deep depends upon the missionary. If he unwisely gathers his converts, as he is strongly tempted to do, in a village under his own surveillance, where they will be removed largely from the contamination of paganism, where they will look to him, and not to their chiefs, as their leader and guide in all things, and where they adopt European clothes and manner of living, the tribal system is inevitably shaken to its foundations. This is specially so when the Chiefs keep to their old ways.

It is a situation of this kind that Mr. Temple contemplates when he speaks of the Government being forced to restrict the activities of Missions. The principle of ruling the people through their Chiefs and of encouraging development along their own lines, appears to be incompatible with the teaching and practice of missionaries, and to discourage their activities the only consistent course for Government to pursue. We can understand that where the tribal life, with its old moral sanctions, has already been shattered beyond repair, Mr. Temple would eagerly support the missions for the sake of the new ethic they bring. But can the Christian Church accept restriction of its work to these folk? Some missionaries are frankly opposed to the Government's ideal; they would break down the tribal system—without considering perhaps what should take its place. Others as frankly identify themselves with the Government's ideal, and believe that Christianity, if presented as it should be, so far from being a hindrance to its realization provides (in Mr. Temple's words) the bulwark of native administration. They claim, moreover, that their belief is warranted by past experience.

Instances will presently be adduced to show that while some amount of temporary confusion has attended the introduction of Christianity—confusion that is due, perhaps, more to its presentation than to the Gospel itself—its intention, its tendency, and its achievement on the whole, have been on the side of the integration of African society. Sir Maurice Evans speaks of missionaries as being the only people who are consciously undertaking this very necessary task, and earnestly asks their detractors what they would suggest in substitution. Practically every Commission that has reported on the Native problem in South Africa (where it largely concerns detribalized Africans) has recommended the encouragement of Christian missionary activity as not only the right, but the wise policy for Government to pursue.[1] The Commission of 1903-5, which included some of the leading citizens and most able administrators, said :

> "The Commission considers that the restraints of the law furnish an inadequate check upon this tendency towards demoralisation, and that no merely secular system of morality that might be applied would serve to raise the Natives' ideals of conduct or to counteract the evil influences which have been alluded to, and is of opinion that hope for the elevation of the Native races must depend on their acceptance of Christian faith and morals."

III.

According to Dean Inge, "As a great historical institution Christianity can be characterised only as the religion of the white race. . . . From the second century till the present day, Christianity has been the most European and the least Asiatic of religions. Its great expansion in modern times has been due to the unparalleled expansion of the white race."[2] He uses a vague and inaccurate

[1] EDGAR H. BROOKES, *The History of Native Policy in South Africa* (1924), p. 436.

[2] In *Science, Religion and Reality* (1925), p. 387.

term. Colour is not a certain mark of race; Semites, among whom Christianity arose, and many Indians with darkish skins, are classified by scientists as "white" (or Caucasic). What Dean Inge means is that Christianity has been adopted and naturalized by peoples of Europe and carried by them into other parts of the world which they have colonized. Some years ago Bernard Lucas wrote, "Before India can be Christianized, Christianity must be naturalized."[1] Is not this true of Africa also? If our religion is to become the religion of the Africans, it must surely be translated into the idiom of the African's soul.

I entirely agree with Dr. P. W. Harrison:

> "Missionary work is no enterprise of pity, in which we of the smug and self-satisfied West take a superior religion, and hand it down to poor miserable degraded heathen. The best definition of missionary work I know is found in the book of Revelation, where the writer is speaking of the New Jerusalem. 'They shall bring the glory and honour of the nations into it.' Missionary work is just that, bringing the glory and the honour of the nations into the Kingdom of God."[2]

Our ideal is not a Christian world made of a uniform pattern throughout, but one that preserves within its unity all the diversity that the Almighty has given to the individual peoples. In the essential things let there be agreement, but in the forms which embody them, let there be variety. Christianity is (so to speak) a pure spirit which can extract from its environment multiform bodies.

[1] BERNARD LUCAS, *The Empire of Christ* (1907), p. 19.

[2] In *The International Review of Missions*, July, 1924.

It should not be expected that Christianity will assume a European shape in China and India. Those countries will bring their own honour and glory into the Kingdom and their institutions will be ennobled thereby. Africa is far below them in wealth of culture, and may have to receive more than she can give, but her mite must not be despised. In the measure possible, her institutions should be preserved to enrich the Kingdom, while being in turn enriched by it.

What can be done, then, to naturalize Christianity in Africa? Only a partial answer is possible here. It is necessary to urge that our religion be presented to the Africans, not in antagonism to, but as a fulfilment of their aspirations. In actual practice this means, among other things, cultivation of their languages, conservation and sublimation of all that is of value in their customs and institutions, frank recognition of the measure of truth contained in their religion. It implies, not a paganization of Christianity for the purpose of making it easier to the Africans, but the Christianization of everything that is valuable in the African's past experience and registered in his customs.

That the presentation of Christianity has always followed these lines in the past would be too much to claim. Some eminent missionaries have noted and lamented the fact.

"One is led to ask," writes Dr. S. O'Rorke, lately Bishop of Accra, "have our missionary methods hitherto been sufficiently well-thought out and planned? Has sufficient respect been given to native ideas, not to say 'faith' and age-long custom? It will be here suggested that the answer must be in the negative. We have gone to work in the past upon the unsound foundation that 'The heathen in his blindness, Bows down to wood and stone.'[1] In harmony with this presupposition the heathen has been called upon to make a complete break with his past in every respect."[2]

My old friend the Kasenga blacksmith had (to my mind) a truer conception of the missionary's task and method. "I take," he was wont to say, "an old hoe or the remnant of an axe and of it make a new tool. I do not throw the iron away because in its present form it is no longer usable: I fashion it anew into a thing of use and beauty. That is to say, I *semununa* it. I am a refashioner (*musemunuzhi*), and it seems to me that the missionary is trying to do much as I do. He too is a *musemunuzhi*." In his own idiomatic and picturesque way this thoughtful, intelligent pagan was translating our Lord's own view of His mission, "I come not to destroy but to fulfil." Our Lord, it is true, spoke of not putting new wine into old wine-skins. But in His acted parable at Cana He showed how the new wine of the Gospel was a transformation of the water of the old dispensation. He did not ignore or abolish the Decalogue: He fulfilled it by spiritualizing it. He sanctioned all the truth that had been won by the prophets of Israel.

[1] Dr. Aggrey (who is a Negro) amended the couplet thus, "The heathen *in his hunger*, Bows down to wood and stone."

[2] In his article "Religion in the Gold Coast," *Hibbert Journal*, July, 1924.

History affords no instance, so far as I know, of any people adopting an alien culture, or a new religion, so completely as to retain nothing of the old. A complete wiping out of the past is psychologically impossible. The African's mind is not a *tabula rasa* upon which we can write what we please. Africans are not, as some people imagine, passive recipients of whatever new culture is offered to them. Like our forefathers, they have their own religion and social institutions. If, in teaching the Africans, we demand that they shall surrender all that they have hitherto cherished, we are asking them to do what we Europeans have never done. For the Christianity of to-day is other than essential Christianity—it is an amalgam of elements drawn from many sources. In the Christian festival of Christmas are mingled many elements which come from the cults of Teuton or Celt and the paganism of classical antiquity. Our Easter took the place of a celebration of the death and resurrection of a pagan god at the spring equinox. The names of the days are names of heathen deities. As Christianity adopted the vocabulary of paganism and spiritualized it, so in consecrating them it also transformed many pagan institutions. If, then, we insist upon the African taking our institutional Christianity as it stands, and surrendering all his past, what we are really requiring of him is that, in addition to the pure essence of our religion, he should also take over what it has absorbed from its European environment. It is, of course, extremely difficult to do otherwise.

We go to Africa not merely as Christians but as European Christians, with a strong natural prejudice in favour of everything that is European and a corresponding disdain for everything else. But we ought to recollect that there is a distinction not only between Christianity and civilization, for large tracts of our civilization are not Christian, but decidedly unchristian; there is also a distinction between vital, essential Christianity and the organized, historical institution that embodies it. Somebody has truthfully said that our Lord's Commission does not read, "Go into all the world and teach the English language"; nor does He bid us convey to the Africans every European accretion upon the Gospel. Our aim must be to make of the Africans not European Christians but Christians, and to Europeanize them as little as we can in the process—to implant the Gospel of Christ deep within their hearts, and allow them to organize their faith in a manner suited to their traditions and environment.

It is needless to say that this is not to advocate the extreme accommodation with paganism that transformed the Virgin Artemis into the Ephesian Mother of God, and the cult of ancestors into worship of the saints. In view of much in the history of Christianity in Europe and Asia, and of Islam in Africa to-day, we need to hear Sir W. M. Ramsay's warning:

> "You may in outward appearance convert a people to a new and higher faith; but if they are not educated up to the level of intellectual and moral power which that higher

faith requires, the old ideas will persist in the popular mind, all the stronger in proportion to the ignorance of each individual; and those ideas will seize on and move the people, especially in cases of trouble and sickness and the presence or dread of death."[1]

IV.

If Christianity is to become truly indigenous in Africa, there are two mistakes which the missionary must avoid, viz., an iconoclastic attitude to the old manner of life, and an excessive individualism.

It goes without saying that he will find a great deal that is repugnant to his Christian feelings. It is not to be expected that he should acquiesce in these things, but it is necessary that he should be prudent and patient. As the new life gains in power in the hearts of the people, what is evil will slough off, as old leaves are shed from vigorous trees. African social customs are so closely articulated that external interference is like interference with the balance of animate nature. On this point one of the ablest and most experienced of African missionaries, Bishop Hine, has something to say. Referring to the "highly organized system" of the Ba-ila, he insists upon the necessity of proceeding with caution and wisdom "lest we destroy that which has in it much that is good, and seek to replace it by laws and rules which are antagonistic to the native sense of fitness or custom."

[1] SIR W. M. RAMSAY, *Pauline and other studies*, p. 157.

He continues :—

> ". . . . . there is a reason for the law, very evident and binding to the native mind. At any rate, before he 'wipes away all such nonsense' the Christian teacher should know why the law exists and what it means to the hearer. The whole question is intricate and wonderful, and it needs indeed the spirit of wisdom and understanding, of counsel and knowledge on the part of those who teach the Gospel of Christ and the True Way of Life, that they may act with prudence and not with haste, lest they only upset and destroy much that is useful and fail to replace it by anything that is of lasting worth."[1]

The missionary must apply himself to a close, accurate, detailed, prolonged study of the people, and even when he knows them thoroughly should abstain from trying to put down customs by the weight of his authority; let the people themselves decide, in the strength of their enlightened conscience, what course to take in regard to the old ways. In the meantime, let him exercise his soul in patience and believe in the ultimate victory of the Gospel. In particular, let him respect the tribal authority and teach his people to do so. In the light of experience in Africa the wisdom of St. Paul's view is manifest, "Let every soul be in subjection to the higher powers, for there is no power but of God, and the powers that be are ordained of God." And if there are occasions when for conscience' sake the Christians must respectfully but firmly refuse to obey the behest

[1] The Rt. Rev. J. E. Hine, M.D., D.D. (Bishop of Grantham, formerly Bishop of Nyasaland, of Zanzibar and of Northern Rhodesia), reviewing *The Ila-Speaking Peoples* in *Central Africa*, April, 1921.

of a pagan chief,[1] let them cheerfully accept the consequences without calling for the intervention of the European magistrate, and let them on all other occasions display an unmistakable and enthusiastic zeal for the institutions of their people and thereby convince them of their patriotism.

If one thing is more characteristic than another of the African, it is his strong social sense, seen in his intense loyalty to his Chiefs and in the solidarity of the clan. It is a very difficult thing for the missionary to realize the strength of this. He has been reared in the creed of individualism that prevailed alike in Church and State from the eighteenth well on into the nineteenth century, and even now has not altogether lost its grip. The whole tendency of the modern impact of civilization upon the African is to make him into an individualist, and missionaries, even more than others perhaps, because of their interest in men as men, are liable to accelerate the process. The mission of Christianity looks beyond the individual to the formation of a Society, and this aspect of it, if rightly presented to the Africans, ought to make a very strong appeal to their keen social sense.

Since the African is accustomed to act as a member of a group, it would seem wise for the missionary to aim at, and expect, movements in the mass towards Christianity. As a matter of

[1] An illuminating instance is related by the Rev. W. T. Balmer in the Wesleyan magazine, *The Foreign Field*, February, 1926.

fact, such movements have often taken place, and sometimes on a very large scale, as, for example, in West Africa under the preaching of the native prophet Harris, a free-lance who gathered whole communities, numbering many thousands in all. Such accessions demand careful attention on the part of the missions lest the last state of these converts be worse than the first. But when a whole community moves in this way the advantage is offered of avoiding the schism that is so dangerous. Missionaries of a severely individualistic temperament and creed may suspect such mass movements, seeing that the conversion of the majority may not be very profound, but, after all, it was largely in this way that our Teutonic forefathers were brought into the Church.

The same African characteristic should, and unquestionably does, make for the strength of the organized institutions of the Church. The essence of his clan consists in the subordination of the individual to the interests of the brotherhood, a mutual-aid society whose members are also members of each other. No doubt from our pronounced individualistic point of view the system lacks much—some observers would trace the mental stagnation of the African to its influence. But there can be no doubt that the brotherliness of the clan is more in keeping with the genius of Christ's Gospel than is the selfishness of our individualistic civilization. This sentiment of brotherhood, this capacity of self-sacrifice on behalf of others, this solidarity which swallows up all egoistic competition that can thrive only on harm done to one's fellows,—these are the very qualities that should characterize Christians. It is to this aspect of African character that Islam makes its strongest appeal, and if Christianity is to win Africa it must, in the spirit of Christ, outbid Islam in its offer of a real brotherhood.

Surely it is in this direction that the criterion for judging the success of missionary enterprise should be sought. Statistics, I must confess, arouse no enthusiasm in me; John Wesley was right, numbers are an inconsiderable circumstance. The true measure of the Church's success is the degree to which it has built up Christian communities—not of denationalized folk, but of Africans, organized on lines congenial to the native mind; not alienated from the mass of the people, but animated with a true spirit of brotherliness towards all; not disdainful of outsiders, but exercising a wide and elevating influence over the whole tribe or nation, and ever drawing into their circle those who have remained without, until the religious society becomes co-extensive with the civil community. In other words: a branch of the Church Catholic, in all essential things united with the disciples of Christ throughout the world, but self-supporting, self-governing, self-propagating, and truly African. Such a society is a very powerful agency in the adjustment of old ways to new, and in establishing an enlightened group-morality in place of the old, worn-out ethic.

Such branches of the Christian Church are in

fact being formed in Africa, and prove by their measure of success that the social sense of the Africans can be utilised for high purposes. Take as an example, the Church in Uganda.[1] As the British have built up the administration of the Protectorate by including the indigenous governments in a larger framework, so the Church Missionary Society has organized the Church on the lines of the native civil system. The organization reaches out to the little village societies which form the units and are grouped into districts and pastorates. The whole culminates in the Synod which is representative of the two thousand local churches of the diocese. The system rests upon the principle that Africa is to be evangelized by Africans and that the Church must be built up by its own sons. The English clergy, headed by the Bishop, are few in number (too few to meet the needs); the overwhelming majority of clergy are Africans, trained locally, living in native style, dressed in native garments, supported financially by their own people. From the beginning, the Christians have been taught to regard the Church not as a foreign institution, but their own—that it is their business to extend it and to support it by their contributions.

Such a society meets the African's need for fellowship. He does not stand alone: the clan-feeling is sublimated in the Church. When representatives go from little obscure village

[1] The Rt. Rev. J. J. Willis, D.D., Bishop of Uganda, *An African Church in building* (1925).

churches to the great assemblies and return to report what they have seen and done, the members realize that they form part of a large and growing group. The Uganda diocese covers the whole of the four kingdoms included in the Protectorate. Each kingdom has its own civil council, but the Church Council, i.e., the Synod, represents the whole Protectorate and thus binds all the provinces in a larger unity. Attended by many of the native rulers and leaders, besides commoners, and all as delegates from lower courts, this assembly is an ordered, responsible, governing body whose decisions carry great weight and whose unifying influence is very great. The members of the Church are all literate. Nobody would claim that the ethical standard is of the highest ; yet the Church numbers its saints and martyrs, and the Christians are not to be judged by our measure but by the depth of the pit from which they were dug. The Church in Uganda is not yet fifty years old, and it is doubtful whether the Church in England was any better at that age.

There is no need to insist upon the material and educational benefits the peoples of Uganda have received through the introduction of Christianity. It is sufficient to allude again to the fact that the cotton-growing, for which the country is gaining fame, was started by missionaries. Nor do I wish to forget that the Roman Catholics have made their own contribution to the national life. My purpose here has been to show the Protestant Church as a great unifying agency, which has trained rulers and the commonalty in civic virtue.

No doubt the Church Missionary Society had many advantages in Uganda, for it found intelligent peoples organized under capable leaders, many of whom became Christians, and it was able to establish the Church firmly before European invasion began. In other parts of Africa the Missions have had to do with broken and scattered remnants of tribes and have played no small part in their re-organization. In Basutoland and Nyasaland, to name no other territories, and scarcely to a less degree than in Uganda, Christianity has exerted, and still exerts, a tremendous social influence. It has not only redeemed individuals from barbarism and implanted within them new ideals of personal conduct, it has done much for the tribes corporately, and has gone a long way towards making them nations. Through their medical work the missionaries have combated the evils that threaten depopulation; by example and precept they have elevated the conception of home; they have introduced industries; they have liberated intellectual powers and started into life the ambition to advance. Moreover, they have reduced languages to writing and produced the beginnings of a literature, thus conserving for the peoples what is both one of the greatest of social bonds, and an instrument of future progress. They have also, in a few instances, standardized differing dialects and thus brought closer together peoples who before were separated. The Christian Church has in these ways shouldered in Africa her distinctive responsibility of renewing the mind and will of peoples by moral and spiritual influence. In co-operation with Governments, wherever it is permitted, she is helping to make strong nations and resisting the contrary tendencies towards disintegration. The end is not yet and before the goal is reached there will be many a mighty struggle. But a beginning has been made. We claim no more.

V.

In regard to African social customs there is more than one possible attitude to take. The course commonly adopted, it is to be feared, is to repress them, as wholly unworthy of Christians. In view of our desire to establish an indigenous African Christianity, the best way of dealing with them is summed up in the word "sublimation." As used by psychologists this describes the process of utilizing the primary instinctive tendencies of mankind as a great fund of energy available for the higher ends of life: "the superposition of man's higher moral and intellectual capacity upon a basis of animal instincts."[1] To sublimate the pugnacious instinct, for example, means to transmute the fighting capacities of men into "moral equivalents for war." Applied to our missionary work, the word may be used analogously of the process of

[1] W. McDougall, *Introduction to Social Psychology*, pp. 404, *seq.*

utilizing for Christian ends the experiences registered in African practices and beliefs. The customs have grown up out of some felt need and represent something of value to the people. Not all of them are unclean and false; very often in the heart of a false and unclean custom there is something admirable, and Africans will admit that many of the repugnant elements are not really essential. To sublimate means not to transplant the whole of any custom, good or bad, but to seek out the good kernel in things evil and to make it serve the interests of a higher moral and spiritual life. All that is best in the African's past experience should be enlisted into the service of Christ and His Church.[1]

Without pretending to be in any way exhaustive, I will illustrate what is meant.

The pagan African is eminently religious and carries his religion into all his activities. If Christianity is to be true to his genius and meet his needs it too must be infused into all his life.

The native religious ceremony of giving a name to the new-born child can readily be transmuted into Christian baptism. And in giving names to children and to adult converts, why should we pursue the senseless custom of always bestowing Scriptural names? The desire of Christian Natives to take new names to symbolize their new birth deserves sympathy, but why *Zakariya, Zefaniya, Hezekiya, Sofoniya*? If they will prefer names

[1] It is instructive to read what is being done on these lines in Ceylon. See PAUL GIBSON's article in *The International Review of Missions*, January, 1925.

taken from the Bible why not give them the vernacular equivalents? In the Xosa language *Nanziwe* means "Delightsome" and is surely more suggestive and musical than the Hebrew equivalent, *Hephzibah,* the meaning of which they do not know. My own children were baptized by the names given them by Africans and I want no sweeter names then *Thabo* ("Joy") and *Matsediso* ("The mother of Consolation"). The Africans have a genius for making or choosing euphonious and meaningful names; why not encourage them to continue the practice? [1]

The large question of recreation cannot here be dealt with in any fullness. It has become a pressing problem in view of the restrictions imposed upon hunting in some parts and the killing off of the game in others. Missionaries need to encourage the natives in pastimes as well as in work. In the schools they should, while introducing foreign games (cricket and football), foster also the playing of native games, of which a great variety exists. Too often has dancing been banned. Many native dances are lascivious, but not all, and it is better to select and to purify what is after all a healthful exercise. David danced before the Lord with all his might and the Psalmist urged the people to praise God's name in the dance. We cannot imagine an Anglo-Saxon dancing as a religious

[1] See CANON GODFREY CALLAWAY'S article in *The South African Outlook*, February 2, 1925. "Upon that genius our heavy feet have trampled with disastrous results. I include myself in the number of offenders and I am amazed as I think of my own blindness and stupidity."

exercise, but I can readily conceive of an African doing so. And why not? The African's natural histrionic gifts could well be utilized in his general and religious education. Miracle Plays would appeal to them very strongly. In all these matters missionaries are too apt to take a repressive attitude.

The Africans have also a distinct musical talent—it may well be, indeed, they will prove to be among the most gifted peoples in this respect. A negro musician of real genius, who has taken a degree in America, is now engaged in studying the indigenous music in Africa. It is to be hoped that some day this will be, at least partially, substituted for Western music in African Churches. Indeed it is already used to a small extent. In Nyasaland, Dr. Donald Fraser says, "the old war-songs are used to-day to stir not the warlike but the missionary spirit; the old dance-tunes inciting to vice and wickedness express the most tender emotions of religion."

Among the African institutions which might well be sublimated is the initiation ceremony through which boys and girls pass at puberty. Undoubtedly many features of it merit the disapproval of missionaries. It is a thing to which the Africans are very much attached, for it is regarded as the entrance into tribal life, and a young person who is not initiated loses status. That there is some good in it may be gathered from the fact that in planning the Boy Scout code Sir R. Baden Powell followed, as he has said, "the principles adopted by Zulus and other African tribes which reflected some of the ideas of Epictetus and the methods of the Spartans and of the ancient British and Irish for training their boys."[1] Some of the instruction given in the initiation schools has a high moral tone. Mr. Emile Torday, for example, records the following rules given to the Bushongo youths.[2]

> "To respect and obey the king, members of the royal family, mother and father; to avoid offending the parents' feeling of propriety; to avoid obscene language; to respect woman's modesty; to be just to one's enemy, to rescue him when in danger, and not to try to get him into trouble; not to permit several to attack a single person; not to steal; if they covet a thing to ask for it and if they cannot get it honestly to do without it; to respect other people's wives; not to tell lies to a tribesman."

I rejoice in the extension of the Boy Scout Movement to Africa. Much of the training given forms an excellent sublimation of the initiation ceremonies. The Church might well go further and establish a kind of rite which would be accepted by the tribal authorities as equivalent to the ancient ceremony in giving an entrance into the tribe. Experiments have already been made along these lines with, it appears, some success. It would be a considerable gain to Christianity in Africa if this ancient custom could be sublimated. Merely to ignore it, or to repress it by stringent prohibitions, is not only to court trouble in the future but to

[1] See SIR R. BADEN POWELL's article in *The Daily Telegraph*, July 19, 1921.

[2] EMILE TORDAY, *On the Trail of the Bushongo*, pp. 185, 186. The teaching given to Ba-ila youths is outlined in *The Ila-speaking peoples of Northern Rhodesia*, Vol. II, pp. 31, *seqq.*

neglect a valuable means of Christianizing African life.[1]

In no department of native life does the missionary need to act more circumspectly than in regard to marriage. It is fatally easy to do almost irreparable injury to African social life by unwise interference.

Among Europeans (including missionaries) there is no more common superstition regarding Africans than that these buy wives. It is high time that this misrepresentation ceased. In some regions the Natives have been so often told that they purchase wives that they have come to believe it, and now regard the "dowry" as a purchase. But in the eyes of the true Africans, the cattle or other goods handed over by the bridegroom's clan to the bride's do not constitute a purchase. The man does not acquire the proprietary rights that he gets when he purchases a slave. The *chiko* (or marriage-fee) is a guarantee of good treatment for one thing, and is regarded by women as a token of honourable marriage. Women for whom it has not been presented are not regarded as married. Why missionaries have refused to countenance this excellent native custom is difficult to understand. A much wiser course has been taken by the North Rhodesian Missionary Conference. They have asked the Government to bring in an Ordinance making Christian marriage dependent on the

[1] What trouble may be caused is shown by the recent experience of the Baptist Mission in the Yakusu district of the Congo. The better way is indicated in the experiments conducted by the U.M.C.A. (See *Central Africa*, June, 1922, pp. 126-128 and October, 1923, pp. 218, 219.)

observance of the essentials of native custom, and one of the things they suggest the Native Commissioner should satisfy himself about before granting a license for Christian marriage is that "where demanded by native custom, some payment from the family of the bridegroom to the family of the bride has been made, unless the omission of this custom is agreed to by the representatives of both parties."[1]

Most missionaries perhaps regard polygamy as a closed question, and would be horrified by a suggestion that the Christian Church should seem in any way to countenance the custom. But a suggestion for reconsideration of this attitude ought not to be thrust aside lightly. Monogamy is the only form of marriage consonant with Christian morality. Yet there are worse things than polygamy; prostitution is worse. The surreptitious concubinage practised by large numbers of professing African Christians is worse than polygamy—it inflicts a greater wrong upon the women. To demand that before a man can enter the Church he must discard all wives but one, is to debar from the privileges of Church membership many men who are desirous of being Christians, but who cannot bring themselves to send away the women whom they have honourably married and

[1] *Proceedings of the General Missionary Conference of Northern Rhodesia*, 1924, pp. 82-85. The Rev. B. J. Ross, while asking "What thing under heaven, we may ask, are missionaries in South Africa for if it is not to work against the stream of Native life?" is one of the missionaries who support the custom. (*South African Outlook*, December 1, 1925, p. 281.)

who are the mothers of their children; it is also a direct incentive to loose living on the part of the discarded women. Under present conditions there is no place for unmarried women in the tribe—they are almost bound to live immorally. Slavery is also an abominable evil. Yet St. Paul never set up a Church rule against the owners of slaves: he even sent a slave back to his master. St. Paul's teaching, based upon his Master's, made it certain that ultimately the Christian conscience would revolt against and abolish slavery. To my mind, our attitude towards polygamy should be the same. Let us go on inculcating the Christian view of the relation of the sexes, let us insist upon monogamist marriages for the young converts, and in good time the African's conscience, aided by the pressure of economic laws, will wipe away polygamy, with other evil things.

In regard to marriage, our Christian ceremony should take over some of the traditional African forms. Let us by all means continue the use of the wedding ring with its beautiful symbolism, but let us also adopt the African symbols. Where, for example, the native rite includes the partaking by bride and bridegroom of a plate of porridge in common—a symbol of the close union on equal terms of man and woman—this is too precious a thing to be lost, and it could easily be made an attractive and impressive part of the ceremony in church.

The limits of space will not allow me to write in detail about other customs susceptible of Christianization. It has been insisted that the African's whole attitude towards life is religious. If a man goes hunting, his first act after killing game is to offer a portion of the meat in sacrifice. All the agricultural processes are hallowed by religion. I would sublimate all this by boldly converting the pagan ceremonials. At the right season the people could be called together to ask God's blessing upon the land to be cultivated and the seed to be sown; there should be regular Christian festivals of the firstfruits and harvest. Their fishing and hunting would be similarly consecrated—every act of the people, individual and corporate. We are too apt to lead our converts to associate religion only with Sunday. The pagan Africans have the advantage of a better conception of the place religion should occupy in life: and Christians should be not less, but more religious than the pagans.

There are many things in the African's religion which can be made the basis of Christian teaching. His ideas of God, for example. Even in the seemingly irrational taboos there is a precious element, for many of these testify to a deep-rooted desire for purification from what these people regard as evil.

The plea here put forth is that we should present Christianity to the Africans, not in antagonism to, but as a fulfilment of their former aspirations. Then our religion will not come to them as a white man's creed, and their old faith and social system will not appear as a mass of unmitigated evil to be spurned as a false and unclean thing, but as a premonition of truth. Christianity will become deeply grounded in their past life,—not an exotic, but a living plant rooted in their racial experience.

Perhaps the greatest obstacle in the way of adopting this attitude to-day is found in the resistance of African Christians. "The best Christians we have had," says a missionary, "are those who cut clean away from native customs. . . . . Many, if not most, cases of arrested development and breakdown of character are directly traceable to failure to make this clean-cut." But this intransigent attitude and these lapses, are they not due in large measure to the teaching of the missionaries that all the old life was of the devil? Nobody wishes to encourage what is positively evil, but why ban everything indiscriminately? Good Christian and educated Africans such as Dr. Aggrey and Mr. D. T. Jabavu lament the unsympathetic attitude of missionaries in the past. The fact is that our Evangel to the African has consisted too much of a long series of *Don'ts*: and we have in some respects merely substituted new taboos for the old we have destroyed.[1]

Ultimately the attitude they will adopt towards the past experience of their race will be determined by the Natives themselves. Missionaries are not a permanent factor in the life of Africa—they will

[1] On this subject Chapters 4 and 5 on discipline, in *La Psychologie de la Conversion* (Vol. 2), by RAOUL ALLIER, should be carefully studied. I had not read them when I wrote this chapter. This brilliant author's conclusions, I fear, are in general contrary to the views I have put forward.

one day (the sooner the better) disappear because no longer needed. It is not their business to decide what form African Christianity shall take, but to lay the foundations securely and well. In a century's time, many Africans will want to know about their great-grandfathers and the only place where they will be able to learn of their manner of life will be the books written by anthropologists and missionaries. They will not thank us when they come to know how many valuable things in African life have been allowed to pass into oblivion.

CHAPTER XI.

WHEREIN THE EDUCATION OF THE AFRICAN IS CONSIDERED.

I

WHETHER the Africans shall be educated or not is beside the question to-day. As Lord Selborne has truly said, "The very moment that a Native comes into contact with the white man his education has begun, if it is only with the storekeeper in the Government location." Every white man in Africa is, whether he realizes it or not, an educator of the black.

To counteract the too often deleterious effects of European civilization, to fit the African for his new environment, and to give him a chance of

NOTE ON LITERATURE.—The following are the most important publications dealing with the subject of this chapter :—

(1) CHARLES T. LORAM, *The Education of the South African Native* (1917). [Quoted as "Loram."]

(2) T. J. JONES, *Education in Africa* (1922) [E. A.]; *Education in East Africa* (1925) [E. E. A.]. Reports of the two Education Commissions under the auspices of the Phelps-Stokes Fund.

(3) *Educational Policy in British Tropical Africa.* Memorandum by the Advisory Committee on Native Education (1925) Cmd. 2374. [E. P.] *The Place of the Vernacular in Native Education.* Memo. No. 3 of the Advisory Committee (1925). [P. V.]

developing what is in him, a purposive education is necessary such as is given in schools. This is the subject of the present chapter. From the white man's point of view, the question is not "Can we afford to educate the Native?" but rather, "Can we afford *not* to educate him?"[1]

In the dialogue[2] where Plato sets the stage for a discussion on education, the end of which is the improvement of the soul of youth, Socrates asks, "Is this a slight matter about which you and Lysimachus are deliberating? Are you not risking the greatest of your possessions? For children are your riches; and upon their turning out well or ill depends the whole order of their father's house." Socrates knew, as we know, that great care is required in this matter, for education may be either a curse or the greatest of blessings. Knowledge is the food of the soul, said Socrates on another occasion;[3] "if you have understanding of what is good and evil, you may safely buy knowledge of Protagoras or of any one . . . there is far greater peril in buying knowledge than in buying meat and drink . . ." We Britons (and it is with British Africa that this chapter deals particularly) have, in effect, adopted some millions of Africans as our children, and it is no exaggeration to say that their welfare and our own depends largely upon our success in educating them well.

[1] LORAM, p. 45.

[2] *Laches*, Jowett's translation, Vol. I, p. 92.

[3] *Protagoras*. Jowett's translation, Vol. I, p. 135.

The task is a huge one. Approximately 50,000,000 Africans live under the British flag and we may estimate one-fifth of them to be children of school-age. If for the time being we pass over the question of adult education, our problem thus presents itself: How to educate nearly 10,000,000 young Africans? Allowing one teacher to fifty pupils, this means an army of 200,000 teachers. Where are these to come from—who is to train them? Who is to provide the money necessary to build and maintain the schools?

Missionaries have been the pioneers of education in Africa. They have regarded schools, not as a helpful adjunct merely, but as part and parcel of their work—an essential element in it. Even to-day, we are told on good authority, "at least nine-tenths of all the schools which exist in Tropical Africa are mission schools."[1] Throughout Africa, Protestant missions report over 19,000 institutions with about a million pupils; Roman Catholic missions report approximately the same numbers. These schools have been criticized—sometimes with good reason, but often unfairly. At least the missions may take credit for having borne the burden hitherto of what is really an Imperial task. Out of their scanty funds, provided largely

[1] Dr. Garfield Williams, I.R.M., January, 1925, p. 12. Figures are given in I. R. M., October, 1924. These show 102 Government schools in British Tropical Africa. The Muslim schools are excluded from these calculations (there are 26,000 Koranic schools in Northern Nigeria), probably because they are not accounted worthy of the name. "In the Belgian Congo and in Portuguese Africa the work of education is almost entirely in the hands of missions."

by the generosity of poor people in the Homeland, they began and have carried on the work in spite of indifference, and often opposition, on the part of Governments and settlers; they persevered in the days when Africans saw no good in going to school, and if to-day the Africans are clamouring for education it is largely due to the incentive they have given. What faults the mission schools have are due to the fact that, in common with their generation, the missionaries had inadequate ideals of education. But they are not alone to blame. They carried to Africa the system under which themselves were trained at home. Many of the deficiencies have been forced upon the missionaries by Government—as in South Africa. Other faults are due to lack of money. When all is said, the missionaries, on the testimony of the Phelps-Stokes commissions, have no cause to be ashamed of their work.[1]

But the position to-day is that the enormous task of educating the African is beyond the unaided powers of the Church. A few figures taken from Dr. Jesse Jones' second report will suffice to demonstrate the inadequacy of their efforts. Of about 200,000 native children distributed throughout Northern Rhodesia, not more than 50,000 attend

[1] DR. GARFIELD WILLIAMS, who accompanied the second commission ("I have gone quite definitely as a critic"), says: "in general the work accomplished by missionaries in their schools in the past in Africa is simply staggering in its magnitude and in the general excellence of its quality if one studies it scientifically—that is taking account of all the facts." Much of it he pronounces "a positively superb piece of educational work." I. R. M., January, 1925, p. 14.

school—all but 600 are in mission schools. In Nyasaland the proportion of pupils is larger: 146,800 out of 240,000—all of them, be it noted, in mission schools. There are said to be 800,000 children of school-age in Tanganyika, of whom 5,000 attend the sixty-five Government schools, and 115,000 the mission schools. In Uganda the children number approximately 640,000 and those receiving instruction, 157,000.

While these figures show how much remains to be done, they do not tell all the tale. A large proportion of the children attend (very irregularly) little out-schools where the teaching is given often by untrained men and is ineffective from the educational point of view. It is said that even in Uganda, out of the 157,000 pupils only 500 have reached the third or fourth (English) standards, and not more than 100 a higher standard than the fourth.

While the exchequers of the missionary societies are taxed to exhaustion in maintaining their schools (in spite of the fees they may receive from parents), the Governments of British territories are drawing huge sums from the Africans in the form of taxes, but, whether in supporting mission schools, or in maintaining their own, are spending a very small proportion of that revenue on educating the Africans. Happily they have now awakened to the necessity of doing more. In 1925 the Advisory Committee on Native Education, appointed by the Secretary of State for the Colonies, on the initiative of the missionary societies, submitted recommendations which were accepted as its policy by the Imperial Government. In their memorandum they declared:

> "The rapid development of our African Dependencies on the material and economic side demands and warrants a corresponding advance in the expenditure on education. Material prosperity without a corresponding growth in the moral capacity to turn it to good use constitutes a danger. The well-being of a country must depend in the last resort on the character of its people, on their increasing intellectual and technical ability, and on their social progress. A policy which aims at the improvement of the condition of the people must therefore be a primary concern of Government and one of the first charges on its revenue."[1]

No controlling power that acknowledged the responsibility of Trusteeship for the moral advancement of the native population could adopt a different attitude.

As an earnest of what is to be, the Government of the Gold Coast is spending £400,000 on the erection of the great institution at Achimota, which is to bear the name of the Prince of Wales, and has appointed the Rev. A. Fraser as Principal, with Dr. Aggrey, a native of the Colony, as Assistant Vice-Principal. Other local administrations are taking up the matter with considerable energy.

II.

We are thus confronted with these two facts. On the one hand, the missions which have laid the

[1] E. P., p. 5.

foundations of an educational system find themselves unable to provide all the necessary schools. On the other hand, the Governments are now prepared to spend a larger proportion of their revenues on educating the people. What is to follow? The Advisory Committee declare that "Co-operation between Government and other educational agencies should be promoted in every way."[1] And again, "Government welcomes and will encourage all voluntary educational effort which conforms to the general policy. But it reserves to itself the general direction of educational policy and the supervision of all educational institutions, by inspection and other means." The Committee look to the giving of grants-in-aid to efficient schools, adding: "Provided that the required standard of educational efficiency is reached, aided schools should be regarded as filling a place in the scheme of education as important as the schools conducted by Government itself." From this it appears that the Advisory Committee comtemplate that the Governments will where necessary build their own schools, and give the missions grants-in-aid on condition that their schools attain a standard set by Government.

Most of the missions have in the past been willing to accept grants where offered on such

[1] Mr. Ormsby-Gore, the Under-Secretary of State for the Colonies, said in a speech, "The Government is out for co-operation with all the missionary societies. . . We cannot do without them. We have seen their magnificent work and we want to do our share in the service of Africa as a whole—for the African, body, soul and spirit." (*East Africa*, January 14, 1926.)

terms. A few have preferred to work quite independently, on the ground that they teach religion and that the Church ought not to accept money from the State for this purpose ; or because they do not wish to be interfered with in their curriculum. There is much to be said for this attitude of independence. When Governments pay the piper they naturally claim to call the tune. Where educational ideals conflict, the missions must either lower their flag or risk the starvation of their schools. If the two parties are to co-operate in any real sense they must come to an agreement as to the aims and processes of education. If no agreement can be reached, then the missions are justified in refusing grants rather than surrender their principles. In that case they must either provide more money, or be prepared to see their schools suffer in the competition with the more wealthy Government institutions.

The chief difficulty in the way of co-operation is the question of religion in the schools. The controversies that this has raised in England are well known. In Africa, few men who know the people would dispute that they are eminently religious and that the education we give should pay due regard to that side of their life—indeed any education that is in accordance with African genius will make religion colour every phase of life.[1] Any system of instruction in industry and

[1] M. Louis Franck (Belgian Colonial Minister) puts the case thus : " Pour l' éducation morale c' est sur l' évangélisation qu' il faut surtout compter. On ne fera rien de permanent sans elle. Cette conviction est indépendante de toute considération

science alone would make the Africans a nuisance and a menace to the world—would ruin them. We have no use for secular education in Africa. That Government schools must necessarily be destitute of religious training is not true; in Southern Nigeria, for example, they follow the same syllabus as the mission schools. As long as Mr. Fraser and Dr. Aggrey and their colleagues are in charge of Achimota college the atmosphere and instruction will be religious. But some Government schools exclude religion—in Sierra Leone, for example. Of the Tanga institution in Tanganyika Dr. Jesse Jones notes, "no provision is made for religious instruction, and this is also the case in the Government district schools." The comment made by the headmaster is significant: "Moral training from the religious standpoint is outside our province, but I would like to suggest that if facilities were given officially in any creed to take place in the school curriculum, we would get a better type of boy in the school and better results . . . the task of forming character divorced from a definite code of morals is not likely to succeed."

India has much to teach Africa—by her mistakes. Bishop Whitehead, who spent nearly forty years there, says that the genius of India has always

de foi ou de dogme. Elle est basée sur cette observation que la vie indigène est profondément pénétrée de religiosité, et dominée par le mystère. . . . . Seul un autre sentiment religieux, plus élevé, mais aussi profond, paraît capable de remplacer ces influences traditionnelles, et d' amener la moralité indigène à un plan supérieur." *Etudes de Colonisation comparée* (1924), p. 123.

expressed itself in religion and that a system of education for India which leaves out religion is like "Hamlet" without Hamlet. The Government has maintained "quite rightly" a strict neutrality in regard to religious teaching. This policy "has tended to repress India's genius rather than to develop it, and to substitute politics for religion as the main preoccupation." From an educational point of view, as regards the training of character, the decreased interest in religion is a great loss.[1]

It cannot cause surprise if missionaries, who are supremely concerned with religion, should view with apprehension the establishment of Government schools on the ground that they might follow the example of India. Happily, the Advisory Committee have re-assured them. They say:

> "Since contact with civilization—and even education itself—must necessarily tend to weaken tribal authority and the sanctions of existing beliefs, and in view of the all-prevailing belief in the supernatural which affects the whole life of the African it is essential that what is good in the old beliefs and sanctions should be strengthened and what is defective should be replaced. The greatest importance must therefore be attached to religious teaching and moral instruction. Both in schools and in training colleges they should be accorded an equal standing with secular subjects."[2]

Such a declaration, while suggesting some questions, means that in Africa the British Government does not intend to maintain, as in India, an attitude of strict neutrality as regards religion.

[1] *Indian Problems* (1924), pp. 147, 149.

[2] E. P., p. 4.

Another apprehension is removed by the Advisory Committee's decision that Advisory Boards of Education should be set up in each Dependency, to include government officials, missionaries, traders, settlers and representatives of native opinion. This is eminently satisfactory, since if there is to be co-operation, missionaries should have some voice in the formation of educational policy. It would have been better to give these Boards executive as well as advisory powers, but in practice it will be found that missionaries of experience and character will exercise very great influence over the decisions taken. These boards have already been set up in most of the dependencies.

With the removal of these misapprehensions, it will be advisable for the missionary societies to enter into co-operation with the Governments. But let them not make any mistake. They must do their part in providing adequate staffs for their schools and training institutions. The Governments are evidently determined to go ahead, and it rests with the missions to decide whether they will keep step, or be left behind.

III.

We can wisely adapt means to an end only if we know what goal we desire to reach. In dealing with the education of Africans we must ask therefore, What is it we are aiming at? What do we desire that they should become?

Africans can no longer live an isolated existence. Over a large part of Africa they have to live side by side, more or less, with Europeans. Even in segregated areas, such as Basutoland, their economic life depends largely upon white men. The resources of the country can only be developed by harmonious co-operation of the races. Should this fact supply the regulative principle of our educational scheme? Is it our aim to make the African a more useful person to the European? That is the theory held more or less explicitly by many people. Educate the African, they say, because by doing so you will increase his wants; he will work harder, whether on his own lands to produce exportable things, or on the mines and plantations to earn wages; in either case he will be in a position to purchase greater quantities of European goods and that will provide more work for our factories in England and put more money in our pockets. It is quite obvious both that to increase the purchasing power of 50,000,000 British Africans must be beneficial to the mother-country and that education must have this effect. But is this to be our motive, and is it to determine the kind of education we shall give the African?

In territories such as South Africa, is it our aim to prepare the detribalised African for political rights equal to those of the European? Or looking ahead, are we to prepare the Africans for the possible eventuality that, as the Romans abandoned Britain, so the Europeans will leave Africa—a time when the Africans will stand alone? Or are we to envisage native states included in the British commonwealth of nations, and are we to prepare the future citizens?

It is better to approach the subject from the standpoint of the C.O.P.E.C. Commission on Education. Our aim should be to develop the African's personality on all sides and to the fullest extent to which it is capable. We do not know what the future of the African is to be. But there is every reason to believe that he possesses a nature that is rich and capable of great development. If he is given the chance to develop his personality we shall be preparing him for whatever his destiny may be. If we can make of him a worthy citizen of the Kingdom of God, he will also become an efficient and useful citizen of the British Commonwealth, fitted in the future to take his place beside his European peers, and useful to them as well as to his fellow-Africans.

IV.

The personality of the African is rooted in the past—the past of the African's own race. He cannot be treated as if he were a European who happened to be born black. He ought not to be regarded as if he were a building so badly constructed that it must be pulled down, its foundations torn up and a new structure erected on the site, on a totally new plan and with entirely new materials. Any such attitude is psychologically absurd.

Education has been defined as the causing of people to develop according to the laws of their own nature. The first requisite in an educator is that he understand the nature of the educand. It is a trite saying that the verb "to teach" governs a double accusative: to teach Jack arithmetic the teacher must know Jack as well as arithmetic. If this simple fact is insisted upon when educator and educand belong to the same race, how much more is it necessary to insist upon it where the teacher is European and the pupil African? In this case Jack has lived in an entirely different environment; his social heritage differs from ours; his ideas, his outlook upon the universe, are diverse from ours. If we are to educate him these facts cannot be ignored. Surely the first thing necessary is to understand the African and his past, and the second is to plan our educational scheme so that he shall develop according to the laws of his own nature.

To ignore these elementary considerations is to prepare for trouble. Here again India has a lesson to teach Africa. When, early in the nineteenth century, the question of education called for settlement, the decision was given against the "Orientalists," who advocated a system conducted on Indian lines with the vernaculars as the medium of instruction (English to be taught in higher grades as a foreign language). The decision was given on grounds of practical and administrative convenience, not on educational principles. Bishop Whitehead does not hesitate to describe Macaulay's minute of 1835 "the evil genius," not the Magna Charta, of Indian education; and the result "a disaster." He does not deny that many blessings have accrued to India through the system finally adopted, but these have been bought at too great a cost. The fact that English is the medium of instruction for all the higher education has placed a tremendous burden on the large majority of the students which they are quite unfitted to bear—the double burden of mastering their subjects and of thinking in a foreign language is far too great a strain. The vicious system demoralizes both teachers and students. Mechanical learning, which is the result of using a foreign and imperfectly acquired tongue, inevitably divorces words from realities, and widens the gulf between the educated class and the mass of the people. The education becomes aggressively English, its avowed object being (as Macaulay said) to make Indians English "in taste, in opinions, in morals and in intellect." So it has tended to repress India's genius rather than to develop it.[1] One of Mr. Gandhi's grievances against the system is precisely that it makes the Indians lose the treasures of their own language. An English literary education, which has nothing to do with the building up of character, has, he declares, emasculated the youth of India.[2]

My own experience in South Africa leads me to endorse Bishop Whitehead's condemnation of a

[1] BISHOP WHITEHEAD, *op. cit.* I have summarized this indictment from Chapter 10.

[2] ROMAIN ROLLAND, *Mahatma Gandhi* (1924), pp. 10, 105.

system which ignores the roots of personality in the past. I began my missionary career by teaching in two institutions where teachers were trained. The syllabus in both cases was that ordained by the Cape Colony government for white and black students alike. No native language was allowed to be spoken. All teaching was carried on in English, of which the students' knowledge was often pitifully meagre. The very first lesson I gave was in English grammar and the passage set for analysis was the opening of Paradise Lost—those sonorous lines beginning "Of man's first disobedience and the fruit of that forbidden tree." More hours than bear thinking about were spent in teaching the history of the early Saxon kings of England. It was all so nauseatingly false and superficial that I quickly came to loathe the whole system. It was cramming of the vilest kind. So much work had to be done within a fixed time to prepare the pupils for the yearly examination: there was no time really to teach. I understand what Bishop Whitehead says about demoralization. My own fine ideals went by the board—they simply could not be put into practice. The unfortunate victims of the pernicious system simply memorized page after page of the text-books ("to by-heart," say the Indians), which were written, be it remembered, for European students. No use was made of the gardens to teach gardening, hygiene was not thought of, no games were taught. All the educational value of the wonderful African languages was utterly ignored. You can call this system by any name you wish, but it certainly was not education. The effect on the men's minds was deplorable. I knew several students who went mad under the forcing process. Those who survived and passed the examinations (as some of them did) left with a totally false view of education —left to spread it among their pupils. To learn a book and pass a test and thus to become a "teacher" and "an educated man" was the ideal. The pathetic thing was that young men would heroically practise self-denial and labour hard to earn their fees, and would travel immense distances to enter these schools. They became strong opponents of any reform, on the ground that to differentiate between them and English students in a syllabus was to insult native intelligence. Cut off from the past, taught indirectly or directly that everything in their own tribal life was valueless, it is no matter for wonder that they came to depise everything African, or that a deep gulf was opened between these teachers and their "uneducated" tribesmen.

The same evils which existed in South Africa[1] have been rampant elsewhere in Africa, as the Phelps-Stokes Commissions report. The old system was not adapted to the actual needs of the people: it produced an altogether disproportionate number of clerks and such-like persons, who left home and sought employment with Europeans in the

[1] A more enlightened system has, I understand, now been introduced. But Dr. Jesse Jones found the old one still regnant in 1921.

towns. And their most marked characteristic was that they had become what the French call *deracinés*. It is not that we want to repress the African's legitimate ambition to rise. It is not that we want to keep him isolated from the world, and to deny him any knowledge. We want them to be truly Africans, not caricatures of Europeans. "If I were to define denationalization," says A. G. Fraser, "I should say it was irreverence for and ignorance of one's own nation and culture, and of the things now chiefly affecting it."[1] Anything in the schools that leads to such denationalization stands condemned.

One of the links with the past is found in the African's language, and any real education of the African involves the conservation and use of his language in all stages, from the lowest to the highest. I would make my own the words of one of the foremost Africanists of our time, Professor Diedrich Westermann:

> "Language and mental life are so closely connected that any educational work which does not take into consideration the inseparable unity between African language and African thinking is based on false principles and must lead to an alienation of the individual from his own self, his past, his traditions and his people. If the African is to keep and to develop his own soul and is to become a separate personality, his education must not begin by inoculating him with a foreign civilization, but it must be based on the civilization of each people, it must implant respect for the indigenous racial life, it must teach him to love his country and tribe as gifts given by God which are

[1] *Aims of African Education* in I. R. M., October, 1925, p. 517.

> to be purified and brought to full growth by the new divine life. One of these gifts is the vernacular, it is the vessel in which the whole national life is contained and through which it finds expression."[1]

In support of this position the words may be added of a distinguished Belgian—M. Louis Franck :

> "To exclude the native languages from the school of the people in order to impose exclusively a European language is a mistake and an injustice."[2]

The French commit this injustice consistently. Their prevailing colonial policy has been to assimilate their African subjects—to make them Frenchmen, and they therefore teach French. "The day that our North Africa speaks French it will be truly a French land and an extension (*prolongement*) of the fatherland. It will feel and think like France."[3] Some of the writers speak as if the very existence of their country depends upon teaching their language in Africa. M. Aristide Prat, Inspector-General of Education in French West Africa, rebels against this traditional policy; it is an excellent way, he says, to make *déracinés* and rebels. Yet, illogically it seems to me, he clings to the teaching of French and to the total exclusion of indigenous tongues.[4]

The Portuguese have in recent years followed a

[1] *The Place and Function of the Vernacular in African Education*, in I. R. M., January, 1925.

[2] *Etudes de Colonisation comparée* (1924), p. 125.

[3] ALBIN ROZET, quoted by M. VIGNON, *Un programme de politique coloniale*, p. 466.

[4] *Bulletin Périodique* of the Société Belge d' Etudes et d' Expansion, April, 1925.

similar policy, again not on educational, but on political grounds.

I agree with M. Franck, it is not only a mistake from an educational point of view—it is an injustice.

It must be admitted that the ideal of teaching every African in his mother-tongue is difficult to put into practice. Not, however, because the languages are unfitted for the purpose: rich, flexible, expressive, musical, capable of infinite development, these make an excellent medium for instruction. No insuperable difficulty has been encountered in translating the Scriptures into these languages. The educationist's difficulty arises from their multiplicity. There may be a thousand languages spoken in Africa; some of them over wide areas and by millions of people; others mere dialects used by a few hundreds or thousands. In a country like Basutoland where there is a standard language, the problem is simple; whereas in a region like the Bauchi province in Nigeria, where the 750,000 people are divided into 110 tribes and many of the languages are so divergent as to be unintelligible in neighbouring villages,[1] the problem is formidable. The whole question needs careful examination by experts, and this is one object of the projected International Bureau of African languages and literature. Every dialect cannot be perpetuated in literary form. Certain expansive

[1] O. TEMPLE, *Notes on the Tribes of the Northern Provinces of Nigeria* (1919), p. 415. MR. W. N. THOMAS states that over 230 different languages are spoken in Northern Nigeria. (C. K. MEEK, *The Northern Tribes of Nigeria* (1925) Vol. II. p. 132.)

languages will no doubt displace the more local forms of speech. The schools will help the process of selection and perpetuation. It will mean in many cases that pupils will have to learn and be taught through the medium of an African language which is not their own mother-tongue. This is not an ideal arrangement, but a compromise forced upon us by circumstances—the sheer impossibility of producing a literature in so many hundreds of tongues. But this is a very different thing from teaching English, as some people advocate in order to solve the difficulty. To teach a Sicilian in the standard Italian, which is more or less the dialect of Tuscany, does him no real harm; to teach an African in a closely allied tongue, whose vocabulary is much the same and whose genius is identical with his own, is not inflicting a great injury upon him—indeed Africans readily learn neighbouring languages. But to insist upon an African abandoning his own tongue and to speak and read and think in a language so different as English, is like demanding that the various Italian peoples should learn Chinese in order to overcome their linguistic problem.

The Advisory Committee has wisely decided that in all elementary schools, and as a rule (except perhaps in the highest classes) in secondary schools also, the education should be conducted in the vernacular: "the mother-tongue is the true vehicle of mother wit."[1] For the large majority of the pupils it is not necessary to learn English at all.

[1] PV. p. 3.

Those who show extraordinary promise and will become teachers and leaders may be taught English in secondary schools in order to broaden their minds and give them access to the treasures of our literature. Where a secondary school, or normal college has to serve a multi-lingual area, and where no common language exists, it may be found necessary to use English as a medium of instruction.[1] But even there the vernacular should not be neglected; it should be made a regular subject of study together with the native folk-lore and traditions. For it is supremely important that the future leaders and teachers of the people should not be cut off from their fellows, but should be in closest touch with them.

V.

The principle enunciated by the C.O.P.E.C. Commission is the sound one, namely that education should aim at the full and harmonious development of the resources of the human spirit, the making of the perfect man and woman: a completely integrated personality rightly related to the society from which it is inseparable. In other words, as Sanderson of Oundle used to insist: the aim of education is that we may have life and have it more abundantly.

Life unfolds itself under four aspects: Beauty,

[1] In a mission school in the Sudan, thirty young men speak fifteen languages, so distinct that they cannot understand each other. English has become their common speech.

Truth, Usefulness and Goodness; and if the African is to be truly educated all these must be developed in him. These aspects cannot be isolated one from another. You cannot have one class for Beauty and another for Goodness. The whole school-life, within the building and outside, should be so organized that both curriculum and environment lead irresistibly, if insensibly, to the desired end, namely that the pupils love beauty, truth and goodness, and are useful.

It is often said that Africans have no appreciation of beauty. This is not altogether true, but if the æsthetic sense is undeveloped that is all the more reason why we should pay attention to it. The pupils ought to be surrounded with beautiful things. Education should aim at training their taste in such matters as dress and architecture. One only needs to look at much of the costume and many of the habitations of civilized Africans to realize how we have failed to make them love beauty. How much, apart from singing hymns, have the schools done to develop the African's undoubted genius for music? What has been done to train their ability for metal-work, wood-carving, grass-plaiting and clay-moulding? If the Africans are to be truly educated these things must be attended to, not solely for utilitarian ends, but for the purpose of refining and developing their æsthetic sense.

Education is most emphatically not a mere impartation of knowledge: it is not a pouring-in of facts; certainly it is not a pumping-in of a mass of heterogeneous information. There must be much instruction, of course. At the very least the three R's must figure in every elementary school. But it is essential that these, and whatever else we teach in the schools, higher and lower, be related to the life of the people. There is no sense in wasting time by trying to teach things which they cannot assimilate and for which they will never have any use. No door must be closed against an African; he must have liberty to rise as high as he is capable of going. There are now many capable African ministers, physicians and lawyers. In course of time it is to be hoped there will be thousands more of these.[1] But the great bulk of the people will continue to live simple lives, and it is absurd to try and teach them subjects that will never be of any service to them. I have seen an examination paper set (in English) for third year candidates in a normal school in East Africa. Not a single question related to Africa. The last question ran: "What do you know about Homer and the Odyssey, Julius Cæsar, Hannibal, etc.?" It may be good to teach the literature and history of Greece and Rome, but it is assuredly wrong to neglect the literature and history and geography of the pupils' own country. Beginning in junior standards with the folk-tales, many of which have high educational value, the pupils should be made familiar with the laws and institutions of their country, the story of their tribe and chiefs, of the coming of the Europeans

[1] I am not so sure about lawyers.—E. W. S.

and their aims, and of the change which this threatens. In this way they will be led to reflect, and to value whatever there is of good in their traditions. The geography, too, of their country, its resources and its economic needs, are a subject for teaching. These can all be made intensely interesting and of real value, especially if parallels be drawn with the history and geography of England and other countries. A most important subject is the laws of health. In view of what we discovered in a previous chapter it is a matter of first-class importance. But even this instruction is not the main thing. "Truth" in the Copec enumeration does not stand merely for accurate knowledge of facts. Above everything, pupils must be trained to use their minds, to ask questions, to think clearly, to love truth fearlessly and passionately.

Another aspect of life is Usefulness. Under this head we may briefly deal with two subjects, the first of which is technical education. Any system is false in so far as it neglects training of eye and hand. But the reason for giving this training must be clearly comprehended. Some missions teach agriculture and handicrafts, partly in order to render their work self-supporting by the sale of the products. In some instances the missions train carpenters, masons, telegraph-operators, for the Government and settlers. These men turn out some really excellent work, proving the intelligence and manual dexterity of the Africans. But to what extent does this training result in raising the kraalman's standard of life? Do the trained artisans return to their own villages and give their fellows the benefit of their training? As a rule they do not. Some of them are so highly trained that they will not demean themselves to make common objects for humble homes. Some of them are at sea unless they have the elaborate tools to which they were accustomed during their apprenticeship. They generally find employment on European farms and settlements. This is not to be deprecated entirely. The missions fulfil a very useful function in preparing skilled artisans who will assist in developing the resources of the country. All that is now urged is that technical instruction should not stop at producing employés for the Europeans. There is a valid reason for it apart from this. Manual work gives a medium for self-expression, an occasion for teaching accuracy and perseverance, for forming taste, for arousing the joy of creation. It is therefore a means of developing character, and this is its supreme justification. This is an argument for teaching in all schools simple industries which involve the use of easily procurable materials. Above all, we must remember that the Africans are, and will remain, primarily agriculturists—as Dr. Jesse Jones says, they are relatively far more dependent on agriculture than any other people in the world. First of all, the schools must imbue the pupils with a sense of the vital importance of everything that pertains to the soil and the farm: then they must teach better methods of tilling, how to overcome the insect pests, how to grow new plants, how to care for and improve stock, and so on. In a word, the schools must endeavour to put the Africans in a position of economic independence.

The second thing to be said under this head of usefulness is that the schools should be made a means of blessing to the whole community. Too often they stand apart from the everyday life of the village: the boys and girls attend for a few hours a day and then return home: the parents do not see what good it brings *them*. The school should aim not solely at teaching the children but at uplifting the whole life of the community. It should be the centre of social service—spreading abroad, by means of the pupils, present and past, knowledge of sanitary laws and of agriculture, and ideals of cleanliness and purity. What has been done in America, and in recent years in India, points the path in this direction. The extension to all schools of the Boy Scouts' and Girl Guides' movements would be an excellent thing.

Lastly, Goodness. If there is one thing that is recognized more than another by all who are concerned with education in Africa, it is that the primary object to be attained is character in the pupils. Whatever we teach, our aim must be to turn out good men and women. The Supreme Teacher has indicated the ideal: the character we want is that of the man who loves the Lord his God with all his heart, with all his soul, and with all his mind, and his neighbour as himself. Men who are not themselves professing Christians really have that ideal at the back of their mind when they speak of character. To reach that end, religion must take its proper place in the schools of Africa.

And in speaking of religious teaching we do not mean the conventional hour or two allotted to the subject in the curriculum. It means more than an occasional lesson on the Bible and catechism. "Religion," says a Quaker document quoted by the C.O.P.E.C. Commission, "is not a distinct technical department or occupation, but rather that which gives unity and meaning to the whole, a dynamic, embracing and inspiring power." "If this is true, then," the Commission comments, "religion is the vital essence of education, and education is an integral part of the mission of religion."[1] Definite dogmatic instruction there must be—I am a strong believer in a catechism, provided that it be written with direct reference to the religious needs of the African. The Bible must be used and taught regularly. But religion is more than religious instruction. It cannot be imparted as geography and arithmetic are imparted. Religion as life in God flows through a teacher who is himself religious. More depends here upon the teacher than in any other department. And the man or woman who is aflame with love for God and man will set his pupils aflame, and show them how religion can elevate and colour and inspire every phase of life. An oft-quoted passage indicates the place

[1] C.O.P.E.C. Report on Education, p. 49.

that should be taken by religion in the schools of Africa :—

> " Not long ago I met one of our great schoolmasters—a veteran in that high service. ' Where in your time table do you teach religion ? ' I asked him. ' We teach it all day long,' he answered. ' We teach it in arithmetic, by accuracy. We teach it in language, by learning to say what we mean—" Yea, yea, and nay, nay." We teach it in history, by humanity. We teach it in geography, by breadth of mind. We teach it in handicraft, by thoroughness. We teach it in astronomy, by reverence. We teach it in the playground, by fair play. We teach it by kindness to animals, by courtesy to servants, by good manners to one another, and by truthfulness in all things. We teach it by showing the children that we, their elders, are their friends and not their enemies.' "[1]

Happy, indeed, will Africa be when all her schools unite to send out young men and women who shall have been taught in this way that religion is co-extensive with life.

VI.

Two subjects of paramount importance must be referred to, if but briefly. First, the education of African women. It is folly to suppose that Africa can be given a new life if the mothers of the future generation are neglected. The home is even more important than the school as a means of education, and mothers, in Africa as all the world over, are the chief moulders of a people.

To educate the girls is a difficult and delicate

[1] L. P. JACKS, *A Living Universe*, pp. 50, 51.

task. The right way has been shown by Miss Mabel Shaw, of the London Missionary Society. Her notable article in the International Review of Missions for October, 1925, contains matter of the utmost significance. She has demonstrated the possibility of training girls over a number of years, implanting successfully Christian ideals, without removing them from the life of the tribe. How successful her experiment is can be seen from the fact that the old prejudice of the women of the tribe has been broken down.

> "Now that they see the fine, sturdy, happy babies that some of the old girls have, instead of the poor puny mites that girls who have married at fourteen have, they are content to leave their girls in school until they are sixteen, seventeen, even eighteen years old. They see sick children nursed and recovering, whereas in the village they might die; they see the girls clean, strong, healthy, and these things make their impression on the women, and it makes some of them eager to learn the new ways."

Lastly must be emphasized the need for concentrating largely upon the education of the future leaders of the African peoples. The great institutions like that at Achimota have their place —always provided that they do not create too great a gulf between the students and the life of their nation. It is true that the future of Africa lies not so much in these colleges as in the village schools. But the teachers and leaders of the future generation must be trained. The greatest need in Africa to-day is a great corps of intelligent, god-fearing men and women, with eyes open to the future of their race and with reverence for the past, who shall go out to uplift their fellows. To be the trainers of such leaders—Africa has no more useful and attractive task to offer to the Christian men and women of England.

EPILOGUE.

I.

TWENTY-SIX years ago my father delivered the Hartley Lecture.[1] We are supposed to have advanced in many directions during this quarter of a century, and are rather apt perhaps to look upon the previous generation as hopelessly antiquated. But in re-reading my father's book again after so far completing my own, I am struck above all else by its very modern tone. With a vigour and eloquence that I cannot emulate he set forth many of the things advocated in these pages. He defined the aim of the Christian Church in no narrow way. To him (as to myself) the object of the missionary work of the Church is to win for Jesus Christ the moral supremacy of the world.

"I am fully convinced," he said, "that the purely evangelistic method is not sufficient for the complete moral and social transformation of such heathen people or peoples as the Africans. The full work of the Gospel is never completed until its truths and morals are embodied in the customs and laws and institutions of the people at large. This means the formation of a social life which shall be Christian to its very foundation, penetrated by Christian

[1] JOHN SMITH, *Christ and Missions* (1900).

> ideas and aims to its very springs. . . . . The complete transformation of heathen Africa requires all the forces represented by the Christian church, the day-school and the workshop. Any method that aims at accomplishing lasting work must provide for the mental and social training of the young. . . . . The ennoblement of native character and life must come by the eye and hand as well as by the head and heart."

My father insisted upon the cardinal importance of building an indigenous Church in Africa, self-propagating, self-supporting, self-governing, with a native ministry, not Europeanised and not severed from the people. Everything will fail, he urged, unless Christianity be given a real living root in the native soil. He doubted whether the tone of African Christianity will ever be thoroughly healthy until it is the spontaneous product of native thought and energy, working mainly through native channels. He advocated the frank recognition, and even assimilation, of whatever is good in other forms of religion. With all this, as with his noble exposition of the Christian motive, I am in entire and cordial agreement.

My lecture has covered much ground that my father's did not touch. He was always indignant at the wrongs committed against the Africans, but questions of land and population, and some other like matters, did not come within the scope of his theme. I should like my lecture to be considered as a sequel to his. He said what was most necessary to be said in his day—much, indeed, that still needs saying. I have tried to say some of the things that need saying to-day.

II.

In view of what is here set forth, and much it has not been possible to say, what is the duty of Christian people? Their duty is to apply the spirit of Christ fearlessly to the solution of the problems presented by the contact of races and cultures in Africa.

Let us, in the first place, be clear upon some points. Christianity stands for the Kingdom of God, which is not eating and drinking, but righteousness and peace and joy in the Holy Ghost. The Kingdom of God is not the British Empire, nor any other Empire, and Christianity does not exist for the glorification and extension of any earthly power. This is not to belittle the British Empire which in its finest aspects is, in my opinion, one means of bringing in the Kingdom of God. But we must beware of confounding the two. Nor is Christianity synonymous with Western civilization. There are many things that are true and good in this civilization of ours, but many things also that are glaringly unchristian. The Gospel does not exist to be the useful ally of the magistrate in keeping the barbarian quiet—nor to be the trainer of docile servants for the farmer and miner. There is in Christianity a permanent, timeless principle which has no special reference to any particular conjunction of events, to any particular period, to any particular race.

"The claim of Christianity is not that it is one among a number of religions, all of which are good, each for a different set of people, nor indeed that it is primarily a drug for men's diseases at all, in which case we might suppose that there would be different drugs for different diseases; it claims that it is the truth about this world in which we live, and that from it and through it alone can you find in any fullness the knowledge of the God who made and who rules the world, and is guiding it to the fulfilment of His own purpose."[1]

This does not mean that Christianity has nothing to say about the actual problems of Africa. It means that Christianity has the final word to say, and that apart from Christianity there can be no solution. Our Faith is to be vindicated by a practical application of it to every-day life. If God be Love and the Father of all, if He wills that men are to realise their common brotherhood in active acknowledgment of that eternal fact, if truth be on the side of love and not on the side of hate, prejudice and contempt, then this doctrine must be applicable to every problem raised by the contact of races and cultures in Africa, and it is our business as Christian men and women to apply it.

The civilization that is being introduced so rapidly into Africa is deeply saturated with materialism. Upon their claim to be of a superior race, Europeans as a whole base a right to the service of others. They do not look upon human well-being in the highest sense as an object worth toiling for in itself. Increase of knowledge of the world, self-expression in music, art and literature,

[1] The RT. REV. WILLIAM TEMPLE, Bishop of Manchester, *The Universality of Christ* (1921), p. 31.

the following after Truth, Beauty and Goodness, all such spiritual values we subordinate to a search for cotton, gold and copper. We place in the forefront of our aims the growing of products for our factories, and the extension of markets for our merchandise. This pursuit of material ends colours even our professed altruism, as when we press for education of the African and for the saving of life, not so much for the African's own benefit as because our own prosperity will be enhanced thereby. The religion of Jesus Christ cannot tolerate such regard for material ends as the purpose of life. It cannot acquiesce in any scheme that makes the Black a mere instrument for producing wealth—whether for himself or for the White. The rights of personality stand supreme in Christ's estimation of man, and should so stand in ours. Men and women, of whatever race or colour or grade of culture, and altogether apart from their economic value in the market, are God's creatures and of infinite worth in themselves. They are members of one family of which ourselves form a part. Such a conception does not place all men on an equality in capacity and actual acquirement,[1] but it does demand that their manhood be respected, and that they be given a fair chance to develop the utmost that is in them. We who have been dowered with greater privileges must share our heritage with the less privileged, giving of our best with

[1] "With regard to the Negroes I have coined the formula, 'I am your brother, it is true, but your elder brother.'"—ALBERT SCHWEITZER.

unstinted generosity, even though it may mean that our relatively higher position in the industrial and cultural world be diminished thereby. That risk we must take. In a word, Christ's principle demands that we white folk put ourselves by an effort of imagination in the black man's place, and ask ourselves what we would then wish to be done in regard to us. We must do to others as we would be done by.

We Europeans are practical people and demand of every proposal, Will it pay? We ought not to argue matters on these lines. If a thing is right it should be done whatever the consequences. Yet, if our religion be true, its application in the economic sphere will be justified by results, and the cynical maxim "Honesty is the best policy" will be proved correct. We recognize that in our home industries it is not only right but also commercially profitable to treat men as men and not as mere "hands" to be exploited. That the application of the same principle to Africa has the same result has already been proved. The slave-trade was as contrary as anything possibly could be to the spirit of Christ. The great Emancipators based their persuasions for its abolition upon high Christian principle, but they never shrank from declaring that abolition would pay. The abolition, as Mr. Ramsay Muir says, "struck a note of a new era in the history of the British Commonwealth, an era in which ruthless exploitation of primitive peoples would be no longer regarded as permissible." Here was an assertion that Christian principle and not commercial expediency must rule our relations with Africa. Who will deny that it has been justified economically? An unrestrained, unredeemed commercialism, inspired by no motive loftier than that of Mammon, defeats its own ends by leading to the decimation and extinction of its victims. Had the slave-trade continued unchecked, it would by this time have almost, if not quite, depopulated Africa. What would that have meant to the peoples of Europe? What would it have meant to the looms of Lancashire to-day and still more in the near future, had our merchants succeeded in maintaining the trade in men and women? As it is, commerce and industry are still suffering from the effects of the inhuman and impolitic procedure of past centuries. And the unchristian treatment of Africans in many parts of Africa to-day will have to be paid for by commercial failure in the future. You cannot depopulate a country now and expect it to provide labourers and customers for the next generation. If you will kill your goose, you must suffer the loss of golden eggs. On the contrary, to conserve the population, to treat Africans as men should be treated, is to make an investment that will pay handsomely.

This, it is true, is to argue the question on a low level, and yet there are some people to whom only such arguments appeal. Let us press upon them the maxim that what is true religiously is also true economically; that if they will not treat the African as a man from higher motives, at least let them treat him properly for their own sake.

III.

Let people in England remember that in their name the principle of Trusteeship for the well-being of Africans has been solemnly accepted. It is for them to see to it that this be not a mere pious aspiration but carried out in all the acts of Government, and particularly in all economic policy.

Each and everyone of us has personal responsibility in this matter. The burden of Trusteeship rests upon each individual. As Trustees it is our bounden duty to acquaint ourselves with what is being done in Africa. We must strenuously resist the temptation to speak wild and whirling words that have little or no foundation in truth. Indiscriminate denunciation does more harm than good. It is not easy to arrive at a correct estimation of complex and difficult problems. An attempt has been made to do so in this book, but it is possible that here and there failure may be detected notwithstanding an earnest desire to be absolutely just. I would plead with my readers to seek out and study the facts. If they are then convinced that injustice is being done in any matter let them strike and strike hard,—they have many means of making their voices heard. But only in so far as their protests are well-informed will they prevail.

In recent years there has been a noteworthy growth of altruistic regard for the African and other backward peoples. It would be folly, however, to pretend that all members of the white race accept the principle of Trusteeship. There are many Britons who look upon it as sentimental claptrap. A conflict still rages between two opposing conceptions of what our attitude should be towards the Africans. It is part of the warfare between God and Mammon. Mr. Ramsay Muir is undoubtedly correct in his claim that "it was the influence of the missionaries which was to establish the principle that, in the backward regions of the world, it was the duty of the British power to prevent the ruthless exploitation of primitive peoples and to lead them gently into civilised ways of life." Missionaries must continue to stand, as they have stood in the past, as tribunes of the Africans. But let us beware of thinking, or of saying, or of acting as if we believed, that missionaries ever possessed any monopoly of the Christian spirit. This is said deliberately and of purpose, because there is still a tendency in some quarters to suspect the motives of other classes of white men. Many people, not professedly disciples of Christ, are inspired by Christian ideals in their relation to the Blacks. They prove it possible to settle among and to trade with Africans and yet to act justly. There is a widespread and increasing conviction among Europeans in Africa that service and not exploitation is the road we must follow. In my experience, the men who represent Great Britain as administrators are almost uniformly actuated, like the noble fellow to whose memory I have (in part) dedicated this book, by the loftiest motives. These try to live up to the standard sketched for the British Colonial Service by Sir Hugh Clifford in a memorable letter addressed to its members in Nigeria :—

> "Our primary function is not so much to *rule* as to *serve* the populations whose affairs we are administering and the countries whose resources we are helping to develop. Also, loyalty, discipline and devotion to duty should be the very life-blood of the Service ; and among the major tenets of our creed should be that if, as all too frequently befalls, public duty and private interests and affections threaten to clash, precedence must unhesitatingly, nay, instinctively, be accorded to the former; that each of us while serving in the Tropics carries the honour of our country in his hands and must ever be scrupulously regardful of that sacred trust; that every precept of chivalry that lies at the back of the Englishman's inbred love of fair-play—every sympathy which weakness should quicken in the strong and every appeal that impotence can address to power—should make it a point of honour for each of us to be meticulously just and unendingly patient, tolerant and kind in all our doings with the often pathetically defenceless people whose affairs are committed to our charge."[1]

Here indeed is the spirit of Him who came not to be ministered unto but to minister. Let us thankfully recognize it wherever it is found and give these men our cordial and loyal support in their difficult task.

Finally, our duty is to uphold the hands and to increase the numbers of the men and women who go out as our representatives in obedience to the Saviour's command: "Go and make disciples of all nations." Let us not imagine that the task is ended—it is as yet hardly begun. There are immense fields yet to be occupied, and not for

[1] *West Africa*, February 21, 1925.

many long years will the African Church be able to stand alone. The old period of adventurous pioneering in regions unknown is drawing to a close, has indeed closed in many parts of Africa, but the era of steady, quiet building the foundations of the Christian nations to be calls for men and women of like endurance and devotion. We need the best the Church can give—they cannot be too able nor too highly trained. I hope the day will soon come when every central mission station will have its doctor and nurses, with a well-equipped hospital. The most urgent need to-day is for well-qualified educationalists who will train the native teachers and preachers. There is room for hundreds of them. The Christian Church never had a greater opportunity than it now has in Africa of shaping the destiny of nations.

IV.

While these final words are being written there hangs before me in the place of honour in my study the enlarged photograph of Mungalo—one of my friends to whom I dedicate this book. He was an old chief of the Ba-ila at Kasenga. His unbeautiful face was deeply pitted by smallpox; no doubt his soul was deeply stained, he remained pagan to the end: yet if ever two men loved each other they were Mungalo and myself. In a land where the term *mulongo* ("friend") is sacred, he and I were "friends." Nobody ever spoke to me of Mungalo by name: it was always "thy friend." I never spoke of him by name: it was always "my friend," and everybody understood. I can hear even now his ringing tones as he announced himself outside my door by calling me: *Mulongwangu*! ("my friend"); and can see his rugged countenance lighten as he welcomed me to his home with the same word: *Mulongwangu*! Heaven itself will be something less than heaven if I do not hear that greeting—*Mulongwangu*!—when I enter the pearly gates. We spent long hours together, whether in his hut, or in my study, or out in the open. He was a rare companion—the best raconteur I ever knew. We talked freely and frankly, discussing all things on earth and in heaven, so far as our limited experience would allow. Pagan as he was, I rarely have known a man of finer reverence. He was deeply religious. Through the window of Mungalo's soul thrown open so unreservedly to me, I saw the African in all his weakness and strength: a man of like passions with ourselves, capable, as we are, of depths of infamy and of altitudes of nobility. Anyone who has enjoyed the intimate friendship of one African can never think meanly of the race. They have a genius for friendship; they excel in loyalty. No people perhaps are more capable of a deep and constant fidelity to those whom they love—for their sake they will go through fire and water and brave a thousand deaths. A people characterised by such fine faithfulness have in them the making of good citizens—of good followers of the Christ who esteemed so highly this lowly virtue and made it the test of life.

INDEX.